OECD environmental
indicators : towards
2001-

OECD Environmental Indicators

2001

TOWARDS SUSTAINABLE DEVELOPMENT

ORGANISATION FOR ECONOMIC CO-OPERATION AND DEVELOPMENT

ORGANISATION FOR ECONOMIC CO-OPERATION AND DEVELOPMENT

Pursuant to Article 1 of the Convention signed in Paris on 14th December 1960, and which came into force on 30th September 1961, the Organisation for Economic Co-operation and Development (OECD) shall promote policies designed:

- to achieve the highest sustainable economic growth and employment and a rising standard of living in Member countries, while maintaining financial stability, and thus to contribute to the development of the world economy;
- to contribute to sound economic expansion in Member as well as non-member countries in the process of economic development; and
- to contribute to the expansion of world trade on a multilateral, non-discriminatory basis in accordance with international obligations.

The original Member countries of the OECD are Austria, Belgium, Canada, Denmark, France, Germany, Greece, Iceland, Ireland, Italy, Luxembourg, the Netherlands, Norway, Portugal, Spain, Sweden, Switzerland, Turkey, the United Kingdom and the United States. The following countries became Members subsequently through accession at the dates indicated hereafter: Japan (28th April 1964), Finland (28th January 1969), Australia (7th June 1971), New Zealand (29th May 1973), Mexico (18th May 1994), the Czech Republic (21st December 1995), Hungary (7th May 1996), Poland (22nd November 1996), Korea (12th December 1996) and the Slovak Republic (14th December 2000). The Commission of the European Communities takes part in the work of the OECD (Article 13 of the OECD Convention).

Publié en français sous le titre :
INDICATEURS D'ENVIRONNEMENT DE L'OCDE
2001
Vers un développement durable

FOREWORD

Concerns about whether development is sustainable from an economic, environmental and social point of view have prompted a number of countries to further move towards policies focusing on pollution prevention, integration of environmental concerns in economic and sectoral decisions, and international co-operation. There is also increasing interest in evaluating how well governments are implementing their policies and how well they are satisfying their domestic objectives and international commitments. These demands have led to the development of environmental indicators as a tool for decision making and for assessing countries' environmental performance.

As part of their commitment to transparency and accountability, and to better information of the public, OECD Member countries have recently also expressed increasing interest in a reduced number of environmental indicators selected from existing larger sets to draw public attention to key environmental issues of concern and to inform about progress made.

The OECD work programme on environmental indicators has led to several sets of indicators each responding to a specific purpose: an OECD Core Set of environmental indicators to measure environmental progress, and various sets of indicators to integrate environmental concerns in sectoral policies (e.g. energy, transport, agriculture). Indicators are also derived from natural resource and environmental expenditure accounts.

The present report is one of the products of this OECD work programme on environmental indicators. It is updated at regular intervals and includes environmental indicators from the OECD Core Set, as well as selected socio-economic and sectoral indicators having an environmental significance. It further includes a selection of key environmental indicators, endorsed by OECD Environment Ministers at their meeting in May 2001. The report highlights the linkages between environmental indicators, environmental performance and sustainable development, and thus provides a building block for the environmental component of sustainable development indicators.

This report was prepared by the OECD Secretariat, but its successful completion depended on personal or official contributions by many individuals in Member countries, and on the work and support of the OECD Working Group on Environmental Information and Outlooks. This report is published on the responsibility of the Secretary General of the OECD.

Joke Waller-Hunter
Director, OECD Environment Directorate

Data in this report largely come from "OECD Environmental Data - Compendium 1999". These data are harmonised through the work of the OECD Working Group on Environmental Information and Outlooks (WGEIO). Some were updated or revised on the basis of comments from national Delegates on "Key environmental indicators", as received by 30 March 2001.

In many countries, systematic collection of environmental data has a short history; sources are typically spread across a range of agencies and levels of government, and information is often collected for other purposes. When reading this report, one should therefore keep in mind that definitions and measurement methods vary among countries and that intercountry comparisons require great caution. One should also note that indicators presented in this report refer to the national level and may conceal major subnational differences.

TABLE OF CONTENTS

I. INTRODUCTION

THE OECD WORK ON ENVIRONMENTAL INDICATORS

PURPOSES

The OECD programme on environmental indicators has three major purposes:

- keeping track of environmental progress;
- ensuring that environmental concerns are taken into account when policies are formulated and implemented for various sectors, such as transport, energy and agriculture;
- ensuring similar integration of environmental concerns into economic policies, mainly through environmental accounting.

CONCRETE RESULTS[1]

The work on indicators is carried out in close co-operation with OECD Member countries. It has led to:

- agreement by OECD countries to use the pressure-state-response (PSR) model as a common harmonised framework;
- identification and definition of several sets of indicators based on their policy relevance, analytical soundness and measurability;
- measurement and publication of these indicators for a number of countries.

USES

The OECD's environmental indicators are regularly used in *environmental performance reviews*; they are a valuable way to monitor the integration of economic and environmental decision making, to analyse environmental policies and to gauge the results. Beyond their application in OECD environmental performance reviews, these indicators also contribute to follow-up work on the OECD environmental strategy and to the broader objective of *reporting on sustainable development*.

THE OECD SETS OF ENVIRONMENTAL INDICATORS

Work carried out to date includes three categories of indicators, each corresponding to a specific purpose and framework.

TRACKING PROGRESS: THE OECD CORE SET OF ENVIRONMENTAL INDICATORS	The OECD Core Set is a set commonly agreed upon by OECD countries for OECD use. It is published regularly. The Core Set, of about 50 indicators, covers issues that reflect the main environmental concerns in OECD countries. It incorporates major indicators derived from sectoral sets as well as from environmental accounting. Indicators are classified following the PSR model: • indicators of environmental pressures, both direct and indirect; • indicators of environmental conditions; • indicators of society's responses.
PROMOTING INTEGRATION: OECD SECTORAL INDICATORS	In addition, OECD sets of sectoral indicators focus on specific sectors. Indicators are classified following an adjusted PSR model: • sectoral trends of environmental significance, • their interactions with the environment (including positive and negative effects); • related economic and policy considerations.
PROMOTING INTEGRATION: ENVIRONMENTAL ACCOUNTING	Environmental indicators are also derived from the OECD work on environmental accounting focusing on i) physical natural resource accounts, related to sustainable management of natural resources, and ii) environmental expenditure. Examples of these indicators are the intensity of natural resource use and the level and structure of pollution abatement and control expenditure.

---

[1]. *For further details on the OECD framework for environmental indicators, see page 131.*

LINKS WITH NATIONAL AND OTHER INTERNATIONAL INITIATIVES

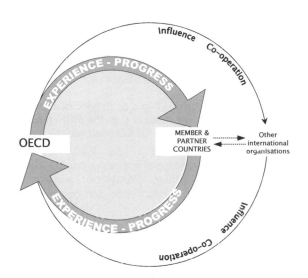

The development of environmental indicators has built on OECD experience in environmental information and reporting and has benefited from strong support from Member countries, and their representatives in the OECD Working Group on Environmental Information and Outlooks (formerly Working Group on the State of the Environment).

Results of OECD work, and in particular its conceptual framework, have in turn influenced similar activities by a number of countries and international organisations. Continued co-operation is taking place in particular with: UNSD, UNCSD and UN regional offices; UNEP; the World Bank, the European Union (Commission of the European Communities, Eurostat, EEA) and with a number of international institutes.

Co-operation is also taking place with non OECD countries, and in particular with Russia and China.

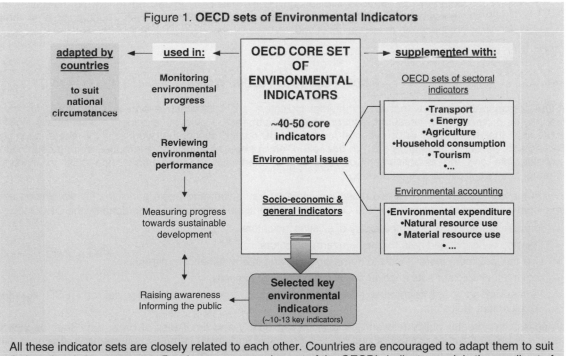

Figure 1. **OECD sets of Environmental Indicators**

All these indicator sets are closely related to each other. Countries are encouraged to adapt them to suit their national circumstances. One important new element of the OECD's indicator work is the small set of key indicators intended to raise public awareness and to focus attention on key issues of common concern.

THE 2001 PUBLICATION

CONTENT

The present publication is an update of the 1998 publication "Towards sustainable development – Environmental indicators". It presents major indicators from the <u>Core Set</u> (Part II) as well as selected <u>socio-economic and sectoral indicators</u> with environmental significance (Part III). It highlights links among environmental indicators, environmental performance and sustainable development.

Each section of indicators in Parts II and III includes:
- a brief statement on the issue referred to and its importance for environmental performance and sustainable development;
- an overview of related OECD work and references, including a schematic description of the conceptual framework in which the indicators are placed (i.e. the PSR model for OECD Core Set indicators and the adjusted PSR model for OECD sectoral indicators);
- a summary of major trends.

The publication further includes a small set of <u>key environmental indicators</u> published at the occasion of the OECD meeting of Environment Ministers (Paris, 16 May 2001) and endorsed by Ministers as a tool for use in OECD work and for public information and communication by OECD (Part IV).

INTERPRETATION

The indicators in this publication are those that are regularly used in the OECD's analytical work and for which data are available for a majority of OECD countries. They are of varying relevance for different countries and have to be interpreted in context.

DATA AND INDICATORS

The data used to calculate the indicators are based on those published in "OECD Environmental Data – Compendium 1999". They come from the OECD SIREN database, which is regularly updated with information from Member countries (through biennial data collection using the OECD/Eurostat questionnaires on the state of the environment and on pollution abatement and control expenditure), from internal OECD sources and from other international sources. No unique choice has been made as to the normalisation of the indicators; different denominators are used in parallel (e.g. GDP, number of inhabitants) to balance the message conveyed.

PROSPECTS AND FUTURE WORK

The OECD experience shows that environmental indicators are cost-effective and powerful tools for tracking environmental progress and measuring environmental performance. However, experience also shows significant lags between the demand for environmental indicators, the related conceptual work and the actual capacity for mobilising and validating underlying data. In the field of environmental statistics, differences among countries may be considerable and the establishment of reliable and internationally comparable data calls for continuous monitoring, analysis, treatment and checking.

Following the conceptual work that laid down the common framework and basic principles for developing sets of international environmental indicators in the OECD context, continued efforts are being done by the OECD to:
- Improve the quality and comparability of existing indicators.
- Develop concepts and data for medium term indicators.
- Link the indicators more closely to domestic goals and international commitments.
- Expand the indicator sets to cover social-environmental aspects.
- Further integrate environmental and sectoral indicator sets in the broader set of OECD sustainable development indicators.

This necessitates greater policy relevance and increased quality and timeliness of basic data sets, as well as a closer link between environmental data and existing economic and social information systems. It also necessitates more work to complement the indicators with information reflecting sub-national differences.

II. ENVIRONMENTAL INDICATORS

CLIMATE CHANGE

Industrialisation has increased emissions of greenhouses gases (GHG) from human activities, disturbing the radiative energy balance of the earth-atmosphere system. These gases exacerbate the natural greenhouse effect, leading to temperature changes and other potential consequences for the earth's climate. Land use changes and forestry also contribute to the greenhouse effect by altering carbon sinks. Climate change is of concern mainly as relates to its impact on ecosystems (biodiversity), human settlements and agriculture, and possible consequences for other socio-economic activities that could affect global economic output.

Climate change could have major or significant effects on sustainable development. Performance can be assessed against domestic objectives and international commitments. The main international agreement is the United Nations Framework Convention on Climate Change (FCCC) (Rio de Janeiro, 1992). The FCCC has been ratified by 186 parties. Industrialised countries, including those in transition to market economies, committed to taking measures aimed at stabilising GHG emissions by 2000 at 1990 levels. Its 1997 Kyoto Protocol establishes differentiated national or regional emission reduction or limitation targets for industrialised countries for 2008-12 and for the base year 1990. The targets are comprehensive, covering CO_2, CH_4, N_2O, PFCs, HFCs and SF_6. The main challenge is to stabilise GHG concentrations in the atmosphere at a level that would prevent dangerous anthropogenic interference with the climate system and to further de-couple GHG emissions from economic growth.

Indicators presented here relate to:

♦ *CO_2 emissions from energy use, showing total emissions as well as emission intensities per unit of GDP and per capita, and related changes since 1980. CO_2 from combustion of fossil fuels and biomass is a major contributor to the greenhouse effect and a key factor in countries' ability to deal with climate change. All emissions presented here are gross direct emissions, excluding sinks and indirect effects. In the absence of national inventories that provide a complete and consistent picture of all GHG emissions, energy-related CO_2 emissions are used to reflect overall trends in direct GHG emissions. Information on fossil fuel share and intensity is given to reflect, at least partly, changes in energy efficiency and energy mix, which are key in efforts to reduce atmospheric CO_2 emissions.*

♦ *atmospheric concentrations of the greenhouse gases covered by the FCCC (CO_2, CH_4, N_2O) and of selected ozone depleting substances controlled by the Montreal Protocol (page 19) that also play a role in the greenhouse effect (CFC-11, CFC-12, total gaseous chlorine). Data are from various monitoring sites that provide an indication of global concentrations and trends.*

These indicators should be read in conjunction with other indicators from the OECD Core Set and in particular with indicators on energy efficiency and on energy prices and taxes. Their interpretation should take into account the structure of countries' energy supply, the relative importance of fossil fuels and of renewable energy, as well as climatic factors.

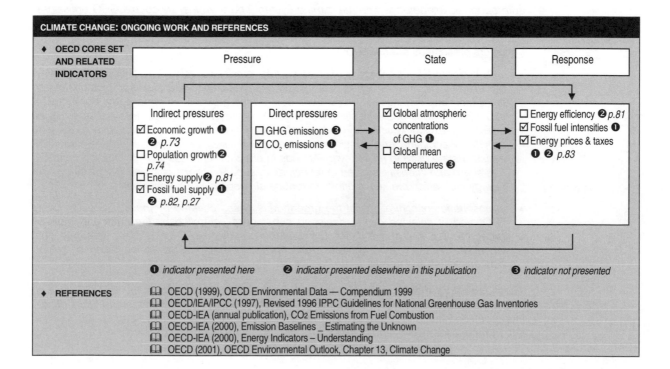

CLIMATE CHANGE: ONGOING WORK AND REFERENCES

♦ **OECD CORE SET AND RELATED INDICATORS**

Pressure	State	Response

Indirect pressures
- ☑ Economic growth ❶ ❷ *p.73*
- ☐ Population growth❷ *p.74*
- ☐ Energy supply❷ *p.81*
- ☑ Fossil fuel supply ❶ ❷ *p.82, p.27*

Direct pressures
- ☐ GHG emissions ❸
- ☑ CO₂ emissions ❶

State
- ☑ Global atmospheric concentrations of GHG ❶
- ☐ Global mean temperatures ❸

Response
- ☐ Energy efficiency ❷ *p.81*
- ☑ Fossil fuel intensities ❶
- ☑ Energy prices & taxes ❶ ❷ *p.83*

❶ *indicator presented here* ❷ *indicator presented elsewhere in this publication* ❸ *indicator not presented*

♦ **REFERENCES**
- 📖 OECD (1999), OECD Environmental Data — Compendium 1999
- 📖 OECD/IEA/IPCC (1997), Revised 1996 IPPC Guidelines for National Greenhouse Gas Inventories
- 📖 OECD-IEA (annual publication), CO₂ Emissions from Fuel Combustion
- 📖 OECD-IEA (2000), Emission Baselines _ Estimating the Unknown
- 📖 OECD-IEA (2000), Energy Indicators – Understanding
- 📖 OECD (2001), OECD Environmental Outlook, Chapter 13, Climate Change

CO₂ EMISSION INTENSITIES [1]

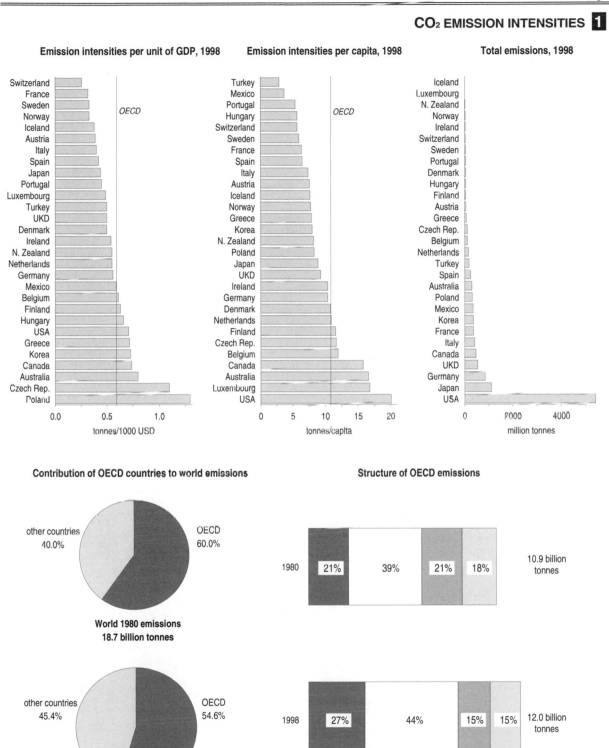

Emission intensities per unit of GDP, 1998

Switzerland
France
Sweden
Norway
Iceland
Austria
Italy
Spain
Japan
Portugal
Luxembourg
Turkey
UKD
Denmark
Ireland
N. Zealand
Netherlands
Germany
Mexico
Belgium
Finland
Hungary
USA
Greece
Korea
Canada
Australia
Czech Rep.
Poland

OECD

0.0   0.5   1.0

tonnes/1000 USD

Emission intensities per capita, 1998

Turkey
Mexico
Portugal
Hungary
Switzerland
Sweden
France
Spain
Italy
Austria
Iceland
Norway
Greece
Korea
N. Zealand
Poland
Japan
UKD
Ireland
Germany
Denmark
Netherlands
Finland
Czech Rep.
Belgium
Canada
Australia
Luxembourg
USA

OECD

0   5   10   15   20

tonnes/capita

Total emissions, 1998

Iceland
Luxembourg
N. Zealand
Norway
Ireland
Switzerland
Sweden
Portugal
Denmark
Hungary
Finland
Austria
Greece
Czech Rep.
Belgium
Netherlands
Turkey
Spain
Australia
Poland
Mexico
Korea
France
Italy
Canada
UKD
Germany
Japan
USA

0   2000   4000

million tonnes

Contribution of OECD countries to world emissions

other countries
40.0%

OECD
60.0%

**World 1980 emissions
18.7 billion tonnes**

other countries
45.4%

OECD
54.6%

**World 1998 emissions
22.7 billion tonnes**

Structure of OECD emissions

1980   21%   39%   21%   18%   10.9 billion tonnes

1998   27%   44%   15%   15%   12.0 billion tonnes

■ Transport sector   ▨ Industry
□ Energy transformation   ▫ Others

1 CO2 EMISSION INTENSITIES

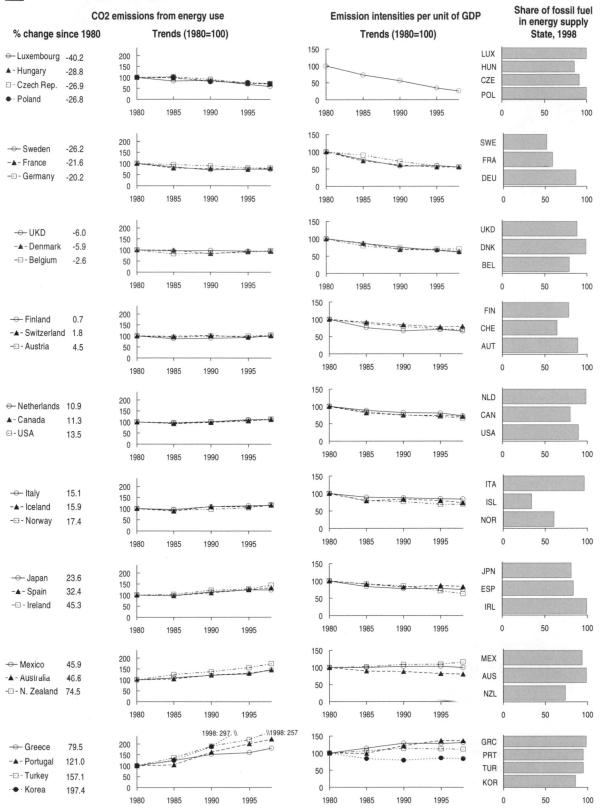

	CO2 emissions from energy use	Emission intensities per unit of GDP	Share of fossil fuel in energy supply
% change since 1980	**Trends (1980=100)**	**Trends (1980=100)**	**State, 1998**

Luxembourg -40.2
Hungary -28.8
Czech Rep. -26.9
Poland -26.8

Sweden -26.2
France -21.6
Germany -20.2

UKD -6.0
Denmark -5.9
Belgium -2.6

Finland 0.7
Switzerland 1.8
Austria 4.5

Netherlands 10.9
Canada 11.3
USA 13.5

Italy 15.1
Iceland 15.9
Norway 17.4

Japan 23.6
Spain 32.4
Ireland 45.3

Mexico 45.9
Australia 46.6
N. Zealand 74.5

Greece 79.5
Portugal 121.0
Turkey 157.1
Korea 197.4

1998: 297.
1998: 257

CO₂ EMISSION INTENSITIES **1**

	CO₂ emissions from energy use						Fossil fuel supply		Real end-use energy prices	GDP
	Total			Emission intensities			Share of total supply	Intensity		
				per unit of GDP		per capita		per unit of GDP		
	million tonnes 1998	% change since 1980	% change since 1990	t./1 000 USD 1998	% change since1980	tonnes/cap. 1998	% change since1980	% 1998	Toe/1 000 USD 1998	% change since 1980	% change since 1980
Canada	477	11	13	0.74	-29	15.8	-10	80	0.29	-10	57
Mexico ♦	356	46	20	0.59	0	3.7	6	94	0.23	229	46
USA	5410	14	12	0.71	-34	20.1	-4	90	0.26	-43	71
Japan	1128	24	8	0.44	-25	8.9	14	81	0.16	-49	65
Korea	370	197	59	0.73	-16	8.0	144	85	0.28	-22	254
Australia	311	47	20	0.80	-19	16.6	15	99	0.27	-3	82
New Zealand	31	75	27	0.55	16	8.2	47	74	0.23	-27	50
Austria	62	4	5	0.39	-30	7.6	-2	89	0.16	-36	49
Belgium	122	-3	15	0.61	-30	12.0	-6	79	0.23	-33	39
Czech Rep.	121	-27	-20	1.10	..	11.7	-27	91	0.34	35	..
Denmark	57	-6	12	0.50	-37	10.8	-9	99	0.18	-23	50
Finland	60	1	12	0.63	-34	11.6	-7	79	0.27	-25	53
France	376	-22	2	0.32	-44	6.4	-28	59	0.13	-26	41
Germany	857	-20	-11	0.56	-45	10.4	-24	87	0.19	-37	44
Greece	83	79	18	0.72	31	7.9	65	98	0.23	-34	37
Hungary	57	-29	-15	0.66	..	5.7	-25	86	0.25	-16	..
Iceland	2	16	5	0.38	-27	7.7	-3	34	0.16	..	58
Ireland	38	45	19	0.54	-37	10.4	33	99	0.19	-40	132
Italy	426	15	6	0.40	-16	7.4	13	96	0.15	-5	38
Luxembourg	7	-40	-31	0.40	-74	16.8	-49	100	0.19	-38	134
Netherlands	171	11	9	0.55	-27	10.9	0	99	0.23	-8	53
Norway	34	17	21	0.33	-31	7.8	9	60	0.15	12	70
Poland	320	-27	-8	1.30	..	8.3	-33	100	0.39	..	..
Portugal	54	121	36	0.45	37	5.4	117	95	0.17	-40	62
Spain	254	32	20	0.42	-17	6.5	26	84	0.16	-13	59
Sweden	54	-26	3	0.33	-45	6.0	-31	52	0.17	-13	33
Switzerland	41	2	-1	0.26	-20	5.7	-9	64	0.11	-54	27
Turkey	188	157	36	0.50	12	2.9	76	95	0.18	..	130
UKD	550	-6	-4	0.50	-39	9.3	-11	89	0.19	-29	53
OECD ♦	12017	11	9	0.59	-30	10.9	-3	86	0.22	-34	62
World	22726	22	7	..	..	3.8	-8	91	..	..	..

♦ *See Technical Annex for data sources, notes and comments.*

STATE AND TRENDS SUMMARY

CO₂ and other GHG emissions are still growing in many countries and overall. Since 1980, CO₂ emissions from energy use have grown more slowly in OECD countries as a group than they have worldwide. Individual OECD countries' contributions to the greenhouse effect, and rates of progress, however, vary significantly.

A number of OECD countries have de-coupled their CO₂ emissions from GDP growth through structural changes in industry and in energy supply and the gradual improvement of energy efficiency in production processes. Most countries, however, have not succeeded in meeting their own national commitments.

CO₂ emissions from energy use continue to grow, particularly in the OECD Asia-Pacific region and in North America. This can be partly attributed to energy production and consumption patterns and trends, often combined with overall low energy prices. In OECD Europe CO₂ emissions from energy use fell between 1980 and 1995, as a result of changes in economic structures and energy supply mix, energy savings and, in some countries, decreases in economic activity over a few years. Recently however, these emissions have started to increase again.

2 GREENHOUSE GAS CONCENTRATIONS

Gases controlled under the Framework Convention on Climate Change

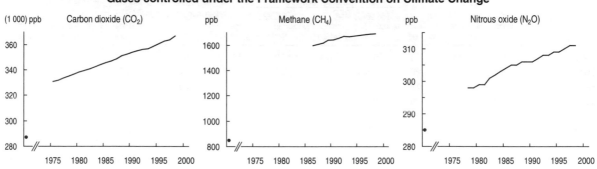

Gases controlled under the Montreal Protocol (subst. depleting the ozone layer)

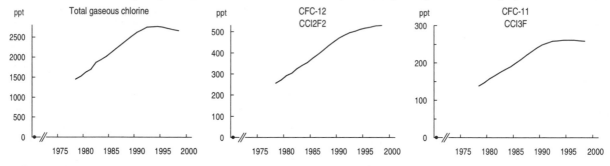

• - Preindustrial level

STATE AND TRENDS SUMMARY

Since the beginning of industrialisation, human activity has substantially raised atmospheric concentrations of GHG. Global CO_2 concentrations have increased along with world population. According to the IPCC (2001), global mean surface air temperature has increased by between 0.4 and 0.8 degree Celsius over the 20th century and is expected to rise 1.4° to 5.8°C by 2100 relative to 1990.

Trends also show large increases in concentrations of ozone depleting substances (ODS) in the atmosphere. A number of ODS play a role in the greenhouse effect. However, growth rates of CFC concentrations have decreased since 1989 as a result of the Montreal Protocol and its amendments. (see also page 19).

OZONE LAYER DEPLETION

The release into the atmosphere of certain man-made substances containing chlorine and bromine endangers the stratospheric ozone layer, which shields the earth's surface from ultraviolet radiation. The main ozone depleting substances (ODS) are CFCs, halons, methyl chloroform, carbon tetrachloride, HCFCs and methyl bromide. These are man-made chemicals which have been used in air conditioning and refrigeration equipment, aerosol sprays, foamed plastics, and fire extinguishers. They are also used as solvents and pesticides.

The depletion of the ozone layer could have major or significant effects on sustainable development. It remains a source of concern due to the impacts of increased UV-B radiation on human health, crop yields and the natural environment. Performance can be assessed against domestic objectives and international commitments. The major international agreements are the Convention for the Protection of the Ozone Layer (Vienna, 1985), the Montreal Protocol (1987) on substances that deplete the ozone layer and subsequent London (1990), Copenhagen (1992), Montreal (1997) and Beijing (1999) Amendments. The protocol and amendments set out timetables for phasing out ODS. The Montreal Protocol has been ratified by 175 parties, including all OECD countries. Countries are developing alternatives to or substitutes for ODS, recovering and recycling ODS and regulating the emissions of ODS. The main challenges are to phase out the supply of methyl bromide and HCFCs (by 2005 and 2020 respectively) in industrialised countries, and to reduce international movements of existing CFCs.

Indicators presented here relate to:

♦ *ozone depleting substances, i.e. the production and consumption of CFCs, halons and HCFCs, and the production of methyl bromide, as listed in the Montreal protocol. Basic data are weighted with the ozone depleting potentials (ODP) of the individual substances.*

♦ *stratospheric ozone levels expressed as the values of total ozone in a vertical atmospheric column over selected stations in OECD cities, presented with a zonal average (from 70N to 70S) taken from satellite data to put trends from individual stations in a global context.*

When interpreting these indicators it should be kept in mind that they do not reflect actual releases to the atmosphere and that individual substances vary considerably in their ozone-depleting capacity. These indicators should be read in connection with other indicators of the OECD Core Set and in particular with indicators on ground-level UV-B radiation.

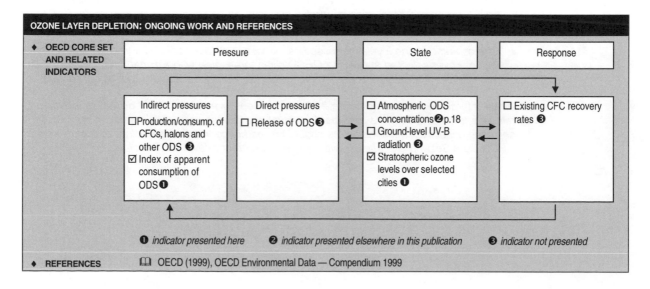

OZONE LAYER DEPLETION: ONGOING WORK AND REFERENCES

♦ **OECD CORE SET AND RELATED INDICATORS**

| Pressure | State | Response |

Indirect pressures
☐ Production/consump. of CFCs, halons and other ODS ❸
☑ Index of apparent consumption of ODS ❶

Direct pressures
☐ Release of ODS ❸

☐ Atmospheric ODS concentrations ❷ p.18
☐ Ground-level UV-B radiation ❸
☑ Stratospheric ozone levels over selected cities ❶

☐ Existing CFC recovery rates ❸

❶ *indicator presented here*   ❷ *indicator presented elsewhere in this publication*   ❸ *indicator not presented*

♦ **REFERENCES**   📖 OECD (1999), OECD Environmental Data — Compendium 1999

OZONE DEPLETING SUBSTANCES 3

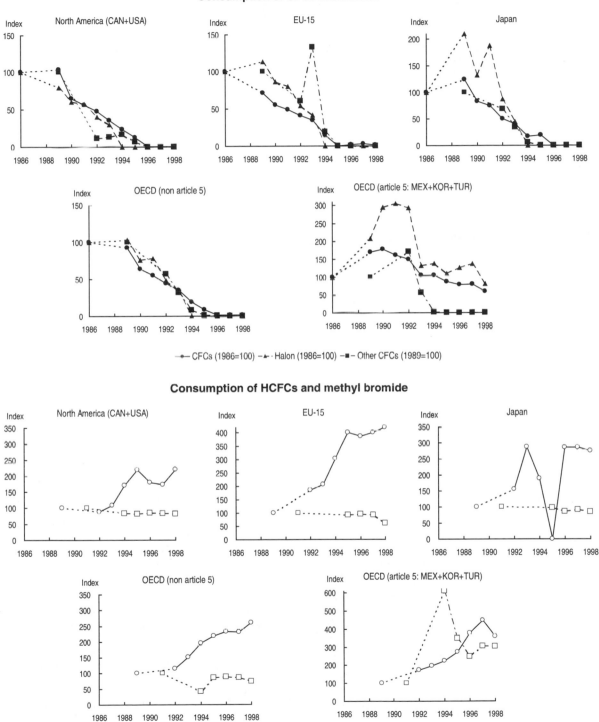

Consumption of CFCs and halons

North America (CAN+USA)

EU-15

Japan

OECD (non article 5)

OECD (article 5: MEX+KOR+TUR)

CFCs (1986=100) · Halon (1986=100) · Other CFCs (1989=100)

Consumption of HCFCs and methyl bromide

North America (CAN+USA)

EU-15

Japan

OECD (non article 5)

OECD (article 5: MEX+KOR+TUR)

HCFC (1989=100) · Methyl bromide (1991=100)

Article 5: Parties operating under article 5 of the Montreal Protocol entitling them to delay compliance with certain measures.

3 OZONE DEPLETING SUBSTANCES

	Production						Consumption						Consumption per capita		
	CFCs		Halons		HCFCs		CFCs		Halons		HCFCs		CFCs	HCFCs	Total
	ODP tonnes 1998	Change (%) 1986-98	ODP tonnes 1998	Change (%) 1986-98	ODP tonnes 1998	Change (%) 1989-98	ODP tonnes 1998	Change (%) 1986-98	ODP tonnes 1998	Change (%) 1986-98	ODP tonnes 1998	Change (%) 1989-98	1998 kg/cap.	1998 kg/cap.	1998 kg/cap.
Canada	-	-100	-	..	58	- 76	42	- 100	-	- 100	907	148	-	-	0.03
Mexico	5 252	-39	-	..	239	15	3 483	- 61	213	82	475	247	0.04	-	-
USA	243	-100	-	- 100	14 986	128	2 521	- 99	-	- 100	13 855	118	-	-	0.05
Japan	- 59	-100	-	- 100	3 995	144	- 208	- 100	-	- 100	4 008	175	-	-	0.03
Korea	5 528	293	2 162	..	550	323	5 299	- 38	2 162	- 26	754	238	0.11	0.05	0.02
Australia	-	-100	-	..	-	- 100	2	- 100	-	- 100	22	- 85	-	-	-
New Zealand	-	..	-	..	-	..	-	- 100	-	- 100	29	24	-	-	-
Austria	-	..	-	..	-	..	..	..	..	..	..	..	..	..	..
Belgium	-	..	-	..	-	..	-	..	-	..	-	..	-	-	-
Czech Rep.	6	-100	-	..	-	..	8	- 100	-	- 100	7	270	-	-	-
Denmark	-	..	-	..	-	..	-	..	-	..	-	..	-	-	-
Finland	-	..	-	..	-	..	..	..	..	..	..	..	..	..	..
France	- 131	-100	-	- 100	6 314	697	-	..	-	..	-	..	-	-	-
Germany	-	-100	-	- 100	682	33	-	..	-	..	-	..	-	-	-
Greece	765	-95	-	..	512	583	-	..	-	..	-	..	-	-	-
Hungary	-	..	-	..	-	..	1	- 100	-	- 100	90	..	-	-	-
Iceland	-	..	-	..	-	..	-	- 100	-	- 100	7	40	-	-	0.03
Ireland	-	..	-	..	-	..	-	..	-	..	-	..	-	-	-
Italy	7 578	-87	-	- 100	701	108	-	..	-	..	-	..	-	-	-
Luxembourg	-	..	-	..	-	..	-	..	-	..	-	..	-	-	-
Netherlands	15 049	-64	-	..	1 145	123	-	..	-	..	-	..	-	-	-
Norway	-	..	-	..	-	..	- 16	- 101	-	- 100	64	25	-	-	0.01
Poland	-	..	-	..	-	..	314	- 94	-	- 100	89	61	-	-	-
Portugal	-	..	-	..	-	..	-	..	-	..	-	..	-	-	-
Spain	5 570	-83	-	..	915	90	-	..	-	..	-	..	-	-	-
Sweden	-	..	-	..	-	..	..	..	-	..	-	..	..	..	..
Switzerland	-	..	-	..	-	..	- 28	- 100	-	- 100	31	72	-	-	-
Turkey	-	..	-	..	-	..	3 985	- 3	203	62	143	616	0.06	-	-
UK	3 316	-97	-	- 100	1 314	94	-	..	-	..	-	..	-	-	-
**OECD	32 337	-96	-	- 100	30 622	156	6 978	- 99	-	- 100	27 087	161	-	-	0.03

• *See Technical Annex for data sources, notes and comments.*

STATE AND TRENDS SUMMARY

As a result of the Montreal Protocol, industrialised countries have rapidly decreased their production and consumption of CFCs (CFC 11, 12, 113, 114, 115) and halons (halon 1211, 1301 and 2402). The targets set have been reached earlier than originally called for, and new and more stringent targets have been adopted. Many countries achieved zero level by 1994 for halons and by end of 1995 for CFCs, HBFCs, carbon tetrachloride and methyl chloroform. Since 1996, there has been no production or consumption (i.e. production + imports - exports) of these substances in industrialised countries except for certain essential uses, but there are still releases to the atmosphere. Efforts are being made to reduce international traffic (legal and illegal) in existing CFCs as well as intentional or accidental releases of existing CFCs. Imports and exports from non-Parties to the protocol are banned. Storage banks for existing halons and CFCs have been created in some countries. New measures have been adopted to phase out the supply of HCFCs and methyl bromide by 2020 and 2005 respectively in industrialised countries.

Global atmospheric concentrations of ODS show important changes. Growth rates of CFC concentrations have decreased since 1989, reflecting the impact of the Montreal Protocol and its amendments (page 18). Growth rates of HCFC concentrations are increasing. HCFCs have only 2 to 5% of the ozone depleting potential of CFCs, but under current international agreements they will not be phased out for at least 20 years and will remain in the stratosphere for a long time. Stratospheric ozone depletion remains a source of concern due to the long time lag between the release of ODS and their arrival in the stratosphere.

STRATOSPHERIC OZONE 4

Total column ozone* over selected cities

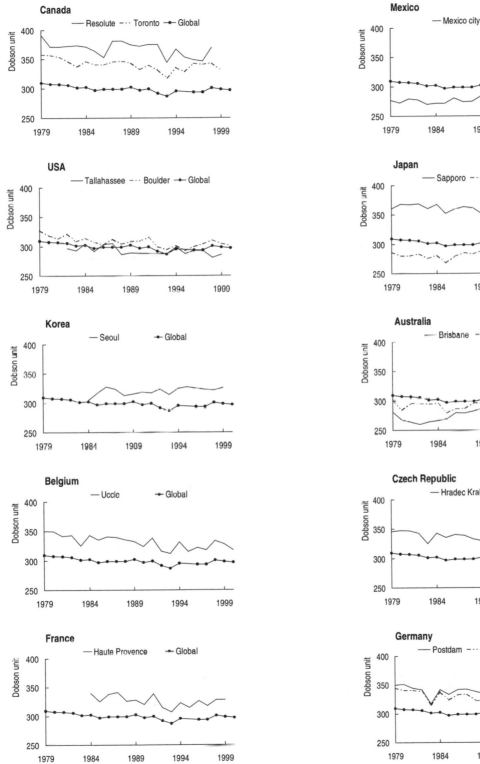

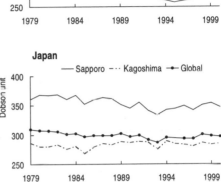

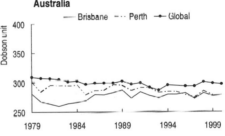

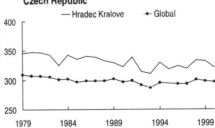

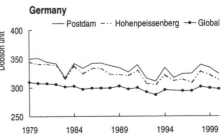

OECD Environmental Indicators 2001

4 STRATOSPHERIC OZONE

Total column ozone* over selected cities

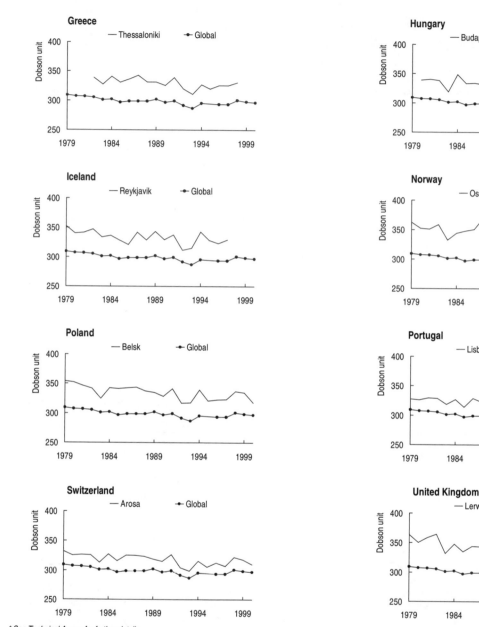

* See Technical Annex for further details.

STATE AND TRENDS
SUMMARY

Since 1979, the amount of stratospheric ozone over the entire globe has decreased. The eruption of Mount Pinatubo in June 1991 caused levels to sink to record lows in 1992 and 1993. Trends also show a decrease in ozone levels over a number of cities. These trends, however, need continued monitoring and careful interpretation, due to possible interference with ground-level ozone.

AIR QUALITY

Atmospheric pollutants from energy transformation and energy consumption, but also from industrial processes, are the main contributors to regional and local air pollution. Major concerns relate to their effects on human health and ecosystems. Human exposure is particularly high in urban areas where economic activities are concentrated. Causes of growing concern are concentrations of fine particulates, NO2, toxic air pollutants, and acute ground-level ozone pollution episodes in both urban and rural areas. Air pollution may also damage ecosystems, buildings and monuments, for example through acid precipitation and deposition.

Degraded air quality can result from and cause unsustainable development patterns. It can have substantial economic and social consequences, from medical costs and building restoration needs to reduced agricultural output, forest damage and a generally lower quality of life. Performance can be assessed against domestic objectives and international commitments. In Europe and North America, acidification has led to several international agreements. For example, under the Convention on Long-Range Transboundary Air Pollution (Geneva, 1979), protocols to reduce emissions of sulphur (Helsinki, 1985, Oslo, 1994, Gothenburg, 1999), nitrogen oxides (Sofia, 1988, Gothenburg, 1999) and VOCs (Geneva, 1991, Gothenburg, 1999) have been adopted. Two other protocols are aimed at reducing emissions of heavy metals (Aarhus 1998) and persistent organic pollutants (Aarhus 1998). The main challenges are to further reduce emissions of NOx and other local and regional air pollutants in order to achieve a strong de-coupling of emissions from GDP and to limit the exposure of the population to air pollution.

Indicators presented here relate to:

- *SOx and NOx emissions and changes in them over time, as well as emission intensities expressed as quantities emitted per unit of GDP and per capita, presented with related changes in economic growth and fossil fuel supply. These indicators should be supplemented with information on the acidity of rain and snow in selected regions, and the exceedance of critical loads in soils and waters which reflect the actual acidification of the environment.*

- *air quality expressed as trends in annual SO2 and NO2 concentrations for selected cities. In the longer term, indicators should focus on population exposure to air pollution. They should be complemented with information on ground-level ozone and on other air pollutants.*

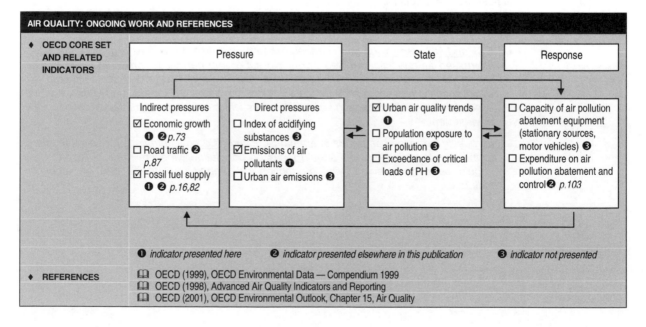

AIR QUALITY: ONGOING WORK AND REFERENCES

♦ OECD CORE SET AND RELATED INDICATORS

Pressure		State	Response

Indirect pressures
- ☑ Economic growth ❶ ❷*p.73*
- ☐ Road traffic ❷ *p.87*
- ☑ Fossil fuel supply ❶ ❷ *p.16,82*

Direct pressures
- ☐ Index of acidifying substances ❸
- ☑ Emissions of air pollutants ❶
- ☐ Urban air emissions ❸

- ☑ Urban air quality trends ❶
- ☐ Population exposure to air pollution ❸
- ☐ Exceedance of critical loads of PH ❸

- ☐ Capacity of air pollution abatement equipment (stationary sources, motor vehicles) ❸
- ☐ Expenditure on air pollution abatement and control ❷ *p.103*

❶ *indicator presented here*   ❷ *indicator presented elsewhere in this publication*   ❸ *indicator not presented*

♦ REFERENCES
- 📖 OECD (1999), OECD Environmental Data — Compendium 1999
- 📖 OECD (1998), Advanced Air Quality Indicators and Reporting
- 📖 OECD (2001), OECD Environmental Outlook, Chapter 15, Air Quality

AIR EMISSION INTENSITIES 5

Sulphur oxide (SOₓ) emissions

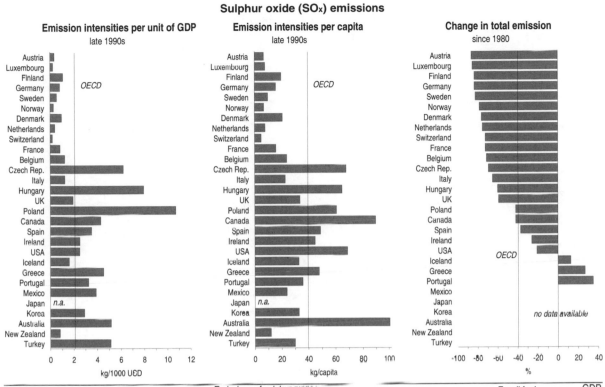

Emission intensities per unit of GDP
late 1990s

Emission intensities per capita
late 1990s

Change in total emission
since 1980

		Total		Emissions of sulphur oxides Intensities per unit of GDP		Intensities per capita		Fossil fuel supply	GDP
		1 000 t. late 1990s	% change since 1980	kg/1 000 USD late 1990s	% change since 1980	kg/cap. late 1990s	% change since 1980	% change since 1980	% change since 1980
Canada	♦	2691	-42	4.3	-62	90	-52	16	57
Mexico		2162	..	3.9	..	24	..	43	46
USA	♦	18481	-21	2.5	-52	69	-33	14	71
Japan		..	..	..	..	..	..	30	65
Korea	♦	1500	..	2.9	..	33	..	248	254
Australia	♦	1842	..	5.2	..	101	..	50	82
New Zealand	♦	46	..	0.8	..	12	..	91	50
Austria	♦	57	-86	0.4	-90	7	-87	20	49
Belgium		240	-71	1.3	-78	24	-72	7	39
Czech Rep.	♦	701	-69	6.2	..	68	-69	-20	..
Denmark	♦	109	-76	1.0	-84	21	-77	5	50
Finland	♦	100	-83	1.1	-88	20	-84	14	53
France	♦	947	-72	0.8	-79	16	-74	-8	41
Germany	♦	1292	-83	0.8	..	16	-84	-13	..
w. Germany		604	-81	0.5	-86	9	-82	..	40
Greece	♦	507	27	4.6	-4	48	16	69	37
Hungary	♦	657	-60	8.0	..	65	-58	-24	..
Iceland	♦	9	13	1.6	-29	33	-6	41	58
Ireland	♦	165	-26	2.5	-65	45	-31	56	132
Italy		1322	-65	1.3	-73	23	-65	20	38
Luxembourg		4	-85	0.2	-94	8	-87	-16	134
Netherlands	♦	125	-75	0.4	-83	8	-77	13	53
Norway		30	-78	0.3	-87	7	-79	30	70
Poland		2368	-42	10.8	..	61	-47	-22	..
Portugal		359	35	3.3	-7	36	34	119	62
Spain		1927	-37	3.5	-56	49	-40	45	59
Sweden	♦	91	-82	0.6	-86	10	-83	-5	33
Switzerland		33	-72	0.2	-77	5	-75	16	27
Turkey	♦	1900	..	5.2	..	30	..	126	130
UK	♦	2028	-59	2.0	71	34	-60	7	53
OECD	♦	42498	-40	2.1	-59	39	-47	16	62

♦ *See Technical Annex for data sources, notes and comments.*

OECD Environmental Indicators 2001

5 AIR EMISSION INTENSITIES

Trends in SOx emissions, Index 1980 = 100

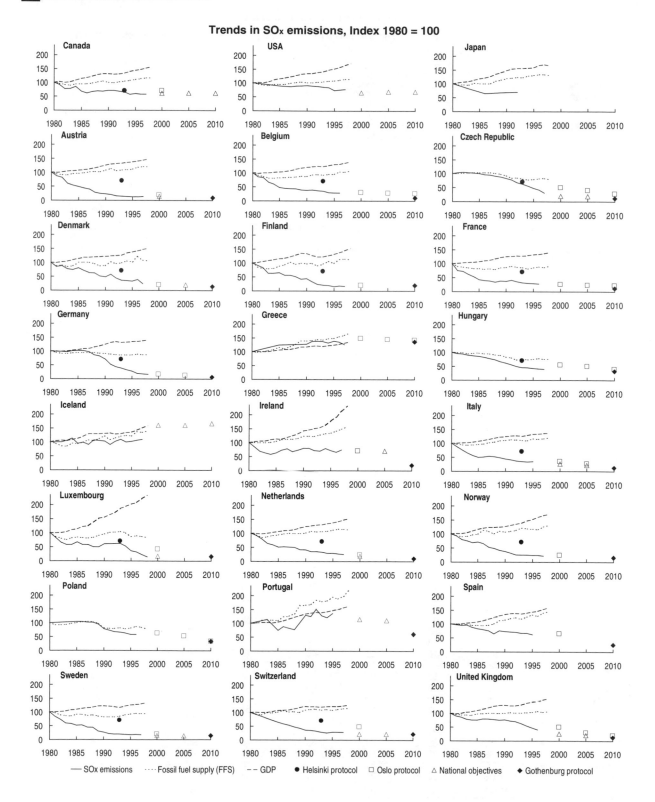

— SOx emissions   ···· Fossil fuel supply (FFS)   – – GDP   ● Helsinki protocol   □ Oslo protocol   △ National objectives   ◆ Gothenburg protocol

AIR EMISSION INTENSITIES 5

Nitrogen oxide (NOx) emissions

Emission intensities per unit of GDP
late 1990s

Emission intensities per capita
late 1990s

Change in total emission
since 1980

	Emissions of nitrogen oxides							Fossil fuel supply	GDP
	Total			Intensities per unit of GDP		Intensities per capita			
	1 000 t. late 1990s	% change since 1980	% change since 1987	kg/1 000 USD late 1990s	% change since 1980	kg/cap. late 1990s	% change since 1980	% change since 1980	% change since 1980
Canada	2011	3	-5	3.4	-30	68	-15	16	57
Mexico	1526	..	..	2.8	..	17	..	43	46
USA	21394	-5	4	2.9	-42	80	-19	14	71
Japan	..	..	..	..	..	..	..	30	65
Korea ♦	1258	..	50	2.5	..	28	..	248	254
Australia ♦	2166	..	..	6.1	..	118	..	50	82
New Zealand	173	..	..	3.1	..	46	..	91	50
Austria ♦	172	-26	-19	1.1	-48	21	-30	20	49
Belgium	334	-24	-1	1.8	-42	33	-27	7	39
Czech Rep.	423	-55	-48	3.8	..	41	-55	-20	..
Denmark ♦	248	-9	-21	2.2	-38	47	-12	5	50
Finland ♦	260	-12	-10	2.9	-39	51	-18	14	53
France ♦	1698	3	21	1.5	-23	29	-5	-8	41
Germany	1780	-47	-46	1.2	..	22	-49	-13	..
w. Germany	1606	-39	-37	1.2	-53	24	-43	..	40
Greece	369	70	..	3.3	29	35	56	69	37
Hungary	197	-28	-25	2.4	..	19	-24	-24	..
Iceland ♦	28	30	15	5.2	-14	102	9	41	58
Ireland ♦	124	50	8	1.9	-30	34	39	56	132
Italy	1768	8	-2	1.7	-19	31	6	20	38
Luxembourg	17	-27	..	1.2	-67	40	-36	-16	134
Netherlands ♦	445	-24	-26	1.5	-48	28	-31	13	53
Norway	222	18	-1	2.2	-29	51	10	30	70
Poland	1154	-6	-25	5.2	..	30	-13	-22	..
Portugal ♦	373	126	..	3.4	55	38	124	119	62
Spain	1243	18	21	2.3	-18	32	12	45	59
Sweden ♦	337	-25	-23	2.1	-42	38	-29	-5	33
Switzerland	129	-24	-26	0.8	-39	18	-32	16	27
Turkey ♦	925	156	62	2.5	14	15	78	126	130
UK	2060	-16	-20	2.0	-42	05	-20	7	53
OECD ♦	44400	-4	-2	2.2	-41	41	-16	16	62

♦ *See Technical Annex for data sources, notes and comments.*

5 AIR EMISSION INTENSITIES

Trends in NOx emissions, Index 1980 = 100

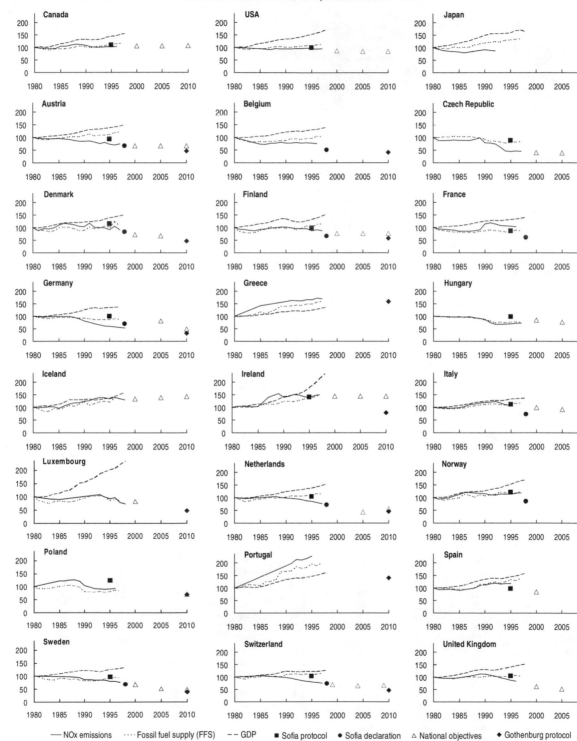

— NOx emissions   ···· Fossil fuel supply (FFS)   – – GDP   ■ Sofia protocol   ● Sofia declaration   △ National objectives   ◆ Gothenburg protocol

AIR EMISSION INTENSITIES 5

STATE AND TRENDS
SUMMARY

SOX EMISSIONS

SO_x emission intensities per capita and per unit of GDP show significant variations among OECD countries. A strong de-coupling of emissions from GDP is seen in many countries. European countries' early commitments to reduce SO_x emissions have been achieved, and new agreements have been adopted in Europe and North America to reduce acid precipitation even further (Gothenburg Protocol).

Emissions have decreased significantly for the OECD as a whole, compared to 1980 levels, as a combined result of:

- structural changes in the economy;
- changes in energy demand through energy savings and fuel substitution;
- pollution control policies and technical progress, including countries' efforts to control large stationary emission sources.

NOX EMISSIONS

NO_x emissions have decreased in the OECD overall compared to 1980, but less than SO_x emissions. Major progress in the early 1990s, particularly in OECD Europe, reflects changes in energy demand, pollution control policies and technical progress. However, these results have not compensated in all countries for steady growth in road traffic, fossil fuel use and other activities generating NO_x. In some European countries the commitment to stabilise NO_x emissions by the end of 1994 to their 1987 levels (Sofia Protocol) has not been met.

Emission intensities per capita and per unit of GDP show significant variations among OECD countries, and a weak de-coupling of emissions from GDP in a number of countries.

6 URBAN AIR QUALITY

Trends in SO₂ concentrations in selected cities, Index 1990 = 100

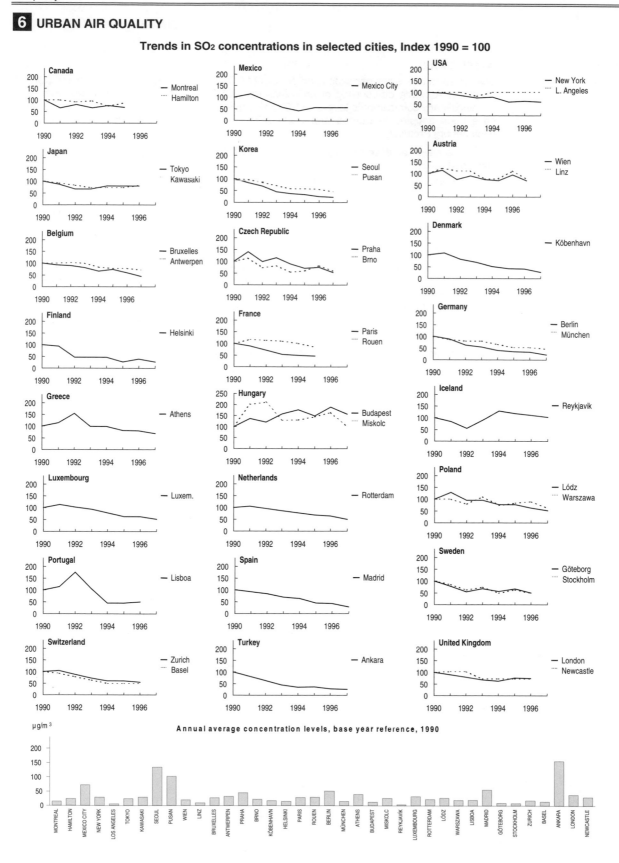

Annual average concentration levels, base year reference, 1990

URBAN AIR QUALITY 6

Trends in NO₂ concentrations in selected cities, Index 1990 = 100

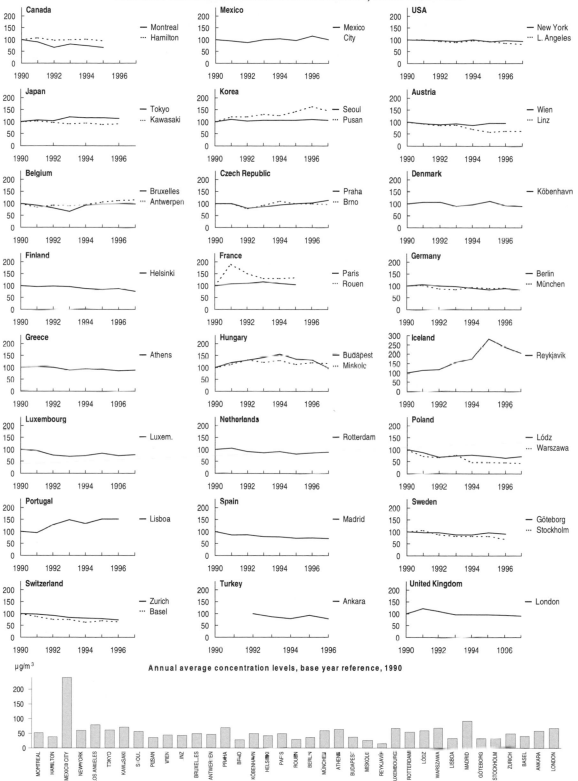

µg/m³ **Annual average concentration levels, base year reference, 1990**

6 URBAN AIR QUALITY

			Annual concentrations of sulphur dioxide						Annual concentrations of nitrogen dioxide					
			base reference ($\mu g/m^3$)	(Index 1990 = 100)					base reference ($\mu g/m^3$)	(Index 1990 = 100)				
			1990	1992	1994	1995	1996	1997	1990	1992	1994	1995	1996	1997
Canada	Montreal	◆	15.0	80	75	67	..	..	52.0	67	74	67	..	..
	Hamilton	◆	24.0	92	73	88	..	..	38.0	97	103	95	..	..
Mexico	Mexico City		71.8	86	43	57	57	57	239.9	88	104	96	115	100
USA	New York		29.0	86	79	59	62	59	60.0	97	100	92	97	93
	Los Angeles		6.0	100	100	100	100	100	79.0	94	96	94	86	81
Japan	Tokyo	◆	24.0	67	79	79	79	..	61.0	103	116	116	113	..
	Kawasaki	◆	29.0	83	72	72	83	..	71.0	97	94	89	92	..
Korea	Seoul		133.5	69	37	33	25	22	56.4	103	107	107	110	107
	Pusan		102.1	85	59	59	56	46	35.7	121	126	142	163	148
Austria	Wien		20.0	75	75	70	95	70	44.0	89	86	95	95	..
	Linz		9.0	111	78	78	111	78	43.0	86	70	58	63	63
Belgium	Bruxelles		27.0	89	67	74	59	44	49.0	82	94	98	100	98
	Antwerpen		32.0	103	84	78	78	72	46.0	93	96	107	113	115
Czech Rep.	Praha		45.0	98	89	71	76	53	69.0	81	94	100	103	114
	Brno		22.0	73	55	59	82	59	28.0	79	111	100	100	96
Denmark	Köbenhavn		17.2	81	51	42	41	27	48.6	107	97	111	93	88
Finland	Helsinki	◆	15.0	47	47	27	40	27	42.0	98	88	83	88	76
France	Paris	◆	28.0	71	50	46	..	..	49.0	110	110	104	..	..
	Rouen		29.0	114	100	86	..	..	29.0	152	131	134	..	..
Germany	Berlin		51.0	63	41	35	33	22	36.0	100	92	83	89	83
	München		15.0	80	67	53	53	47	59.0	88	95	90	92	81
Greece	Athens		39.4	154	99	81	81	69	63.2	100	94	92	86	89
Hungary	Budapest		12.8	120	177	149	189	156	36.8	130	156	135	131	98
	Miskolc		25.9	210	131	145	164	98	25.6	133	130	113	121	118
Iceland	Reykjavík	◆	3.8	55	129	118	111	103	14.8	118	174	281	236	206
Luxembourg	Luxembourg	◆	32.0	103	78	63	63	52	67.0	76	73	84	73	78
Netherlands	Rotterdam	◆	22.0	95	77	68	64	50	54.0	91	91	81	85	89
Poland	Lódz		27.0	96	78	78	63	52	59.0	69	78	73	64	71
	Warszawa		19.0	79	74	84	89	63	68.0	68	47	47	46	44
Portugal	Lisboa	◆	20.0	175	45	45	50	..	33.0	127	133	152	152	..
Spain	Madrid	◆	56.0	84	64	46	43	29	92.0	87	78	72	74	72
Sweden	Göteborg	◆	9.0	55	56	67	50	..	33.0	97	88	97	91	..
	Stockholm	◆	8.0	63	50	63	50	..	33.0	88	82	82	70	..
Switzerland	Zurich		18.1	88	61	61	55	..	49.0	92	82	80	73	..
	Basel		14.1	78	50	50	50	..	41.0	76	63	71	66	..
Turkey	Ankara		156.0	..	35	37	29	27	58.0	..	86	79	93	78
UK	London	◆	38.0	79	63	76	74	..	67.0	110	97	97	94	91
	Newcastle	◆	30.0	103	73	73	73	..	..	..	..	..	..	..

◆ *See Technical Annex for data sources, notes and comments.*

STATE AND TRENDS SUMMARY

Urban air quality has slowly continued to improve, particularly with respect to SO_2 concentrations; but ground-level ozone, NO_2 concentrations, toxic air pollutants and related health effects raise growing concern, largely due to the concentration of pollution sources in urban areas and to the increasing use of private vehicles for urban trips

WASTE

Waste is generated at all stages of human activities. Its composition and amounts depend largely on consumption and production patterns. Main concerns relate to the potential impact from inappropriate waste management on human health and the environment (soil and water contamination, air quality, land use and landscape). Despite achievements in waste recycling, amounts of solid waste going to final disposal are on the increase as are overall trends in waste generation. This raises important questions as to the capacities of existing facilities for final treatment and disposal and as to the location and social acceptance of new facilities (e.g. NIMBY for controlled landfill and incineration plants). Hazardous waste, mainly from industry, is of particular concern since it entails serious environmental risks if badly managed. Also, long-term policies are needed for the disposal of high-level radioactive waste.

Waste management issues are at environmental centre stage in many countries. Responses have been directed mainly towards collection, treatment and disposal. Increasingly, waste minimisation is an aim of <u>sustainable development strategies</u>. This can be achieved through waste prevention, reuse, recycling and recovery. More broadly it is necessary to better integrate environmental concerns into consumption and production patterns. <u>Performance</u> can be accessed against domestic objectives and international commitments. Agreements and regulations on waste in general and transfrontier movements of hazardous waste in particular include directives of the European Union, OECD Decisions and Recommendations, the Lomé IV Convention and the 1989 Basel Convention. The main <u>challenge</u> is to strengthen measures for waste minimisation, especially for waste prevention and recycling, and to move further towards life cycle management of products and extended producer responsibility.

<u>Indicators</u> presented here relate to:

- *<u>waste generation</u>, i.e.:*

  - *total amounts of waste by principal source sector (municipal, industrial and nuclear waste), as well as <u>generation intensities</u> expressed per capita and per unit of GDP. Treatment and disposal shares of municipal waste are shown as complementary information;*

  - *<u>hazardous waste</u> produced per unit of GDP (hazardous waste generation is largely driven by production patterns). This indicator does not reflect toxicity levels or other risks posed by such waste, nor its real impact on the environment. Transfrontier movements are shown as complementary information.*

  Indicators of waste generation intensity are first approximations of potential environmental pressure; more information is needed to describe the actual pressure.

- *<u>waste recycling</u> rates for paper and glass. They present total amounts recycled as percentage of the apparent consumption of the respective material.*

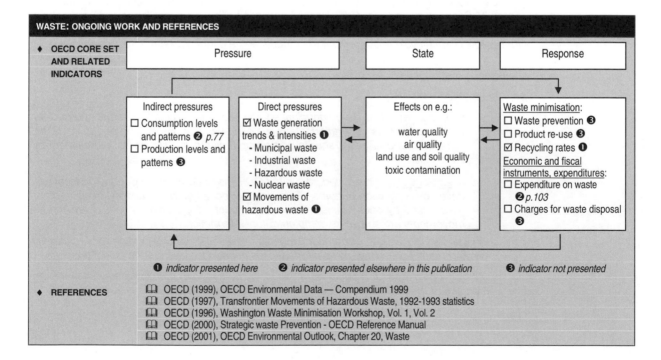

WASTE: ONGOING WORK AND REFERENCES

♦ OECD CORE SET AND RELATED INDICATORS	Pressure	State	Response

Indirect pressures
☐ Consumption levels and patterns ❷ *p.77*
☐ Production levels and patterns ❸

Direct pressures
☑ Waste generation trends & intensities ❶
  - Municipal waste
  - Industrial waste
  - Hazardous waste
  - Nuclear waste
☑ Movements of hazardous waste ❶

Effects on e.g.:

water quality
air quality
land use and soil quality
toxic contamination

Waste minimisation:
☐ Waste prevention ❸
☐ Product re-use ❸
☑ Recycling rates ❶
Economic and fiscal instruments, expenditures:
☐ Expenditure on waste ❷ *p.103*
☐ Charges for waste disposal ❸

❶ *indicator presented here*   ❷ *indicator presented elsewhere in this publication*   ❸ *indicator not presented*

♦ **REFERENCES**
  📖 OECD (1999), OECD Environmental Data — Compendium 1999
  📖 OECD (1997), Transfrontier Movements of Hazardous Waste, 1992-1993 statistics
  📖 OECD (1996), Washington Waste Minimisation Workshop, Vol. 1, Vol. 2
  📖 OECD (2000), Strategic waste Prevention - OECD Reference Manual
  📖 OECD (2001), OECD Environmental Outlook, Chapter 20, Waste

Municipal waste, state

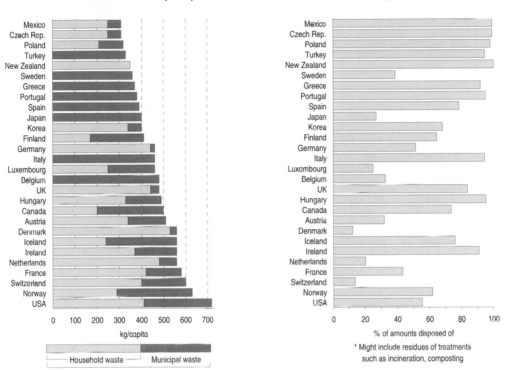

Generation intensities per capita

Landfill disposal shares *

kg/capita

% of amounts disposed of

* Might include residues of treatments
such as incineration, composting

Household waste — Municipal waste

Industrial, nuclear and hazardous waste, state

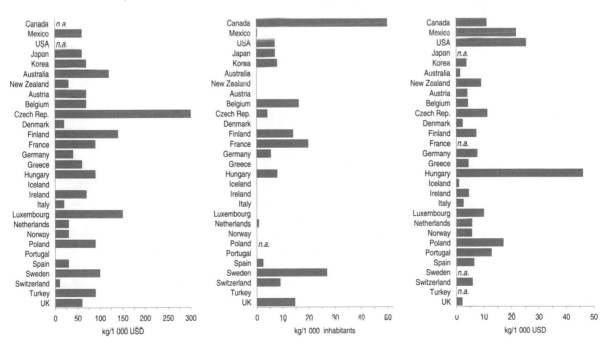

Industrial waste per unit of GDP

Nuclear waste per capita

Hazardous waste per unit of GDP

kg/1 000 USD

kg/1 000 inhabitants

kg/1 000 USD

OECD Environmental Indicators 2001

7 WASTE GENERATION

Municipal waste

	Municipal waste generated per capita		of which: Household waste	Private final consumption expenditure, per capita		Management of municipal waste % of amounts disposed of		
	kg/cap. late 1990s	% change since 1980	kg/cap. late 1990s	1 000 USD/cap. 1997	% change since 1980	Recycling/ compost. late 1990s	Incineration late 1990s	Landfill late 1990s
Canada	500	..	200	11.5	25.1	22	4	74
Mexico	310	..	250	3.8	-0.7	1	-	99
USA	720	20	410	18.1	44.8	27	17	55
Japan	400	5	..	11.3	52.2	4	69	27
Korea	400	..	340	6.2	179.1	26	5	68
Australia	..	..	..	10.9	34.7	..	..	..
New Zealand	..	..	350	9.0	20.7	..	..	100
Austria	510	*55*	340	10.8	37.7	45	16	32
Belgium	480	55	..	10.1	27.4	43	25	32
Czech Rep.	310	..	250	4.9	..	-	-	99
Denmark	560	40	530	9.7	31.4	29	58	12
Finland	410	..	170	8.0	34.0	33	2	65
France	580	*13*	420	10.0	15.2	9	47	43
Germany	460	..	440	10.7	*29.5*	29	17	51
Greece	370	42	..	7.7	36.2	8	..	92
Hungary	490	113	330	4.0	..	-	5	95
Iceland	560	..	240	10.7	25.2	10	11	76
Ireland	560	195	370	9.5	49.8	9	..	91
Italy	460	84	..	10.8	38.9	..	6	94
Luxembourg	460	31	250	16.6	44.9	49	26	25
Netherlands	560	12	480	9.5	25.0	41	31	20
Norway	630	15	290	10.0	6.5	25	13	62
Poland	320	14	210	3.5	..	2	-	98
Portugal	380	90	..	7.4	53.6	5	-	95
Spain	390	44	..	8.3	35.0	17	5	79
Sweden	360	..	..	8.5	9.7	19	42	39
Switzerland	600	36	400	12.4	9.2	40	46	14
Turkey	330	22	..	3.7	26.7	1	..	95
UK	480	..	440	11.6	53.7	7	8	84
* **OECD	500	22	..	11.3	37.1	..	..	..

♦ *See Technical Annex for data sources, notes and comments.*

STATE AND TRENDS SUMMARY

Although municipal waste is only one part of total waste generated, its management and treatment represents more than one third of the public sector's financial efforts to abate and control pollution. The quantity of municipal waste generated in the OECD area has steadily increased since 1980 and reached 540 million tonnes in the late 1990s (500 kg per inhabitant). Generation intensity per capita has risen mostly in line with private final consumption expenditure and GDP, although a slight slowdown has been seen in recent years.

The amount and composition of municipal waste vary widely among OECD countries, being related to levels and patterns of consumption and also depending on national waste management and minimisation practices. In most countries for which data are available, increased affluence, associated with economic growth and changes in consumption patterns, tends to generate higher rates of waste per capita than 20 years ago.

In a number of OECD countries, incineration and recycling are increasingly used to reduce amounts of waste going to final disposal, and particularly to landfill. Landfill nonetheless remains the major disposal method in most OECD countries.

WASTE GENERATION 7

Industrial, nuclear and hazardous waste

| | | Industrial waste | | Nuclear waste | | Hazardous waste | | | | |
| | | Waste from manuf. industry, late 1990s | | Spent fuel arisings, 1998 | | Production | | | Net transfrontier movements | Amounts to be managed |
		Total 1 000 tonnes	per unit of GDP kg/ 1 000 USD	Total tonnes HM	per capita kg/ 1 000 inh.	Year	Total 1 000 tonnes	per unit of GDP kg/ 1 000 USD	Exports-Imports 1 000 tonnes	1 000 tonnes
Canada		..	..	1515	50.0	1991	5 896	11.1	87.9	5 808
Mexico	♦	29570	60	22	0.2	1997	12 700	21.9	- 213.8	12 914
USA	♦	..	..	1900	7.1	1995	172 732	25.5	..	211 075
Japan	♦	139030	60	897	7.1	1995	..	..	2.0	..
Korea	♦	36540	70	370	8.0	1996	1 912	3.7	-	1 912
Australia	♦	37040	120	-	-	1992	426	1.4	3.0	423
New Zealand	♦	1760	30	-	-	1995	479	9.0	- 0.3	479
Austria	♦	10470	70	-	-	1996	606	4.1	19.5	586
Belgium	♦	13730	70	165	16.2	1994	776	4.3	- 317.0	1 093
Czech Rep.	♦	38570	340	43	4.2	1996	1 265	11.3	0.4	1 265
Denmark	♦	2740	20	-	-	1997	254	2.3	59.0	195
Finland	♦	11400	140	72	14.0	1992	559	7.3	16.6	542
France	♦	101000	90	1165	19.8	1995	..	..	- 430.0	..
Germany	♦	63090	40	450	5.5	1993	10 780	7.6	523.0	10 168
Greece	♦	6680	60	-	-	1992	450	4.4	0.1	450
Hungary	♦	6690	90	80	7.9	1994	3 537	46.2	9.6	3 527
Iceland	♦	10	-	-	-	1995	5	1.0	1.0	4
Ireland	♦	3780	70	-	-	1995	248	4.5	16.4	231
Italy	♦	22210	20	-	-	1995	2 708	2.6	..	..
Luxembourg	♦	1440	150	-	-	1997	139	10.0	138.8	-
Netherlands	♦	8810	30	12	0.8	1993	1 520	5.7	- 73.5	1 593
Norway	♦	2880	30	-	-	1994	500	5.6	28.4	472
Poland	♦	22200	90	..	..	1997	4 007	17.0	..	..
Portugal		420	-	-	-	1994	1 365	12.8	- 2.5	1 368
Spain	♦	13830	30	97	2.5	1994	3 394	6.4	- 48.0	3 442
Sweden	♦	13970	100	238	26.9	1995	..	..	- 84.4	..
Switzerland	♦	1500	10	64	9.0	1996	888	5.9	124.0	764
Turkey	♦	28110	90	-	-	..	..	..	..	..
UK	♦	56000	60	865	14.6	93/94	2 077	2.1	- 66.5	1 957
OECD	♦	1496000	80	7955	7.5	..	..	..	..	..

♦ *See Technical Annex for data sources, notes and comments.*

STATE AND TRENDS SUMMARY

Industry has been generating increasing amounts of waste in recent decades. Changes in production patterns and related technologies, and in waste management practices, have altered the composition of such waste.

Generation intensities per unit of GDP reflect wide variations among OECD countries, in particular for hazardous waste.

Nuclear waste is directly related to the share of nuclear power in national energy supply and the types of nuclear technology adopted.

8 WASTE RECYCLING

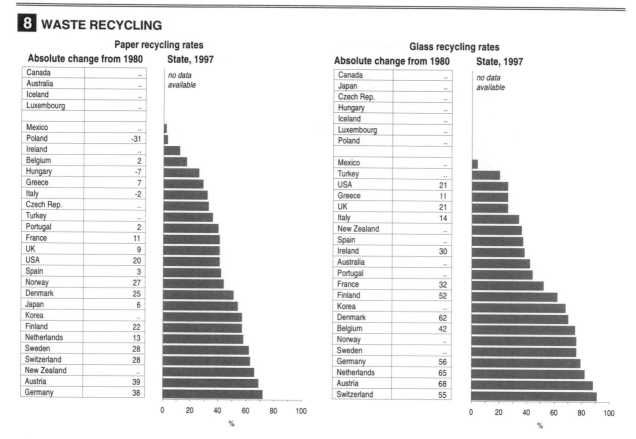

Paper recycling rates — Absolute change from 1980 / State, 1997

Glass recycling rates — Absolute change from 1980 / State, 1997

	Paper and cardboard						Glass				
	Recycling rate, %				Absolute change		Recycling rate, %				Absolute change
	1980	1985	1990	1997	since 1980		1980	1985	1990	1997	since 1980
Canada	20	23	28	..	..	♦	12	12	..	..	..
Mexico ♦	..	..	2	2	..	♦	..	..	4	4	..
USA ♦	21	21	28	41	20	♦	5	8	20	26	21
Japan	48	50	50	54	6	♦	35	47	48	..	..
Korea	..	..	44	57	..		..	..	46	68	..
Australia ♦	..	36	51	..	..		..	..	..	42	..
New Zealand	..	..	..	66	..	♦	..	..	..	36	..
Austria	30	37	52	69	39		20	38	60	88	68
Belgium ♦	15	14	13	17	2		33	42	55	75	42
Czech Rep.	..	..	..	33	..		..	..	..	..	..
Denmark	26	31	35	51	25		8	19	35	70	62
Finland	35	39	43	57	22		10	21	36	62	52
France	30	35	34	41	11	♦	20	26	41	52	32
Germany ♦	34	43	44	72	38	♦	23	43	54	79	56
Greece	22	25	28	29	7		15	15	15	26	11
Hungary	33	42	53	26	-7		..	..	..	..	..
Iceland	..	..	10	..	..		..	..	70	..	..
Ireland	..	10	10	12	..		8	7	23	38	30
Italy	34	25	27	32	-2		20	25	53	34	14
Luxembourg	..	..	..	..	..		..	..	..	..	..
Netherlands	46	50	50	58	13	♦	17	49	67	82	65
Norway	17	16	20	44	27	♦	..	..	22	76	..
Poland	34	34	46	3	-31		..	..	..	..	..
Portugal	38	37	40	40	2		..	10	27	44	..
Spain	39	44	39	42	3		..	26	27	37	..
Sweden	34	..	46	62	28		..	20	44	76	..
Switzerland	35	39	49	63	28		36	46	65	91	55
Turkey ♦	..	..	27	36	..		..	33	31	20	..
UK	32	28	33	41	9	♦	5	12	21	26	21

♦ See Technical Annex for data sources, notes and comments.

STATE AND TRENDS
SUMMARY

Recycling of glass and paper is increasing in most OECD countries as a result of evolving consumption patterns and waste management and minimisation practices.

WATER QUALITY

Water quality, closely linked to water quantity, is of <u>economic, environmental and social importance</u>. It has many aspects (physical, chemical, microbial, biological), and can be defined in terms of a water body's suitability for various uses, such as public water supply, swimming or protection of aquatic life. It is affected by water abstractions, by pollution loads from human activities (agriculture, industry, households), and by climate and weather. Pollution loads from diffuse agricultural sources are an issue in many countries, as is the supply of permanently safe drinking water to the entire population

If pressure from human activities becomes so intense that water quality is impaired to the point that drinking water requires ever more advanced and costly treatment or that aquatic plant and animal species in rivers and lakes are greatly reduced, then the <u>sustainability</u> of water resource use is in question. <u>Performance</u> can be assessed against domestic objectives and international commitments. At national level, countries have set receiving water standards, effluent limits and pollution load reduction targets for a range of parameters (e.g. oxygen, nutrients, micropollutants). In many cases, they are also committed to international agreements such as the OSPAR Convention on the Protection of the North-East Atlantic Marine Environment, the International Joint Commission Agreement on Great Lakes Water Quality in North America or the EU water directives. Protection of freshwater quality and supply is an important part of Agenda 21, adopted at UNCED (Rio de Janeiro, 1992). The main <u>challenge</u> is to protect and restore all bodies of surface and ground water to ensure the achievement of water quality objectives, and to apply an integrated management of water resources based on the ecosystem approach.

<u>Indicators</u> presented here relate to:

- ♦ *<u>river water quality</u>, presenting two parameters (oxygen and nitrate content) for selected rivers. Data are shown for representative sites at the mouth or downstream frontier, giving a summary view of the pollution load and clean-up efforts on the upstream watershed.*

- ♦ *<u>waste water treatment</u>, particularly sewage treatment connection rates, i.e. the percentage of the national resident population actually connected to public waste water treatment plants in the late 1990s. The extent of secondary and/or tertiary (chemical and/or biological) sewage treatment provides an indication of efforts to reduce pollution loads. It does not take into account private facilities, used where public systems are not economic. This indicator should be related to an optimal national connection rate taking into account national specificities such as population in remote areas. Sewerage connection rates and public expenditure on waste water treatment are given as supplementary information.*

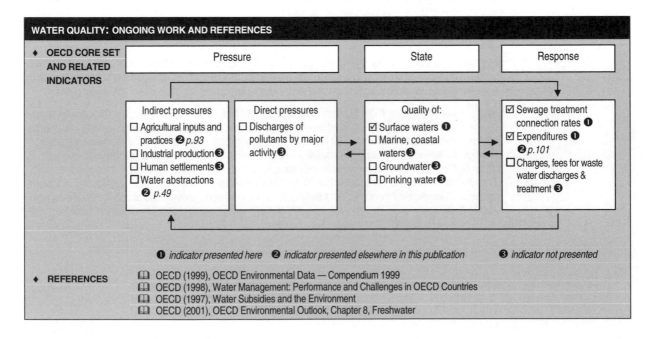

WATER QUALITY: ONGOING WORK AND REFERENCES

♦ **OECD CORE SET AND RELATED INDICATORS**

Pressure	State	Response

Indirect pressures
☐ Agricultural inputs and practices ❷ *p.93*
☐ Industrial production ❸
☐ Human settlements ❸
☐ Water abstractions ❷ *p.49*

Direct pressures
☐ Discharges of pollutants by major activity ❸

Quality of:
☑ Surface waters ❶
☐ Marine, coastal waters ❸
☐ Groundwater ❸
☐ Drinking water ❸

☑ Sewage treatment connection rates ❶
☑ Expenditures ❶ ❷ *p.101*
☐ Charges, fees for waste water discharges & treatment ❸

❶ *indicator presented here* ❷ *indicator presented elsewhere in this publication* ❸ *indicator not presented*

♦ **REFERENCES**
📖 OECD (1999), OECD Environmental Data — Compendium 1999
📖 OECD (1998), Water Management: Performance and Challenges in OECD Countries
📖 OECD (1997), Water Subsidies and the Environment
📖 OECD (2001), OECD Environmental Outlook, Chapter 8, Freshwater

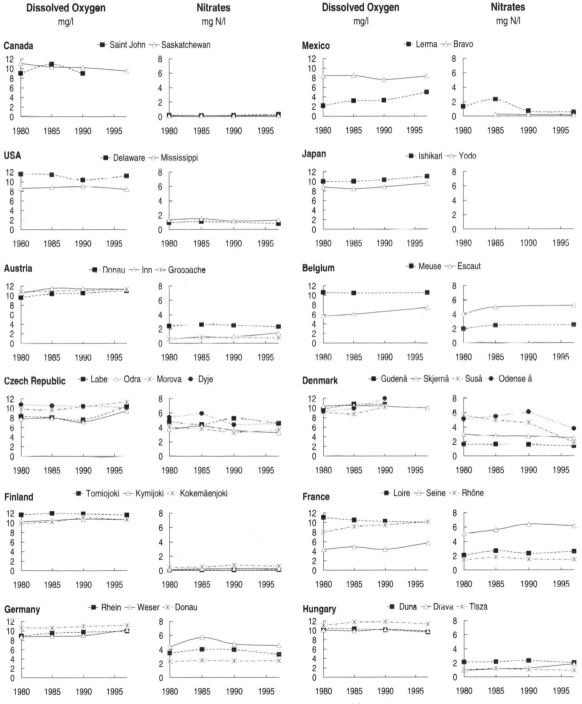

Data refer to averages over three years of average annual concentrations. See Technical Annex for data sources, notes and comments.

9 RIVER QUALITY

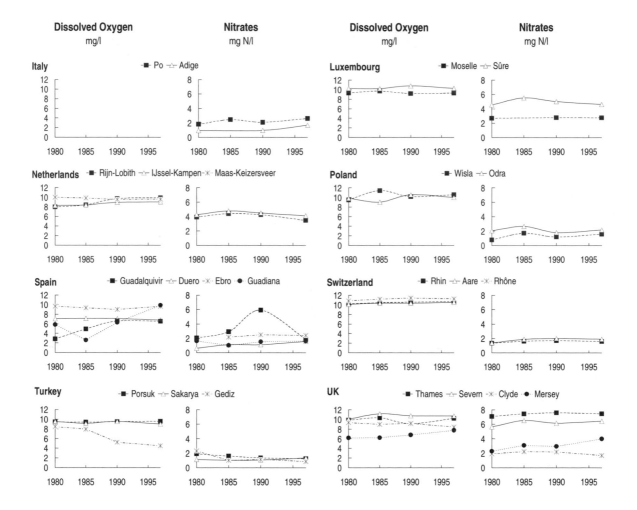

	Dissolved Oxygen mg/l	Nitrates mg N/l	Dissolved Oxygen mg/l	Nitrates mg N/l
	Italy — Po — Adige		**Luxembourg** — Moselle — Sûre	
	Netherlands — Rijn-Lobith — IJssel-Kampen — Maas-Keizersveer		**Poland** — Wisla — Odra	
	Spain — Guadalquivir — Duero — Ebro — Guadiana		**Switzerland** — Rhin — Aare — Rhône	
	Turkey — Porsuk — Sakarya — Gediz		**UK** — Thames — Severn — Clyde — Mersey	

STATE AND TRENDS SUMMARY

Despite significant progress in reducing pollution loads from municipal and industrial point sources through installation of appropriate waste water treatment plants, improvement in surface water quality is not always easy to discern; other factors, such as erosion and pollution from diffuse sources, may continue to reduce water quality. Nevertheless, loads of oxygen demanding substances have diminished: the dissolved oxygen content in the larger rivers is satisfactory for most of the year.

While nitrate concentrations appear to have stabilised locally, probably as a result of nitrogen removal from sewage effluents or a reduction of fertiliser use, in many rivers the trend cannot yet be detected. Furthermore, success in cleaning up the worst polluted waters is sometimes achieved at the cost of failing to protect the few remaining pristine waters, so that all of a country's waters tend to be of average quality.

WASTE WATER TREATMENT 10

Sewerage and sewage treatment connection rates, late 1990s

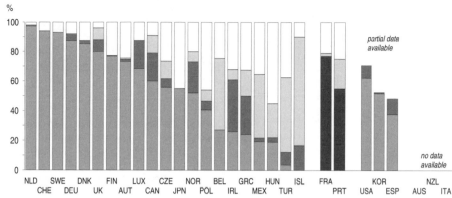

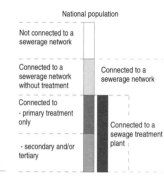

Trends in sewage treatment connection rates
per cent of national population connected

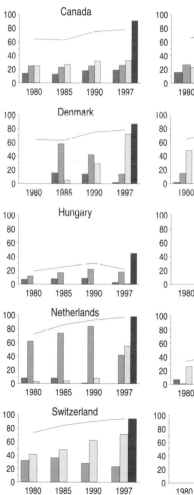

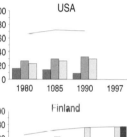

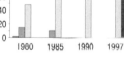

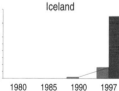

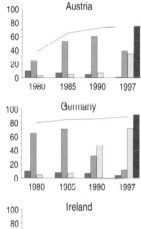

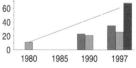

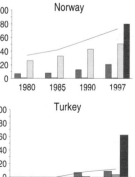

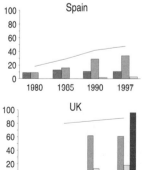

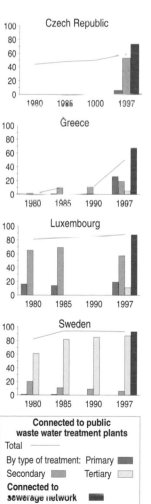

OECD Environmental Indicators 2001

10 WASTE WATER TREATMENT

		Waste water treatment Public sewage treatment connection rates							Sewerage network connection rates late 1990s	Public expenditure on waste water treatment late 1990s	
		early 1980s			late 1990s						
		Total	of which:	Secondary treatment	Tertiary treatment	Total	of which:	Secondary treatment	Tertiary treatment	Total	Total	of which: Investment
		% pop.		% pop.	% pop.	% pop.		% pop.	% pop.	% pop.	USD/capita	%
Canada	♦	64.0		25.0	25.0	78.0		26.0	33.0	91.0	66.7	60
Mexico	♦	..		..	..	21.8		19.2	..	64.6	3.9	39
USA	♦	65.8		27.1	22.8	70.8		32.5	29.8	..	105.0	47
Japan	♦	30.0		30.0	..	55.0		50.0	5.0	55.0	..	..
Korea	♦	8.3		..	..	52.6		51.7	-	..	92.8	82
Australia		..		..	..	..		..	..	..	41.9	68
New Zealand		59.0		49.0	..	..		..	..	82.5	..	..
Austria	♦	38.0		25.0	3.0	74.7		38.6	34.7	75.5	142.8	70
Belgium	♦	22.9		22.9	..	27.1		27.1	-	75.4	38.3	..
Czech Rep.	♦	43.7		..	..	59.2		53.4	-	73.5	57.3	100
Denmark	♦	..		..	..	87.4		13.7	71.6	87.4	105.4	..
Finland	♦	65.0		15.0	48.0	77.0		-	77.0	77.3	52.2	47
France	♦	57.0		..	..	77.0		..	..	79.0	112.8	33
Germany	♦	79.9		64.7	5.0	88.6		12.2	72.3	92.1	75.3	58
Greece	♦	0.5		0.5	..	50.0		19.0	5.0	67.5	17.2	92
Hungary	♦	19.0		12.0	-	22.0		18.0	1.0	45.0	27.7	100
Iceland	♦	..		-	-	16.4		-	-	90.0	31.5	79
Ireland		11.2		11.0	-	61.0		26.0	-	68.0	..	..
Italy		30.0		..	..	..		..	..	60.7	29.4	83
Luxembourg	♦	81.0		65.0	..	87.5		57.4	11.0	87.5	249.2	32
Netherlands	♦	72.4		61.9	2.6	97.4		42.3	55.0	98.0	109.6	30
Norway	♦	34.0		1.0	26.0	73.0		1.0	51.0	80.0	92.1	48
Poland	♦	..		..	..	46.6		31.1	9.5	54.0	35.9	100
Portugal	♦	2.3		..	..	55.0		..	..	75.0	48.5	84
Spain	♦	17.9		9.1	..	48.3		34.4	3.3	..	24.4	65
Sweden	♦	82.0		20.0	61.0	93.0		6.0	87.0	93.0	63.5	44
Switzerland	♦	73.0		32.0	41.0	94.0		23.0	71.0	94.0	101.8	42
Turkey	♦	-		-	-	12.1		3.6	-	62.5	..	..
UK	♦	..		..	..	88.0		61.0	18.0	96.0	11.1	27

♦ *See Technical Annex for data sources, notes and comments.*

STATE AND TRENDS SUMMARY

OECD countries have progressed with basic domestic water pollution abatement: the share of the population connected to a municipal waste water treatment plant rose from 50% in the early 1980s to more than 60% today. Due to varying settlement patterns, economic and environmental conditions, starting dates, and the rate at which the work was done, the share of population connected to waste water treament plants and the level of treatment varies significantly among OECD countries: secondary and tertiary treatment has progressed in some while primary treatment remains important in others. Some countries have reached the economic limit in terms of sewerage connection and must find other ways of serving small, isolated settlements.

The overall amount spent on sewerage and waste water treatment, and the relative shares of investment and operating expenditure within the total, also differ widely among countries. Some countries completed their sewer systems long ago and now face considerable investment to renew pipe networks. Other countries may recently have finished an expansion of waste water treatment capacity and the weight of expenditure has shifted to operating costs. Yet other countries must still complete their sewerage networks even as they build waste water treatment stations. For the OECD as a whole, more than half of public pollution abatement and control expenditure relates to water (sewerage & waste water treatment), representing up to 1% of GDP.

WATER RESOURCES

Freshwater resources are of major <u>environmental and economic importance</u>. Their distribution varies widely among and within countries. When consumers do not pay the full cost of water, they tend to use it inefficiently. This can result in serious problems, such as low river flows, water shortages, salinisation of freshwater bodies in coastal areas, human health problems, loss of wetlands, desertification and reduced food production. Pressures on water resources are exerted by overexploitation as well as by degradation of environmental quality. Relating resource abstraction to renewal of stocks is a central question concerning sustainable water resource management. If a significant share of a country's water comes from transboundary rivers, tensions between countries can arise, especially if water availability in the upstream country is less than in the downstream one.

<u>Sustainable management of water resources</u> has become a major concern in many countries: it can affect human health and the sustainability of agriculture. The efficiency of water use is key in matching supply and demand. Reducing losses, using more efficient technologies and recycling are all part of the solution, but applying the user pays principle to all types of users will be an essential element of sustainable management. Another important element is the application of an integrated approach to the management of freshwater resources by river basin. <u>Performance</u> can be assessed against domestic objectives and international commitments. Agenda 21, adopted at UNCED (Rio de Janeiro, 1992), explicitly considers items such as the protection and preservation of freshwater resources. The main <u>challenge</u> is to ensure a sustainable management of water resources, avoiding overexploitation and degradation, so as to maintain adequate supply of freshwater of suitable quality for human use and to support aquatic and other ecosystems.

<u>Indicators</u> presented here relate to:

- *the <u>intensity of use</u> of water resources, expressed as gross abstractions as % of total available renewable freshwater resources (including inflows from neighbouring countries) as % of internal resources (i.e. precipitations - evapotranspiration) and per capita. When interpreting this indicator, it should be kept in mind that it gives insights into quantitative aspects of water resources and that a national level indicator may hide territorial differences and should be complemented with information at sub-national level.*

- *<u>prices for public water supply</u> to households, expressed in US dollars per cubic metre supplied. Abstractions for public water supply per capita are shown as complementary information.*

These indicators should be read in connection with other indicators of the OECD Core Set and in particular with indicators on the quality of water resources.

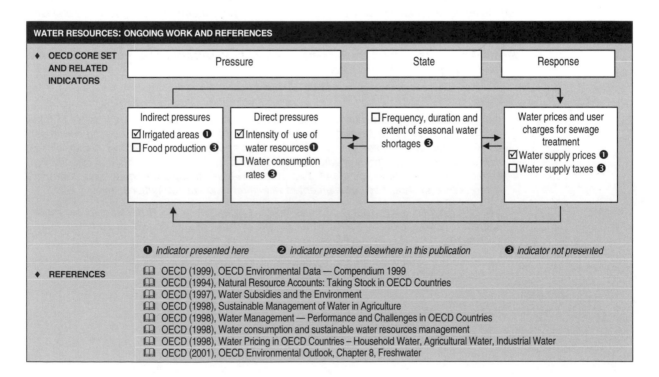

WATER RESOURCES: ONGOING WORK AND REFERENCES

♦ OECD CORE SET AND RELATED INDICATORS

Pressure | State | Response

Indirect pressures
☑ Irrigated areas ❶
☐ Food production ❸

Direct pressures
☑ Intensity of use of water resources ❶
☐ Water consumption rates ❸

☐ Frequency, duration and extent of seasonal water shortages ❸

Water prices and user charges for sewage treatment
☑ Water supply prices ❶
☐ Water supply taxes ❸

❶ *indicator presented here*   ❷ *indicator presented elsewhere in this publication*   ❸ *indicator not presented*

♦ REFERENCES
- OECD (1999), OECD Environmental Data — Compendium 1999
- OECD (1994), Natural Resource Accounts: Taking Stock in OECD Countries
- OECD (1997), Water Subsidies and the Environment
- OECD (1998), Sustainable Management of Water in Agriculture
- OECD (1998), Water Management — Performance and Challenges in OECD Countries
- OECD (1998), Water consumption and sustainable water resources management
- OECD (1998), Water Pricing in OECD Countries – Household Water, Agricultural Water, Industrial Water
- OECD (2001), OECD Environmental Outlook, Chapter 8, Freshwater

INTENSITY OF USE OF WATER RESOURCES 11

Gross freshwater abstractions, late 1990s

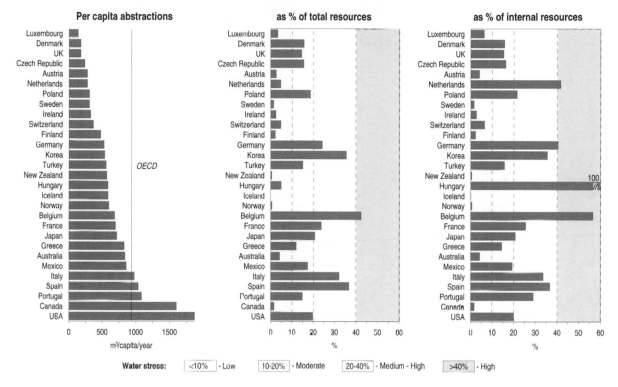

Per capita abstractions

as % of total resources

as % of internal resources

Water stress: | <10% | - Low | 10-20% | - Moderate | 20-40% | - Medium - High | >40% | - High

Freshwater abstractions by major uses

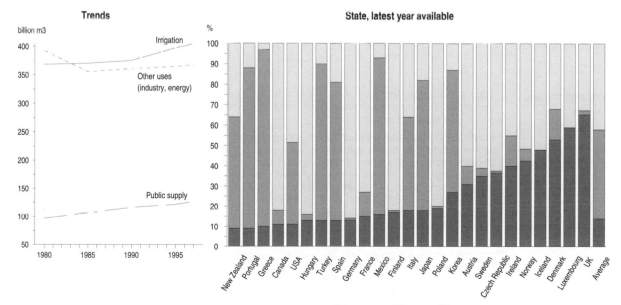

Trends

State, latest year available

■ Public supply ■ Irrigation □ Others

11 INTENSITY OF USE OF WATER RESOURCES

		Intensity of use of water resources				Irrigation		
		abstractions as % of available resources		abstractions per capita		water abstractions per area of irrigated land	Irrigated areas as a share of cultivated land	
		% late 1990s	absolute change since 1980	m3/cap/year late 1990s	% change since 1980	m3/ha/year 1997	% 1997	% change since 1980
Canada	♦	1.7	0.3	1600	6	4435	1.7	13
Mexico	♦	17.4	5.3	860	8	9523	23.8	17
USA	♦	19.9	-1.0	1870	-18	9019	12.0	11
Japan	♦	20.8	0.5	720	-4	21020	62.9	-
Korea	♦	35.6	10.5	540	17	12816	60.5	2
Australia	♦	4.3	1.2	840	14	4376	5.1	53
New Zealand	♦	0.6	0.2	570	50	3860	69.5	72
Austria	♦	2.7	0.1	280	-3	50063	0.3	10
Belgium	♦	42.5	..	690	..	..	3.7	133
Czech Republic	♦	15.6	-7.1	240	-31	583	0.7	..
Denmark	♦	15.7	-4.0	180	-25	291	20.1	36
Finland	♦	2.2	-1.1	480	-38	313	2.6	11
France	♦	23.9	5.7	700	23	3314	8.9	89
Germany	♦	24.4	0.7	530	-2	1297	3.9	7
Greece	♦	12.1	5.1	830	60	5487	35.4	46
Hungary	♦	5.0	1.0	590	31	774	3.9	56
Iceland	♦	0.1	-	590	26	-	-	-
Ireland	♦	2.6	0.2	330	6	..	-	-
Italy	♦	32.2	-	980	-2	9582	24.7	28
Luxembourg	♦	3.4	..	140	..	..	..	..
Netherlands	♦	4.9	-5.2	280	-57	..	57.5	5
Norway	♦	0.7	..	600	..	1495	14.1	55
Poland	♦	18.7	-3.8	310	-23	1096	0.7	3
Portugal	♦	15.0	..	1090	..	13560	21.8	9
Spain	♦	36.8	0.8	1040	-3	7733	18.8	27
Sweden	♦	1.5	-0.8	310	-37	930	4.1	75
Switzerland	♦	4.9	-	370	-10	..	5.4	6
Turkey	♦	15.2	8.3	560	56	6477	15.6	63
UK	♦	14.6	-6.5	180	-25	1323	1.7	-16
OECD	♦	11.8	0.5	970	-6	..	11.8	18

♦ *See Technical Annex for data sources, notes and comments.*

STATE AND TRENDS SUMMARY

Irrigation, industry and household water use are generally pushing up demand for fresh water worldwide. It is estimated that global water demand rose by more than double the rate of population growth in the last century.

Most OECD countries increased their <u>water abstractions</u> over the 1970s in response to demand by the agricultural and energy sectors. Since the 1980s, some countries have stabilised their abstractions through more efficient irrigation techniques, the decline of water intensive industries (e.g. mining, steel), increased use of cleaner production technologies and reduced losses in pipe networks. Agriculture is the largest user of water worldwide. Global abstractions for irrigation have increased by over 60% since 1960. In OECD countries overall, abstractions for irrigation mainly increased in the 1960s and the 1970s. In eight OECD countries, irrigation accounts for more than 50% of total abstractions.

Although at national level most OECD countries show sustainable use of water resources, several countries have extensive arid or semi-arid regions where development is shaped by water scarcity. Indicators of <u>water resource use intensity</u> show great variations among and within individual countries. The national indicator may thus conceal unsustainable use in some regions and periods, and high dependence on water from other basins.

PUBLIC WATER SUPPLY AND PRICE 🖸

Abstractions for public supply per capita, late 1990s

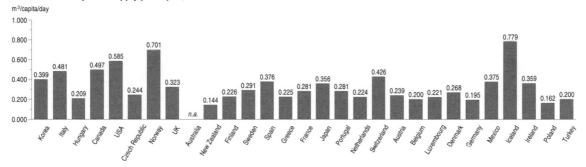

Water prices in major selected cities, 1998

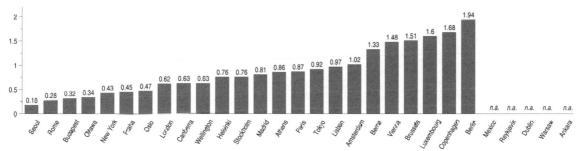

Average prices for public freshwater supply to households, selected cities, 1998

		Price USD/m³			Price USD/m³			Price USD/m³			Price USD/m³
Canada	Ottawa	0.34	Belgium	Brussels	1.51	Hungary	Budapest	0.32	Sweden	Stockholm	0.76
	Toronto	0.31		Antwerp	0.88		Debrecen	0.37		Goteborg	0.59
	Winnipeg	0.73		Liège	1.48		Miskolc	0.44		Malmo	0.54
USA	New York	0.43	Czech Rep.	Praha	0.45	Iceland	Reykjavik ♦	0.61	Switzerland	Berne	1.33
	Los Angeles	0.58		Brno	0.37		Hafnarfjorour ♦	0.51		Geneva	2.14
	Miami	0.36		Ostrava	0.44	Italy	Rome	0.28		Zurich	1.88
Japan	Tokyo	0.92	Denmark	Copenhagen	1.68		Milan	0.13	Turkey	Ankara ♦	0.18
	Osaka	0.68		Aarhus	1.26		Naples	0.57		Canakkale ♦	0.20
	Sapporo	1.13		Odense	1.32	Luxembourg	Luxembourg	1.60		Eskisehir ♦	0.19
Korea	Seoul	0.18	Finland	Helsinki	0.76	Netherlands	Amsterdam	1.02	UK	London ♦	0.62
	Daegu	0.19		Tampere	0.86		The Hague	1.91		Bristol ♦	0.57
	Pusan	0.22		Espoo	1.35		Utrecht	0.94		Manchester ♦	0.55
Australia	Sydney	0.73	France	Paris	0.87	Norway	Oslo ♦	0.47			
	Brisbane	0.68		Bordeaux	1.16		Bergen ♦	1.30			
	Melbourne	0.59		Lyon	1.45		Trondheim ♦	0.80			
N. Zealand	Wellington	0.63	Germany	Berlin	1.94	Portugal	Lisbon	0.97			
	Auckland	0.46		Hamburg	1.74		Coimbra	0.72			
	North Shore City	0.59		München	1.35		Porto	1.02			
Austria	Vienna	1.48	Greece	Athens ♦	0.86	Spain	Madrid	0.81			
	Salzburg	1.43		Thessaloniki ♦	0.55		Barcelona	0.78			
	Linz	1.12		Patras	0.77		Seville	0.57			

♦ *See Technical Annex for data sources, notes and comments.*

STATE AND TRENDS   Policies for pricing water supply and waste water treatment are important in matching supply and demand and improving the cost-effectiveness of water services. Prices charged to domestic and industrial users sometimes include an abstraction tax and increasingly cover full investment and operating costs. Domestic prices vary widely among and within countries. The cost of delivering clean water to urban areas depends, inter alia, on the proximity of water sources, the degree of purification needed and the settlement density of the area served.

FOREST RESOURCES

Forests are among the most diverse and widespread ecosystems on earth, and have many functions: they provide timber and other products; deliver recreation benefits and ecosystem services including regulation of soil, air and water; are reservoirs for biodiversity; and commonly act as carbon sinks. The impact from human activities on forest health and on natural forest growth and regeneration raises widespread concern. Many forest resources are threatened by overexploitation, degradation of environmental quality and conversion to other types of land uses. The main pressures result from human activities: they include agriculture expansion, transport infrastructure development, unsustainable forestry, air pollution and intentional burning of forests.

To be sustainable, forest management must strive to maintain timber value as well as environmental, social and aboriginal values. This includes optimal harvest rates, avoiding excessive use of the resource, and at the same time not setting harvest rates too low (particularly where age classes are unbalanced), which can reduce productive capacity. Performance can be assessed against national objectives and international principles on sustainable forest management adopted at UNCED (Rio de Janeiro, 1992). Other international initiatives are the Ministerial Conferences for the Protection of Forests in Europe (Strasbourg, 1990; Helsinki, 1993; Lisbon, 1998), which led to the Pan-European Criteria and Indicators for Sustainable Forest Management, the Montreal Process on Sustainable Development of Temperate and Boreal Forests; and the UN Forum on Forests. The main challenge is to ensure a sustainable management of forest resources, avoiding overexploitation and degradation, so as to maintain adequate supply of wood for production acitivities, and to ensure the provision of essential environmental services, including biodiversity and carbon sinks.

Indicators presented here relate to:

♦ *the intensity of use of forest resources (timber), relating annual productive capacity to actual harvest. Annual productive capacity is either a calculated value, such as annual allowable cut, or an estimate of annual growth for existing stock. The choice depends on forest characteristics and availability of information. NB: a measure based on a national average can conceal variations among forests. Changes in annual harvest, annual growth and growing stock are given as complementary information.*

♦ *area of forest and wooded land, as a percentage of total land area and per capita, along with changes in the area of forest and wooded land since 1970.*

These indicators give insights into quantitative aspects of forest resources. They present national averages that may conceal important variations among forests. They should be related to information on forest quality (e.g. species diversity, forest degradation), on output of and trade in forest products and be complemented with data on forest management practices and protection measures.

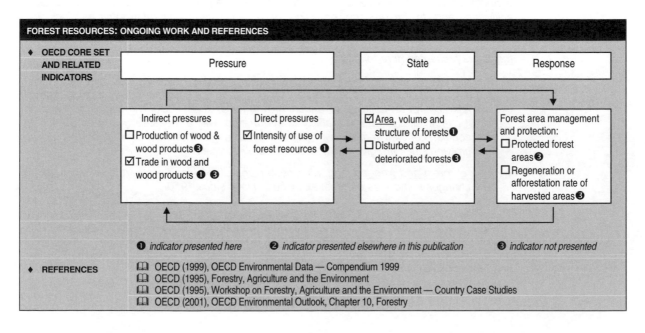

FOREST RESOURCES: ONGOING WORK AND REFERENCES

♦ **OECD CORE SET AND RELATED INDICATORS**

Pressure	State	Response

Indirect pressures
☐ Production of wood & wood products❸
☑ Trade in wood and wood products❶ ❸

Direct pressures
☑ Intensity of use of forest resources ❶

☑ Area, volume and structure of forests❶
☐ Disturbed and deteriorated forests❸

Forest area management and protection:
☐ Protected forest areas❸
☐ Regeneration or afforestation rate of harvested areas❸

❶ *indicator presented here*   ❷ *indicator presented elsewhere in this publication*   ❸ *indicator not presented*

♦ **REFERENCES**
📖 OECD (1999), OECD Environmental Data — Compendium 1999
📖 OECD (1995), Forestry, Agriculture and the Environment
📖 OECD (1995), Workshop on Forestry, Agriculture and the Environment — Country Case Studies
📖 OECD (2001), OECD Environmental Outlook, Chapter 10, Forestry

INTENSITY OF USE OF FOREST RESOURCES 13

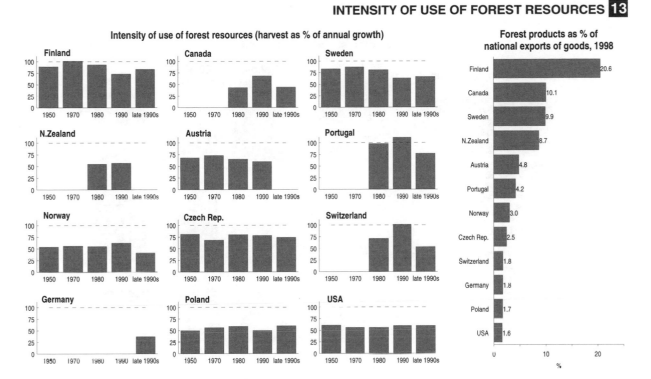

Intensity of use of forest resources (harvest as % of annual growth)

Forest products as % of national exports of goods, 1998

		Intensity of use of forest resources harvest as % of annual growth				Annual harvest % change since 1980	Annual growth % change since 1980	Growing stock % change since 1980	Exports of forestry products % of national exports
		1950s	1970s	1980s	1990s	late 1990s	since 1980	since 1980	since 1980	1998
Canada	♦	..	..	43	68	44	14.6	12.0	34	10.1
Mexico	♦	..	..	23	24	17	-35.1	-10.4	-12	0.3
USA	♦	61	56	56	60	60	10.8	3.6	..	1.6
Japan	♦	..	..	36	35	32	-31.8	-21.2	40	0.4
Korea	♦	..	42	..	7	6	-16.6	..	134	1.0
Australia	♦	..	..	40	..	57	15.7	-17.6	..	1.1
N.Zealand	♦	..	..	55	57	..	74.6	..	..	8.7
Austria	♦	68	73	65	60	..	55.9	..	..	4.8
Belgium	♦	..	..	103	100	85	..	..	16	1.2
Czech Rep.	♦	81	68	80	78	74	-4.4	2.6	8	2.5
Denmark	♦	85	118	75	63	59	-12.3	12.2	..	0.7
Finland	♦	89	101	93	73	83	10.2	23.5	17	20.6
France	♦	..	..	81	82	68	14.3	36.3	21	1.1
Germany		..	..	..	..	37	..	..	..	1.8
Greece	♦	..	..	71	54	60	-12.2	2.9	..	0.3
Hungary	♦	..	60	70	67	57	-12.4	6.5	25	1.0
Ireland		..	20	22	..	65	342.1	51.9	..	0.3
Italy	♦	88	..	74	28	27	-2.7	171.7	101	0.9
Luxembourg	♦	..	..	49	72	52	6.2	-0.2	..	1.2
Netherlands	♦	..	..	41	42	62	..	..	..	1.2
Norway	♦	54	56	55	62	41	3.4	39.8	31	3.0
Poland	♦	50	56	59	50	60	3.9	2.0	26	1.7
Portugal	♦	..	..	98	111	77	..	..	..	4.2
Spain	♦	..	59	46	53	52	94.3	72.7	39	1.1
Sweden	♦	83	87	81	63	66	..	..	..	9.9
Switzerland		..	..	71	101	53	-8.8	21.0	..	1.8
Turkey	♦	..	74	83	51	43	-40.5	13.6	20	0.1
UK	♦	..	..	48	59	68	74.5	23.5	39	0.6
OECD	♦	..	..	56	..	55	9.3	..	..	2.1

♦ *See Technical Annex for data sources, notes and comments.*

STATE AND TRENDS SUMMARY

Intensity of forest resource use does not show an increase for many OECD countries and has decreased in most countries since the 1950s. At national level most OECD countries present a picture of sustainable use of their forest resources in <u>quantitative terms</u>, but with significant variations within countries.

14 FOREST AND WOODED LAND

Area of forest and wooded land

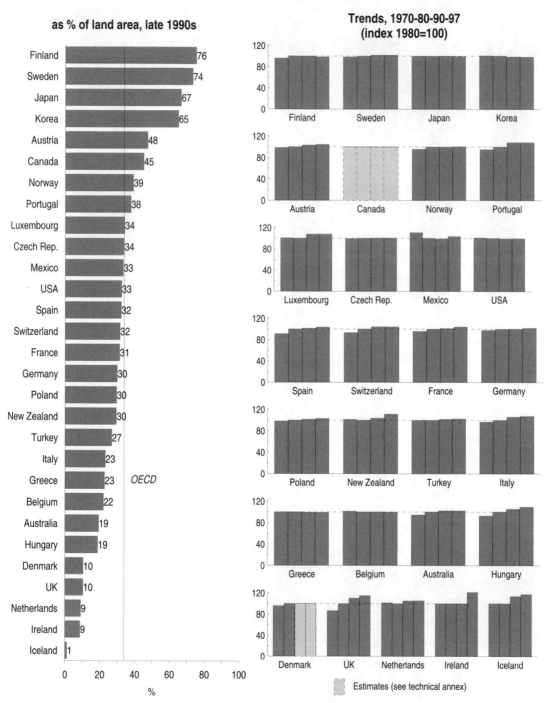

as % of land area, late 1990s

Finland	76
Sweden	74
Japan	67
Korea	65
Austria	48
Canada	45
Norway	39
Portugal	38
Luxembourg	34
Czech Rep.	34
Mexico	33
USA	33
Spain	32
Switzerland	32
France	31
Germany	30
Poland	30
New Zealand	30
Turkey	27
Italy	23
Greece	23
Belgium	22
Australia	19
Hungary	19
Denmark	10
UK	10
Netherlands	9
Ireland	9
Iceland	1

OECD

Trends, 1970-80-90-97
(index 1980=100)

Estimates (see technical annex)

**STATE AND TRENDS
SUMMARY**

The area of forests and wooded land has generally increased or remained stable at national level in most OECD countries and has remained stable in the OECD as a whole, but has decreased at world level.

FISH RESOURCES

Fish play key roles for human food supply and aquatic ecosystems. Main pressures include fisheries, coastal development and pollution loads from land-based sources, maritime transport, and maritime dumping. This affects both freshwater and marine fish stocks and habitats and has consequences for biodiversity and for the supply of fish for consumption and other uses. Aquaculture has been developed to an extent where its dependence on fishmeal products puts it in competition with other commercial markets and could become a limiting factor of aquaculture development.

The sustainable management of fish resources has become a major concern. With continual growth in fish catches, many of the more valuable stocks are overfished and new or less valuable species are being exploited as several fish stocks have collapsed. Unauthorised fishing is widespread. Performance can be assessed against domestic objectives and bilateral and multilateral agreements such as those on conservation and use of fish resources (Atlantic Ocean, Pacific Ocean, Baltic Sea, etc.), the Rome Consensus on world fisheries, the Code of Conduct for Responsible Fishing (FAO, November 1995), the UN Convention on the Law of the Sea and its implementation agreement on straddling and highly migratory fish stocks. Within the framework of the FAO Code of Conduct for Responsible Fishing, plans are being made to address the issue of illegal, unreported and unregulated (IUU) fishing. The main challenge is to ensure a sustainable management of catchment areas so that resource abstraction does not exceed the renewal of the stocks over an extended period.

Indicators presented here relate to:

♦ *national fish catches expressed as per cent of world captures and as amounts per capita, and related changes since 1980. National fish consumption (food supply from fish per capita) is given as additional information.*

♦ *global and regional fish catches and related changes since 1980. Changes in the proportion of fish resources under various phases of fishery development are given as additional information.*

These indicators give insights into quantitative aspects of fish resources; they should be related to information on the status of fish stocks.

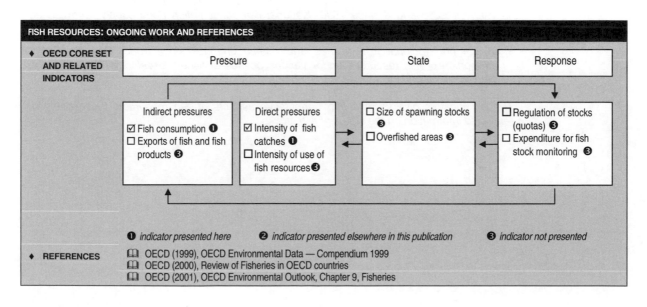

FISH CATCHES AND CONSUMPTION: NATIONAL **15**

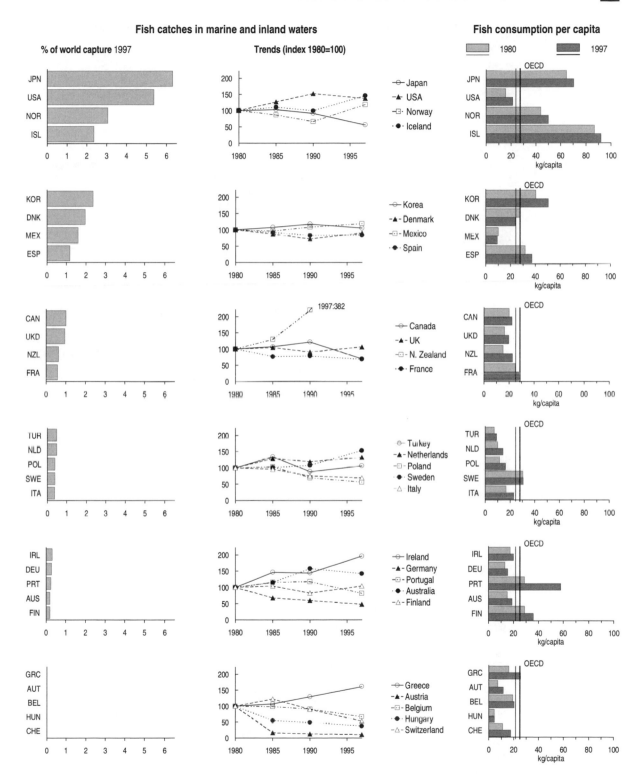

Fish catches in marine and inland waters

% of world capture 1997

Trends (index 1980=100)

Fish consumption per capita

1980   1997

16 FISH CATCHES AND CONSUMPTION: GLOBAL AND REGIONAL

Fish catches, 1980-1997

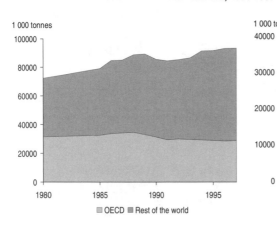

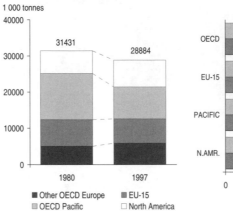

Fish consumption, 1980-1997

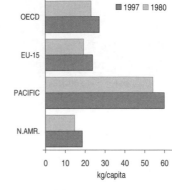

Fish catches by major marine fishing area

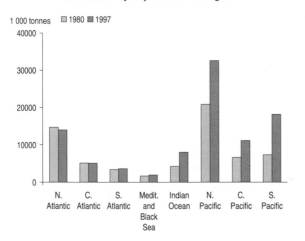

World marine fish resources by phase of fishery development

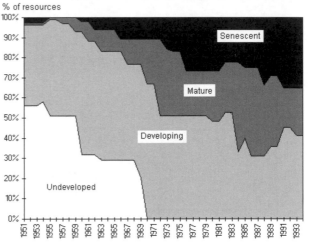

Fish catches by major marine fishing area

	Total		share of world catches		Cod, hake, haddock		Herring, sardine, anchovy		Jack, mullet, saury		Tuna, bonito, billfish, etc.	
	1 000 t. 1997	% change since 1980	% 1980	% 1997	1 000 t. 1997	% change since 1980	1 000 t. 1997	% change since 1980	1 000 t. 1997	% change since 1980	1 000 t. 1997	% change since 1980
Northern Atlantic	14937	1	23	15	3258	-38	3696	79	2126	-23	52	-10
Central Atlantic	5423	5	8	6	26	-50	2578	26	294	-60	387	10
Southern Atlantic	3859	12	5	4	1077	38	491	-51	319	-58	126	70
Mediterr. & Black Sea	1701	0	3	2	72	37	642	-29	119	-13	71	59
Indian Ocean	8551	99	7	9	4	148	839	41	557	65	1190	297
Northern Pacific	35747	71	33	37	5186	20	2641	-18	2283	151	764	56
Central Pacific	11302	70	10	12	1	694	1656	10	1235	101	2199	85
Southern Pacific	15727	115	11	16	741	162	9050	119	3692	177	335	118
Total	97247	52	100	100	10364	-3	21593	40	10626	40	5124	93

• *See Technical Annex for data sources, notes and comments.*

FISH CATCHES AND CONSUMPTION 15&16

	Total fish catches				Marine fish catches	Fish consumption	
	Total		per capita		share of world catches	share of total catches	per capita	
	1 000 t.	% change	kg/cap.	% change	%	%	kg/cap.	% change
	1997	since 1980	1997	since 1980	1997	1997	1997	since 1980
Canada	945	- 30	31.5	-43	1.0	90	22.4	12
Mexico	1 489	19	15.9	-11	1.6	93	9.3	-8
USA	5 010	37	18.8	17	5.4	94	21.3	36
Japan	5 882	- 44	46.6	-48	6.3	94	70.6	9
Korea	2 204	5	47.9	-13	2.4	99	50.5	25
Australia	188	42	10.1	13	0.2	98	18.7	25
New Zealand	596	282	158.5	220	0.6	100	22.7	49
Austria	-	- 89	0.1	-90	-	n.app.	11.5	61
Belgium	31	- 33	2.9	-36	-	98	20.4	5
Czech Rep.	3	..	0.3	..	-	n.app.	4.9	26
Denmark	1 827	- 10	345.7	-13	2.0	100	23.9	-14
Finland	180	4	35.0	-3	0.2	63	35.9	24
France	542	- 31	9.3	-37	0.6	99	27.8	10
Germany	259	- 52	3.2	-54	0.3	90	15.5	19
Greece	170	61	16.2	48	0.2	90	25.5	61
Hungary	13	- 63	1.2	-61	-	n.app.	4.4	2
Iceland	2 206	46	8143.0	23	2.4	100	92.2	6
Ireland	293	96	80.0	82	0.3	98	20.0	15
Italy	350	- 31	6.1	-32	0.4	97	23.0	37
Netherlands	452	33	28.9	20	0.5	99	14.4	44
Norway	2 857	19	650.3	10	3.1	100	49.9	14
Poland	362	- 44	9.4	-48	0.4	93	16.4	44
Portugal	222	- 18	22.3	-19	0.2	99	57.9	101
Spain	1 102	- 16	28.0	-20	1.2	99	37.2	17
Sweden	357	54	40.4	44	0.4	99	30.7	1
Switzerland	2	- 47	0.3	-52	-	n.app.	17.5	59
Turkey	455	7	7.1	-26	0.5	95	9.1	26
UK	887	6	15.0	1	1.0	100	19.9	21
OECD	28 884	- 8	26.4	-10	30.9	96	27.1	17
World	93 329	29	16.0	-2	100.0	92	15.9	37

• *See Technical Annex for data sources, notes and comments... not available   - nil or negligible   n.app. not applicable*

STATE AND TRENDS SUMMARY

Of 441 marine stocks fished worldwide, more than 28% are estimated to be overfished (18%), depleted (9%) or recovering (1%), while about 47% are fully exploited.

Trend analysis shows large differences among OECD countries and among fishing areas, with high increases in some areas (e.g. the Pacific and Indian Oceans) and decreases in others (e.g. the North Atlantic).

Only a few of the fish stocks in areas closest to OECD countries have significant potential for additional exploitation; the North Atlantic and parts of the Pacific areas are already being overfished.

The intensity of national catches per unit of GDP and per capita varies widely among OECD countries, reflecting the share of fisheries and associated industries in the economy.

Catches from capture fisheries are generally growing at a slower rate than 30 years ago; they are even in decline in a number of countries, whereas aquaculture is gaining in importance. While aquaculture helps to alleviate some of the stress from capture fisheries, it also has negative effects on local ecosystems.

BIODIVERSITY

Biodiversity can be defined as the variety of and variability among living organisms; it covers both diversity at the ecosystem and species levels and genetic diversity within species. Conservation of biodiversity has become a key concern nationally and globally. Pressures on biodiversity can be physical (e.g. habitat alteration and fragmentation through changes in land use and land cover conversions), chemical (e.g. pollution from human activities) or biological (e.g. alteration of population dynamics and species structure through the release of exotic species or the commercial use of wildlife resources).

The conservation and sustainable use of biodiversity form an integral part of sustainable development, encompassing the integration of biodiversity concerns into economic policies as well as measures to protect areas, habitats and species. Protection levels range from full to partial protection in actual protected areas to promotion of biodiversity conservation outside such areas (e.g. on farms or in forests). Performance can be assessed against domestic objectives and international agreements such as: the Convention on Biological Diversity (Rio de Janeiro, 1992), the Convention on the Conservation of Migratory Species of Wild Animals (Bonn, 1979), the Convention on International Trade in Endangered Species of Wild Fauna and Flora (CITES, Washington, 1973), the Convention on Wetlands of International Importance (Ramsar, 1971) and the Convention on the Conservation of European Wildlife and Natural Habitats (Bern, 1979). The main challenge is to maintain or restore the diversity and integrity of ecosystems, species and genetic material and to ensure a sustainable use of biodiversity.

Indicators presented here relate to the conservation of biodiversity and concern:

♦ *the number of threatened or extinct species compared to the number of known species. "Threatened" refers to the "endangered" and "vulnerable" categories, i.e. species in danger of extinction and species soon likely to be in danger of extinction. Data cover mammals, birds, fish, reptiles, amphibians and vascular plants. Other major groups (e.g. invertebrates, fungi) are not covered at the present time.*

♦ *protected areas, i.e. land areas under management categories I to VI of the World Conservation Union (IUCN) classification, which refer to different levels of protection. Categories I and II (wilderness areas, strict nature reserves and national parks) reflect the highest protection level. Protected areas are a form of defence against change in land use and in other human activities, which, if unsustainable, can pose a threat to ecosystems and landscapes, and lead to biodiversity changes including natural habitat loss.*

These indicators need to be complemented with indicators on the sustainable use of biodiversity as a resource, and should be read in connection with information on the density of population and of human activities.

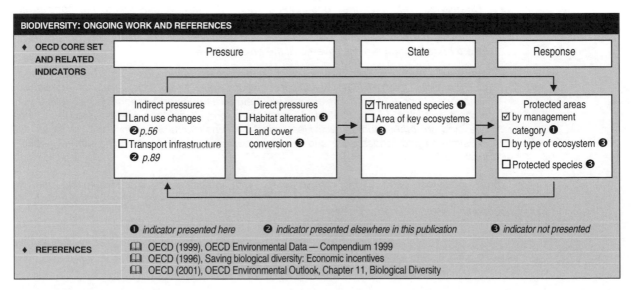

BIODIVERSITY: ONGOING WORK AND REFERENCES

♦ OECD CORE SET AND RELATED INDICATORS	Pressure		State	Response

| | Indirect pressures
☐ Land use changes
❷ *p.56*
☐ Transport infrastructure
❷ *p.89* | Direct pressures
☐ Habitat alteration ❸
☐ Land cover conversion ❸ | ☑ Threatened species ❶
☐ Area of key ecosystems ❸ | Protected areas
☑ by management category ❶
☐ by type of ecosystem ❸
☐ Protected species ❸ |

❶ *indicator presented here*   ❷ *indicator presented elsewhere in this publication*   ❸ *indicator not presented*

♦ REFERENCES	📖 OECD (1999), OECD Environmental Data — Compendium 1999 📖 OECD (1996), Saving biological diversity: Economic incentives 📖 OECD (2001), OECD Environmental Outlook, Chapter 11, Biological Diversity

THREATENED SPECIES 17

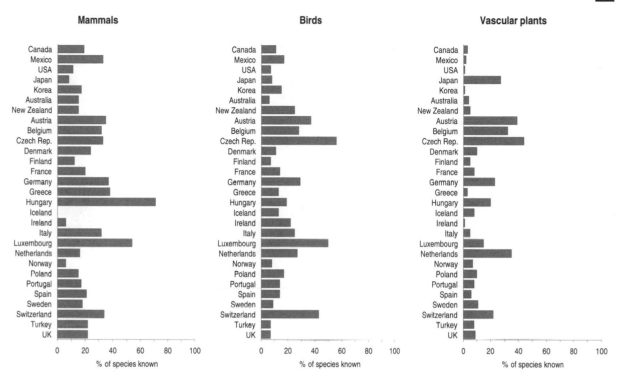

Mammals		Birds		Fish		Reptiles		Amphibians		Vascular plants	
species known	species threatened	species known	species threatened	species known	species threatened	species known	species threatened	species known	species threatened	species known	species threatened
number	%	number	%	number	%	number	%	number	%	number	%
Canada ♦	103	19	426	11	1021	8	42	33	42	21	4120	3
Mexico ♦	491	33	1054	17	2122	6	704	18	290	17	18000	2
USA ♦	466	11	1090	7	2640	2	368	7	222	4	22200	1
Japan ♦	183	0	652	8	198	11	98	20	64	23	6998	27
Korea ♦	100	17	394	15	901	1	26	12	15	13	3971	1
Australia	315	15	777	6	4195	-	770	7	203	14	25000	4
New Zealand ♦	46	15	170	25	1048	1	61	18	4	25	2400	5
Austria ♦	82	35	219	37	58	66	16	88	21	100	2950	39
Belgium ♦	57	32	167	28	46	54	4	50	13	31	1202	32
Czech Rep. ♦	90	33	220	56	65	29	11	100	21	100	2520	44
Denmark ♦	50	24	170	11	33	18	5	-	14	29	1200	10
Finland ♦	59	12	240	7	59	12	5	20	5	20	1838	5
France ♦	119	20	357	14	426	7	36	17	37	30	4762	8
Germany ♦	79	37	240	29	66	68	14	79	21	57	3301	23
Greece ♦	116	38	422	13	107	24	59	7	20	-	5700	3
Hungary ♦	83	71	373	19	81	32	16	100	16	100	2500	20
Iceland ♦	4	-	75	13	5	-	-	-	-	-	485	8
Ireland ♦	31	6	193	22	27	33	3	33	3	33	1309	1
Italy ♦	118	32	473	25	85	..	58	22	38	24	5599	5
Luxembourg ♦	61	54	130	50	34	38	6	100	13	100	1054	15
Netherlands ♦	64	16	170	27	28	82	7	86	16	56	1392	35
Norway ♦	51	6	222	6	195	-	5	20	6	50	1195	7
Poland ♦	84	15	235	17	48	27	9	33	18	100	2300	10
Portugal ♦	98	17	313	14	43	19	34	9	17	-	3095	8
Spain ♦	118	21	368	14	68	29	56	20	25	16	8000	6
Sweden ♦	66	18	245	9	55	13	7	-	13	54	1900	11
Switzerland ♦	79	34	197	43	47	45	14	79	17	94	2617	22
Turkey ♦	135	22	450	7	192	10	106	16	22	14	3072	8
UK ♦	63	22	517	7	54	11	7	43	7	29	2230	9

♦ *See Technical Annex for data sources, notes and comments*

18 PROTECTED AREAS

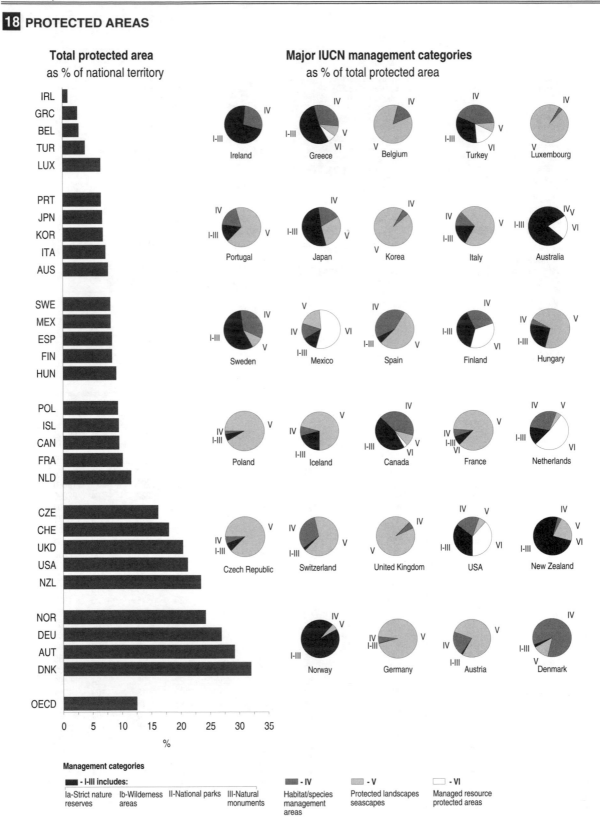

Total protected area
as % of national territory

Major IUCN management categories
as % of total protected area

Ireland · Greece · Belgium · Turkey · Luxembourg

Portugal · Japan · Korea · Italy · Australia

Sweden · Mexico · Spain · Finland · Hungary

Poland · Iceland · Canada · France · Netherlands

Czech Republic · Switzerland · United Kingdom · USA · New Zealand

Norway · Germany · Austria · Denmark

Management categories

■ - I-III includes:

| Ia-Strict nature reserves | Ib-Wilderness areas | II-National parks | III-Natural monuments |

■ - IV — Habitat/species management areas

▨ - V — Protected landscapes seascapes

□ - VI — Managed resource protected areas

PROTECTED AREAS 18

		Major protected areas, 1997				Strict nature reserves, wilderness areas, national parks, 1997			
		Number of sites	Total size 1 000 km²	% of territory	per capita km²/1 000 inh.	Number of sites	Total size 1 000 km²	% of territory	per capita km²/1 000 inh.
Canada		3224	953	9.6	31.8	1676	433	4.3	14.4
Mexico	♦	152	160	8.2	1.7	47	20	1.0	0.2
USA	♦	3333	1988	21.2	7.5	849	645	6.9	2.4
Japan		96	26	6.8	0.2	30	13	3.5	0.1
Korea		30	7	6.9	0.1	-	-	-	-
Australia	♦	5606	598	7.7	32.3	2650	470	6.1	25.4
New Zealand		235	63	23.5	16.8	67	44	16.4	11.8
Austria		695	25	29.2	3.0	5	0.4	0.4	-
Belgium		70	0.9	2.8	0.1	-	-	-	-
Czech Rep.		1790	13	16.2	1.2	5	0.9	1.1	0.1
Denmark	♦	220	14	32.0	2.6	31	0.2	0.6	-
Finland		270	28	8.4	5.5	50	11	3.2	2.1
France	♦	434	56	10.1	1.0	53	4	0.7	0.1
Germany		1398	96	26.9	1.2	3	0.4	0.1	-
Greece		83	3	2.6	0.3	13	2	1.3	0.2
Hungary	♦	186	8	9.1	0.8	5	2	2.2	0.2
Iceland		79	10	9.5	36.2	5	2	1.7	6.5
Ireland		72	0.7	0.9	0.2	5	0.5	0.7	0.1
Italy		422	22	7.3	0.4	18	4	1.2	0.1
Luxembourg	♦	19	0.2	6.5	0.4	-	-	-	-
Netherlands	♦	85	5	11.6	0.3	15	0.5	1.2	-
Norway	♦	198	94	24.2	21.3	138	89	23.0	20.2
Poland		500	29	9.4	0.8	16	2	0.5	-
Portugal	♦	59	6	6.6	0.6	8	0.8	0.9	0.1
Spain	♦	329	42	8.4	1.1	39	2	0.5	0.1
Sweden		350	37	8.1	4.1	90	21	4.0	2.3
Switzerland		211	7	18.0	1.1	1	0.2	0.4	-
Turkey	♦	81	30	3.8	0.5	36	10	1.3	0.2
UK	♦	515	50	20.4	0.8	-	-	-	-
OECD		20765	4372	12.6	4.0	5858	1779	5.1	1.6
World		30350	13232	9.9	2.3	8582	5921	4.4	1.0

♦ *See Technical Annex for data sources, notes and comments.*

STATE AND TRENDS SUMMARY

Protected areas have grown significantly since 1980 in almost all countries, reaching 13 per cent of total area for the OECD as a whole.

Actual protection levels and related trends are difficult to evaluate, as protected areas change over time: new areas are designated, boundaries are revised and some sites may be destroyed or changed by pressures from economic development or natural processes. Environmental performance depends both on the designation of the area (e.g. the representativeness of species or ecosystems protected) and on management effectiveness.

III. SOCIO-ECONOMIC INDICATORS

GDP AND POPULATION

Economic activity is a key determinant of <u>sustainable development</u> and its economic, social and environmental dimensions. Economic growth and production patterns have major effects on environmental issues and on environmental <u>performance</u>. They imply use of energy and other natural resource assets, as well as pollutant discharges and waste production. The sustainability of development depends on the evolution of the stock and quality of natural resources or "natural capital" and on pollution constraints. Economic growth also provides opportunities to finance public expenditure for environmental protection and to replace man-made capital, thus introducing cleaner, less resource-intensive technologies and environmentally friendly goods.

Population influences production and consumption patterns, and hence the <u>sustainability</u> of development. It is an important determinant of environmental conditions and trends. Population density implies density of human activity. Overall population growth puts pressure on natural resources and adds to the challenge of providing sanitation and other environmental infrastructure. Population also affects the environment in the ways that its structural elements (age classes, active population, size of households, etc.) influence consumption patterns and waste production.

<u>Indicators</u> presented here relate to:

- *<u>gross domestic product</u> (GDP), in total and per capita, as well as the change in GDP compared to the change in population over the same period.*

- *<u>population growth and density</u>, presenting changes in national resident population, as well as population densities and an "ageing index" (the ratios between the population over 64 and under 15).*

GDP AND POPULATION: REFERENCES

📖 OECD (1999), OECD Environmental Data — Compendium 1999
📖 OECD (biannual publication), OECD Economic Outlook
📖 OECD (annual publication), National Accounts of OECD Countries
📖 OECD (annual publication), Labour Force Statistics
📖 OECD (monthly publication), Main Economic Indicators
📖 OECD (2001), OECD Environmental Outlook, Chapter 4, Economic Development

GROSS DOMESTIC PRODUCT  19

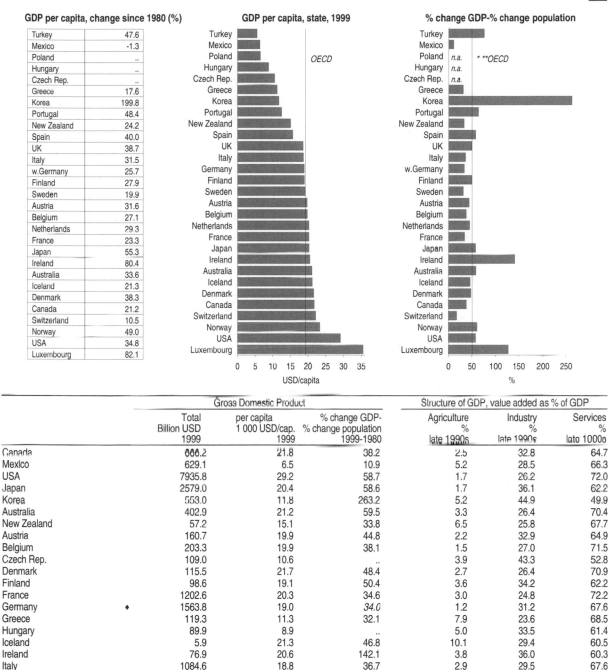

GDP per capita, change since 1980 (%)

Turkey	47.6
Mexico	-1.3
Poland	..
Hungary	..
Czech Rep.	..
Greece	17.6
Korea	199.8
Portugal	48.4
New Zealand	24.2
Spain	40.0
UK	38.7
Italy	31.5
w.Germany	25.7
Finland	27.9
Sweden	19.9
Austria	31.6
Belgium	27.1
Netherlands	29.3
France	23.3
Japan	55.3
Ireland	80.4
Australia	33.6
Iceland	21.3
Denmark	38.3
Canada	21.2
Switzerland	10.5
Norway	49.0
USA	34.8
Luxembourg	82.1

GDP per capita, state, 1999 — OECD

% change GDP-% change population — * **OECD

	Gross Domestic Product			Structure of GDP, value added as % of GDP		
	Total Billion USD 1999	per capita 1 000 USD/cap. 1999	% change GDP- % change population 1999-1980	Agriculture % late 1990s	Industry % late 1990s	Services % late 1990s
Canada	666.2	21.8	38.2	2.5	32.8	64.7
Mexico	629.1	6.5	10.9	5.2	28.5	66.3
USA	7935.8	29.2	58.7	1.7	26.2	72.0
Japan	2579.0	20.4	58.6	1.7	36.1	62.2
Korea	553.0	11.8	263.2	5.2	44.9	49.9
Australia	402.9	21.2	59.5	3.3	26.4	70.4
New Zealand	57.2	15.1	33.8	6.5	25.8	67.7
Austria	160.7	19.9	44.8	2.2	32.9	64.9
Belgium	203.3	19.9	38.1	1.5	27.0	71.5
Czech Rep.	109.0	10.6	..	3.9	43.3	52.8
Denmark	115.5	21.7	48.4	2.7	26.4	70.9
Finland	98.6	19.1	50.4	3.6	34.2	62.2
France	1202.6	20.3	34.6	3.0	24.8	72.2
Germany ◆	1563.8	19.0	34.0	1.2	31.2	67.6
Greece	119.3	11.3	32.1	7.9	23.6	68.5
Hungary	89.9	8.9	..	5.0	33.5	61.4
Iceland	5.9	21.3	46.8	10.1	29.4	60.5
Ireland	76.9	20.6	142.1	3.8	36.0	60.3
Italy	1084.6	18.8	36.7	2.9	29.5	67.6
Luxembourg	15.3	35.5	127.3	0.7	20.1	79.2
Netherlands	320.6	20.3	45.7	3.0	26.7	70.3
Norway	103.9	23.4	61.8	2.3	35.7	62.0
Poland	255.0	6.6	..	3.9	35.8	60.2
Portugal	125.7	12.6	64.8	3.8	30.5	65.7
Spain	621.6	15.8	59.1	3.9	30.4	65.7
Sweden	171.0	19.3	31.6	2.0	29.1	68.8
Switzerland	158.5	22.2	16.9	1.6	30.3	68.1
Turkey	370.0	5.6	76.7	15.5	29.7	54.8
UK	1113.5	18.7	50.4	1.0	29.8	69.2
OECD ◆	20908.1	18.9	50.2	2.5	29.7	67.8

◆ See Technical Annex for data sources, notes and comments.

20 POPULATION GROWTH AND DENSITY

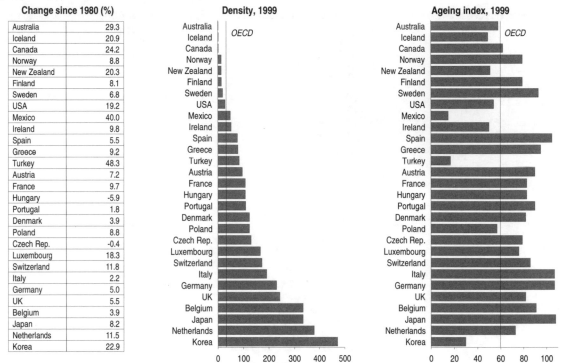

Change since 1980 (%)	
Australia	29.3
Iceland	20.9
Canada	24.2
Norway	8.8
New Zealand	20.3
Finland	8.1
Sweden	6.8
USA	19.2
Mexico	40.0
Ireland	9.8
Spain	5.5
Greece	9.2
Turkey	48.3
Austria	7.2
France	9.7
Hungary	-5.9
Portugal	1.8
Denmark	3.9
Poland	8.8
Czech Rep.	-0.4
Luxembourg	18.3
Switzerland	11.8
Italy	2.2
Germany	5.0
UK	5.5
Belgium	3.9
Japan	8.2
Netherlands	11.5
Korea	22.9

	Population				Unemployment rate
	Total 1 000 inh.	Density inh./km²	Ageing index pop>64/pop<15		% of total labour force
	1999	1999	1999	1980	1999
Canada	30545	3.1	62.4	41.3	7.6
Mexico	97512	49.8	14.9	8.8	2.5
USA	271342	29.0	53.6	50.1	4.2
Japan	126700	335.4	107.6	38.7	4.7
Korea	46858	471.8	29.9	12.1	6.3
Australia	19000	2.5	58.2	38.1	7.2
New Zealand	3781	14.0	51.4	35.7	6.8
Austria	8095	96.5	90.4	75.5	5.3
Belgium	10227	335.0	91.3	71.8	9.0
Czech Rep.	10288	130.4	79.3	57.7	8.8
Denmark	5324	123.5	82.5	69.0	5.5
Finland	5165	15.3	79.1	58.8	10.2
France	59100	107.6	82.6	62.2	11.1
Germany	82200	230.2	107.1	85.4	9.0
Greece	10533	79.8	95.2	57.6	10.7
Hungary	10078	108.3	83.3	..	7.1
Iceland	276	2.7	49.0	35.9	1.9
Ireland	3734	53.1	50.4	35.3	5.5
Italy	57701	191.5	106.6	62.8	11.5
Luxembourg	432	167.0	76.1	73.5	2.9
Netherlands	15781	380.0	73.0	51.6	3.2
Norway	4445	13.7	79.3	66.6	3.2
Poland	38708	123.8	56.8	41.6	12.0
Portugal	9997	108.7	90.3	44.9	4.4
Spain	39428	77.9	105.2	41.9	15.9
Sweden	8878	19.7	93.3	83.1	5.6
Switzerland	7140	172.9	86.0	70.2	2.7
Turkey	65904	84.6	16.8	12.1	7.3
UK	59428	242.7	81.7	71.2	5.9
OECD	1108599	31.9	60.5	44.4	6.6

◆ *See Technical Annex for data sources, notes and comments.*

CONSUMPTION

Consumption by households and government is a determinant of sustainable development and its economic, environmental and social dimensions. It has important implications for the level and pattern of production and for related demands for natural resources. Growth of private consumption has both positive and negative environmental effects, entailing increased use of private transport, more leisure and tourism, higher energy consumption, increased use of packaged goods and higher waste production, but also demand for environmentally friendly goods.

Agenda 21, adopted at UNCED (Rio de Janeiro, 1992), stresses that changes in consumption and production patterns are necessary to ensure more <u>sustainable development</u>. These can be promoted by increasing consumer awareness and expanding use of approaches such as life cycle analysis of products and extended producer responsibility. Governments can show the way by "greening" their own consumption and operations.

<u>Indicators</u> presented here relate to:

♦ *<u>private consumption</u>, i.e. by households and private non-profit institutions serving households. They present private final consumption expenditure expressed as percentage of GDP and per capita, as well as the structure of private consumption.*

♦ *<u>government consumption</u>, presenting government final consumption expenditure expressed as percentage of GDP and per capita.*

They should be read in conjunction with other indicators in this publication, notably those dealing with energy, transport, waste and water, and should be complemented with information on production patterns and trends.

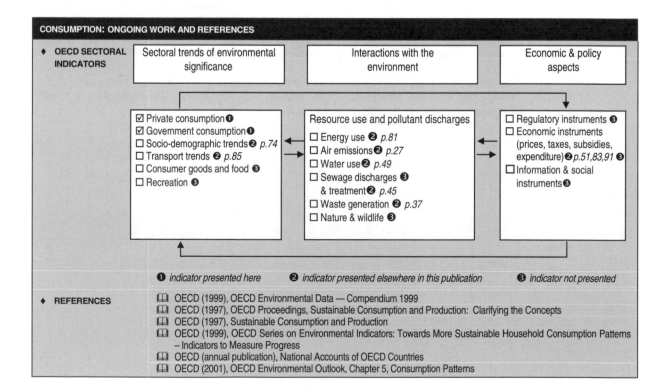

CONSUMPTION: ONGOING WORK AND REFERENCES

♦ **OECD SECTORAL INDICATORS**

Sectoral trends of environmental significance	Interactions with the environment	Economic & policy aspects

☑ Private consumption ❶
☑ Government consumption ❶
☐ Socio-demographic trends ❷ *p.74*
☐ Transport trends ❷ *p.85*
☐ Consumer goods and food ❸
☐ Recreation ❸

Resource use and pollutant discharges

☐ Energy use ❷ *p.81*
☐ Air emissions ❷ *p.27*
☐ Water use ❷ *p.49*
☐ Sewage discharges ❸ & treatment ❷ *p.45*
☐ Waste generation ❷ *p.37*
☐ Nature & wildlife ❸

☐ Regulatory instruments ❸
☐ Economic instruments (prices, taxes, subsidies, expenditure) ❷ *p.51,83,91* ❸
☐ Information & social instruments ❸

❶ *indicator presented here*   ❷ *indicator presented elsewhere in this publication*   ❸ *indicator not presented*

♦ **REFERENCES**

☐ OECD (1999), OECD Environmental Data — Compendium 1999
☐ OECD (1997), OECD Proceedings, Sustainable Consumption and Production: Clarifying the Concepts
☐ OECD (1997), Sustainable Consumption and Production
☐ OECD (1999), OECD Series on Environmental Indicators: Towards More Sustainable Household Consumption Patterns – Indicators to Measure Progress
☐ OECD (annual publication), National Accounts of OECD Countries
☐ OECD (2001), OECD Environmental Outlook, Chapter 5, Consumption Patterns

Private final consumption expenditure, 1999

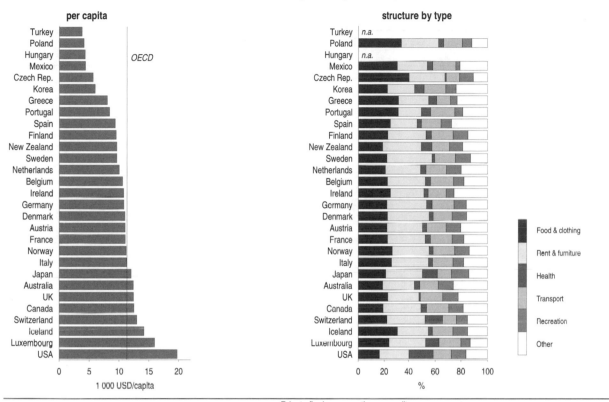

per capita

structure by type

Food & clothing

Rent & furniture

Health

Transport

Recreation

Other

	Private final consumption expenditure								
	Total	per capita		Consumption patterns, by type, %					
	% of GDP 1999	1 000 USD/cap. 1999	% change since 1980	Food & clothing	Rent & furniture	Health	Transport	Recreation	Other
Canada	57	12.5	30.2	19.4	30.3	3.7	17.4	10.7	18.5
Mexico	68	4.4	4.8	30.9	22.6	4.1	18.3	3.0	21.2
USA	68	19.8	57.3	16.1	24.1	18.0	14.5	11.0	16.4
Japan	59	12.1	52.6	21.1	29.4	11.1	11.0	12.9	14.5
Korea	51	6.0	167.7	22.7	21.8	7.4	16.8	7.6	23.7
Australia	59	12.4	42.8	19.1	25.7	3.7	14.3	11.5	25.7
New Zealand	64	9.6	25.3	18.6	30.6	8.0	13.8	10.2	18.7
Austria	56	11.0	42.8	21.9	28.4	3.2	15.5	11.2	19.9
Belgium	53	10.6	34.3	22.7	29.6	4.0	17.7	7.9	18.1
Czech Rep.	54	5.7	..	40.3	27.1	1.3	10.0	10.2	11.0
Denmark	51	11.0	35.9	22.8	33.0	2.5	15.2	10.5	16.0
Finland	50	9.5	43.6	23.3	30.1	3.5	16.8	11.1	15.2
France	54	11.1	23.9	23.0	30.3	3.6	16.9	8.7	17.6
Germany	♦ 57	10.8	*35.0*	22.2	31.5	4.1	17.4	9.3	15.5
Greece	71	8.0	42.2	31.7	23.2	5.8	11.4	4.6	23.3
Hungary	49	4.3	..	..	..	..	..	..	..
Iceland	67	14.2	46.3	30.8	23.9	2.6	15.9	11.4	15.5
Ireland	52	10.8	70.0	24.7	26.3	2.8	14.3	6.5	25.5
Italy	60	11.3	44.1	26.0	29.0	3.2	15.6	7.9	18.3
Luxembourg	45	16.0	48.8	23.6	29.4	9.9	17.4	7.0	12.7
Netherlands	49	10.1	34.2	20.9	28.2	4.0	15.6	11.1	20.1
Norway	48	11.2	43.5	26.8	28.6	2.7	17.0	11.2	13.8
Poland	63	4.2	..	34.4	28.4	4.2	14.3	6.6	12.1
Portugal	67	8.4	68.4	31.7	17.5	6.9	18.9	6.0	18.9
Spain	60	9.4	46.4	25.2	20.6	3.4	15.4	8.4	26.9
Sweden	50	9.7	16.5	22.2	35.4	2.4	16.2	11.0	12.8
Switzerland	59	13.0	13.4	21.8	30.0	13.3	11.2	8.5	15.3
Turkey	69	3.9	19.5	..	..	..	..	..	..
UK	66	12.5	63.6	23.4	24.5	1.2	16.8	11.9	22.2
OECD	♦ 61	11.5	*45.8*	..	..	..	..	..	..

♦ See Technical Annex for data sources, notes and comments.

22 GOVERNMENT CONSUMPTION

Government final consumption expenditure

per capita, 1999

1 000 USD/capita

	Total	per capita	
	% of GDP 1999	1 000 USD/cap. 1999	% change since 1980
Canada	19	4.2	4.8
Mexico	10	0.6	2.4
USA	14	4.1	14.5
Japan	10	2.0	36.3
Korea	9	1.1	74.8
Australia	18	3.8	37.6
New Zealand	16	2.5	13.7
Austria	19	3.9	23.1
Belgium	21	4.1	10.0
Czech Rep.	20	2.1	..
Denmark	26	5.5	28.9
Finland	21	3.9	32.8
France	23	4.8	36.2
Germany ♦	19	3.6	*18.2*
Greece	14	1.6	28.0
Hungary	23	2.0	..
Iceland	19	4.1	61.9
Ireland	13	2.6	19.5
Italy	17	3.3	26.5
Luxembourg	16	5.8	41.3
Netherlands	23	4.6	25.0
Norway	20	4.6	48.9
Poland	15	1.0	..
Portugal	16	2.1	107.8
Spain	17	2.7	93.1
Sweden	25	4.8	11.5
Switzerland	15	3.4	33.7
Turkey	9	0.5	139.8
UK	19	3.5	15.1
OECD ♦	14	2.7	*20.5*

♦ *See Technical Annex for data sources, notes and comments.*

ENERGY

Energy is a major component of OECD economies, both as a sector in itself and as a factor input to all other economic activities. Energy production and use have environmental effects that differ greatly by energy source. Fuel combustion is the main source of local and regional air pollution and greenhouse gas emissions; other effects involve water quality, land use, risks related to the nuclear fuel cycle and risks related to the extraction, transport and use of fossil fuels.

The structure of a country's energy supply and the intensity of its energy use, along with changes over time, are key determinants of environmental performance and sustainability of economic development. The supply structure varies considerably among countries. It is influenced by demand from industry, transport and households, by national energy policies and by national and international energy prices. Environmental performance can be assessed against domestic objectives such as energy efficiency targets, and targets concerning the share of renewable energy sources; and against international environmental commitments that have direct implications for domestic energy policies and strategies (e.g. the United Nations Framework Convention on Climate Change (1992), Convention on Long-Range Transboundary Air Pollution (1979)). The main challenge is to further de-couple energy use and related air emissions from economic growth, through improvements in energy efficiency and through the development and use of cleaner fuels may be necessary.

Indicators presented here relate to:

♦ *trends in energy intensities. Energy intensities, expressed as energy supply per unit of GDP and per capita, reflect, at least partly, changes in energy efficiency and efforts to reduce atmospheric emissions. They also reflect structural and climatic factors.*

♦ *energy mix, i.e. the structure of and changes in energy supply, in terms of primary energy source as a percentage of total energy supply. This is closely related to consumption and production patterns and to environmental effects.*

♦ *energy prices for industry and households, with changes in real energy end-use prices.*

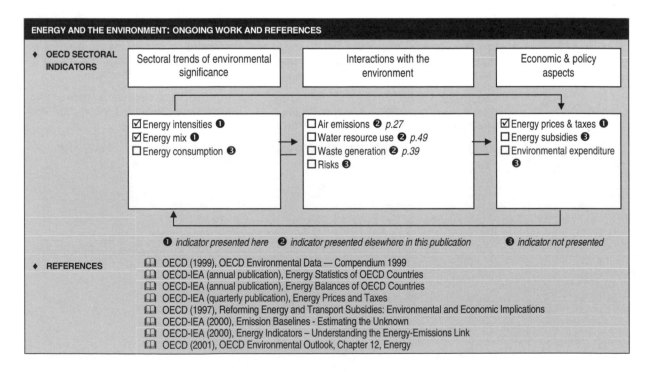

ENERGY AND THE ENVIRONMENT: ONGOING WORK AND REFERENCES

♦ **OECD SECTORAL INDICATORS**

Sectoral trends of environmental significance	Interactions with the environment	Economic & policy aspects

☑ Energy intensities ❶ ☑ Energy mix ❶ ☐ Energy consumption ❸	☐ Air emissions ❷ *p.27* ☐ Water resource use ❷ *p.49* ☐ Waste generation ❷ *p.39* ☐ Risks ❸	☑ Energy prices & taxes ❶ ☐ Energy subsidies ❸ ☐ Environmental expenditure ❸

❶ *indicator presented here*   ❷ *indicator presented elsewhere in this publication*   ❸ *indicator not presented*

♦ **REFERENCES**

📖 OECD (1999), OECD Environmental Data — Compendium 1999
📖 OECD-IEA (annual publication), Energy Statistics of OECD Countries
📖 OECD-IEA (annual publication), Energy Balances of OECD Countries
📖 OECD-IEA (quarterly publication), Energy Prices and Taxes
📖 OECD (1997), Reforming Energy and Transport Subsidies: Environmental and Economic Implications
📖 OECD-IEA (2000), Emission Baselines - Estimating the Unknown
📖 OECD-IEA (2000), Energy Indicators – Understanding the Energy-Emissions Link
📖 OECD (2001), OECD Environmental Outlook, Chapter 12, Energy

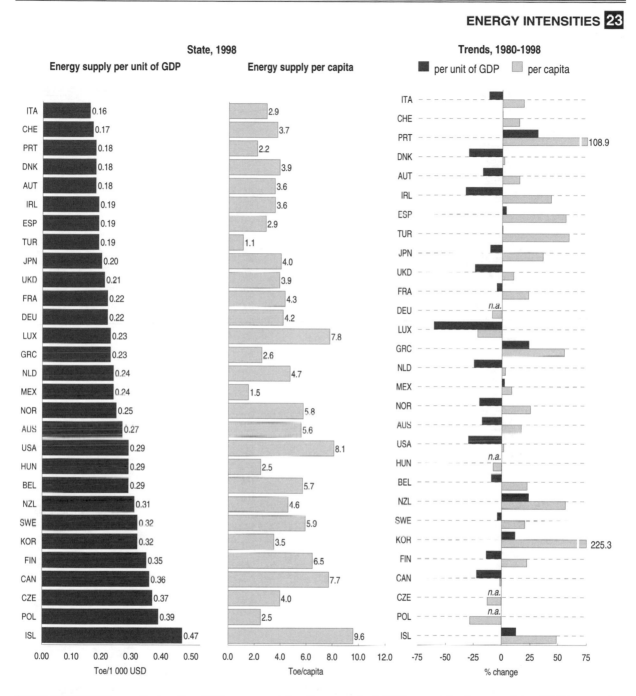

State, 1998

Energy supply per unit of GDP

ITA	0.16
CHE	0.17
PRT	0.18
DNK	0.18
AUT	0.18
IRL	0.19
ESP	0.19
TUR	0.19
JPN	0.20
UKD	0.21
FRA	0.22
DEU	0.22
LUX	0.23
GRC	0.23
NLD	0.24
MEX	0.24
NOR	0.25
AUS	0.27
USA	0.29
HUN	0.29
BEL	0.29
NZL	0.31
SWE	0.32
KOR	0.32
FIN	0.35
CAN	0.36
CZE	0.37
POL	0.39
ISL	0.47

Toe/1 000 USD

Energy supply per capita

2.9	
3.7	
2.2	
3.9	
3.6	
3.6	
2.9	
1.1	
4.0	
3.9	
4.3	
4.2	
7.8	
2.6	
4.7	
1.5	
5.8	
5.6	
8.1	
2.5	
5.7	
4.6	
5.9	
3.5	
6.5	
7.7	
4.0	
2.5	
9.6	

Toe/capita

Trends, 1980-1998

■ per unit of GDP   ☐ per capita

PRT 108.9
KOR 225.3

% change

STATE AND TRENDS SUMMARY

During the 1980s, energy intensity per unit of GDP generally decreased for OECD countries overall as a consequence of economic structural changes and energy conservation measures. In the 1990s, energy intensity did not further improve in most countries, due to decreasing prices for energy resources (oil, gas, etc.). Progress in per capita terms has been much slower, reflecting an overall increase in energy supply and energy demands for transport activities.

Variations among OECD countries are wide (from 1 to 3 per unit of GDP, from 1 to 9 per capita) and depend on national economic structure, geography (e.g. climate) energy policies and prices, and countries' endowment in different types of energy resources.

24 ENERGY MIX

Supply by source, 1998

	Primary energy supply						
	Total (Mtoe)	% change	Structure by source, share of total (%)				
	1998	since 1980	Solid fuel	Oil	Gas	Nuclear	Other
Iceland	3	79	3	31	-	-	66
Luxembourg	3	-9	5	72	22	1	-
Ireland	13	56	23	55	21	-	1
New Zealand	17	85	11	38	24	-	26
Denmark	21	5	34	45	20	-	1
Portugal	22	112	19	72	3	14	5
Hungary	25	-13	18	29	39	-	-
Norway	25	35	9	34	17	-	40
Switzerland	27	28	6	50	9	-	11
Greece	27	69	37	59	3	14	2
Austria	29	23	22	43	23	-	11
Finland	33	32	36	33	10	17	4
Czech Republic	41	-13	52	20	19	8	-
Sweden	52	28	20	30	1	25	12
Belgium	58	27	16	42	21	21	-
Turkey	73	132	40	42	12	11	5
Netherlands	74	14	13	37	48	-	-
Poland	96	-22	71	19	10	-	-
Australia	105	49	48	34	17	-	1
Spain	113	64	19	55	10	36	3
Mexico	148	49	10	62	21	2	5
Korea	163	296	22	56	8	14	-
Italy	168	21	8	57	31	-	4
UK	233	16	18	36	34	11	-
Canada	234	21	17	35	29	8	12
France	256	34	11	35	13	39	2
Germany	345	-4	25	41	21	-	1
Japan	510	47	18	51	12	17	2
USA	2182	20	27	40	23	9	2
OECD	5097	26	24	42	21	11	3

■ Solid fuel	■ Oil	■ Gas	■ Nuclear	□ Other

STATE AND TRENDS SUMMARY

The energy supply mix has a major effect on environmental performance because the environmental impact of each energy source differs greatly.

During the 1980s and early 1990s, growth in total primary energy supply was accompanied by changes in the fuel mix: the shares of solid fuels and oil fell, while those of gas and other sources rose. This trend is particularly visible in OECD Europe. The rates of change, however, vary widely by country.

ENERGY PRICES 25

Trends in real energy end-use prices (Index 1995 = 100)

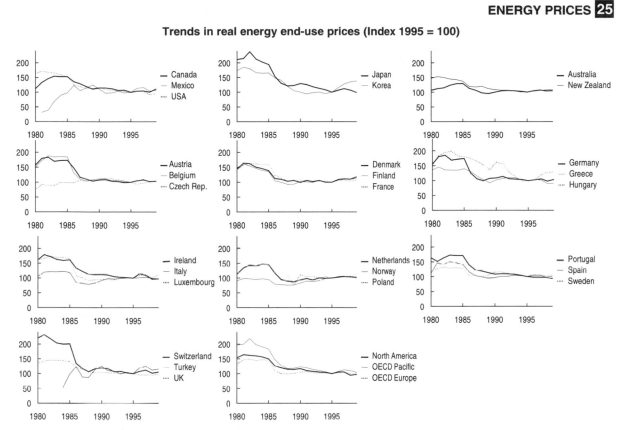

Selected energy prices for industry and households, late-1990s

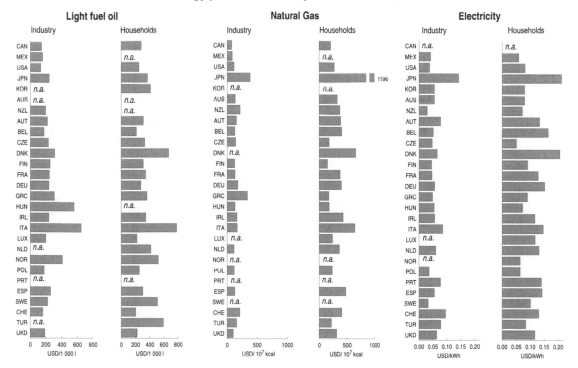

OECD Environmental Indicators 2001

25 ENERGY PRICES

	Industry						Households						Real energy end-use prices
	Oil		Natural gas		Electricity		Oil		Natural gas		Electricity		
	Price USD/1 000 l 1999	Tax (%) 1999	Price USD/10^7 kcal 1999	Tax (%) 1999	Price USD/kWh 1999	Tax (%) 1999	Price USD/1 000 l 1999	Tax (%) 1999	Price USD/10^7 kcal 1999	Tax (%) 1999	Price USD/kWh 1999	Tax (%) 1999	Change (%) since 1980
Canada	145	..	79	..	..	..	281	..	212	..	..	..	-0.5
Mexico ♦	158	-	88	-	0.042	-	..	..	..	..	0.059	13	239.0
USA ♦	134	..	118	..	0.039	..	250	..	277	..	0.082	..	-41.7
Japan	242	5	386	..	0.143	8	372	5	1196	5	0.213	7	-53.0
Korea	..	..	..	..	0.056	..	414	..	..	..	0.080	..	-20.9
Australia ♦	..	..	136	..	0.056	..	..	..	332	..	0.080	..	-2.2
New Zealand	197	-	217	5	0.030	-	..	..	379	14	0.072	11	-26.6
Austria	220	20	155	..	0.078	..	312	43	393	28	0.134	22	-34.6
Belgium	177	8	131	..	0.052	-	214	24	410	..	0.165	..	-32.7
Czech Republic	231	-	143	-	0.048	-	332	31	185	18	0.051	18	40.5
Denmark	311	12	..	..	0.066	20	671	62	655	57	0.207	61	-18.0
Finland	254	28	128	16	0.046	10	310	41	156	31	0.091	26	-24.1
France	244	35	135	-	0.047	-	344	42	384	17	0.129	..	-24.2
Germany	237	25	178	13	0.057	-	275	36	405	19	0.152	14	-33.4
Greece	307	44	342	7	0.049	-	363	52	181	7	0.090	7	-33.1
Hungary	561	56	135	-	0.055	-	x	x	185	11	0.073	11	-14.8
Ireland	238	21	165	-	0.057	-	346	26	435	11	0.117	11	-39.7
Italy	652	66	171	10	0.086	19	782	72	639	47	0.147	26	-6.6
Luxembourg	198	3	..	..	..	..	222	13	245	6	0.118	6	-31.6
Netherlands	..	..	117	9	0.061	2	419	46	369	33	0.132	29	-9.6
Norway	410	14	not app.	not app.	..	..	523	30	not app.	not app.	0.064	36	12.8
Poland	180	11	122	-	0.037	-	253	26	241	18	0.064	18	..
Portugal	not app.	not app.	..	..	0.078	-	not app.	not app.	not app.	not app.	0.141	5	-42.8
Spain	261	32	132	-	0.056	5	303	42	481	15	0.143	18	-10.4
Sweden	222	29	..	..	0.034	..	511	62	..	..	0.101	..	-10.8
Switzerland	164	6	215	1	0.096	-	205	11	412	8	0.131	7	-52.1
Turkey	..	..	162	7	0.079	14	597	65	226	7	0.084	17	..
UK	189	26	106	-	0.064	-	225	26	321	5	0.117	5	-27.3

♦ *See Technical Annex for data sources, notes and comments.*   *.. not available   - nil or negligible not app. not applicable*

**STATE AND TRENDS
SUMMARY**

Energy end-use prices influence overall energy demand and the fuel mix, which in turn largely determine environmental pressures caused by energy activities. They can help internalise environmental costs. Though price elasticities vary considerably by end-use sector, historical and cross-country experience suggests that the overall price effect on energy demand is strong and that increases in energy prices have reduced energy use and hence its environmental impact.

The indicators show a general downward trend in real end-use energy prices in most OECD countries, though rates of change differ greatly among countries. Energy prices and related taxes, whether for industry or households, also vary widely among countries for all types of energy.

TRANSPORT

Transport is a major component of economic activity, both as a sector in itself and as a factor input to most other economic activities. It has many effects on the environment: air pollution raises concern mainly in urban areas where road traffic and congestion are concentrated, though road transport also contributes to regional and global pollution problems such as acidification and climate change; transport infrastructure leads to fragmentation of natural habitats; and vehicles entail waste management issues.

Road transport plays an important role in a country's environmental performance and the sustainability of its development. The volume of traffic depends on the demand for transport (largely determined by economic activity and transport prices) and on transport supply (e.g. the development of road infrastructure). Road traffic, both freight and passenger, is expected to increase further in a number of OECD countries. The main challenge is to reduce the environmental and health effects of transport, particularly regarding air pollution and climate change, by ensuring that efficiency gains from technological developments and demand side management achieve lasting environmental quality improvements.

Indicators presented here relate to:

* *road traffic and vehicle intensities, i.e. traffic volumes per unit of GDP and per kilometre of road, and vehicle numbers per capita and per kilometre of road;*

* *road infrastructure densities, i.e. the length of road and motorway networks per square kilometre of land area;*

* *road fuel prices and taxes, notably the relative price and taxation levels of diesel fuel and leaded and unleaded gasoline.*

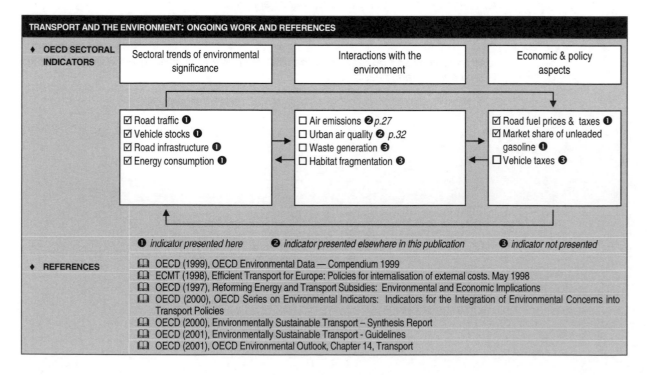

TRANSPORT AND THE ENVIRONMENT: ONGOING WORK AND REFERENCES

♦ **OECD SECTORAL INDICATORS**

Sectoral trends of environmental significance	Interactions with the environment	Economic & policy aspects
☑ Road traffic ❶ ☑ Vehicle stocks ❶ ☑ Road infrastructure ❶ ☑ Energy consumption ❶	☐ Air emissions ❷ *p.27* ☐ Urban air quality ❷ *p.32* ☐ Waste generation ❸ ☐ Habitat fragmentation ❸	☑ Road fuel prices & taxes ❶ ☑ Market share of unleaded gasoline ❶ ☐ Vehicle taxes ❸

❶ *indicator presented here* ❷ *indicator presented elsewhere in this publication* ❸ *indicator not presented*

♦ **REFERENCES**

 📖 OECD (1999), OECD Environmental Data — Compendium 1999
 📖 ECMT (1998), Efficient Transport for Europe: Policies for internalisation of external costs. May 1998
 📖 OECD (1997), Reforming Energy and Transport Subsidies: Environmental and Economic Implications
 📖 OECD (2000), OECD Series on Environmental Indicators: Indicators for the Integration of Environmental Concerns into Transport Policies
 📖 OECD (2000), Environmentally Sustainable Transport – Synthesis Report
 📖 OECD (2001), Environmentally Sustainable Transport - Guidelines
 📖 OECD (2001), OECD Environmental Outlook, Chapter 14, Transport

ROAD TRAFFIC AND VEHICLE INTENSITIES 26

Road traffic intensities
State, 1998
Traffic per unit of GDP

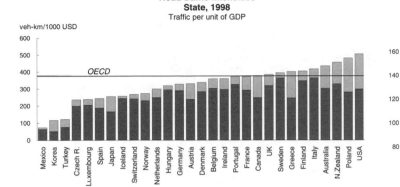

Road traffic intensities
Trends, Index 1980=100
Traffic per unit of GDP

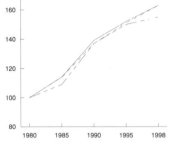

Traffic per network length

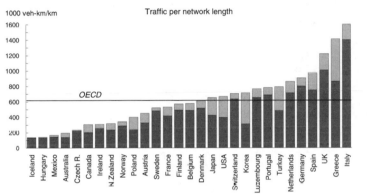

Traffic per network length

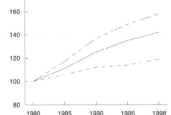

Road vehicle intensities
State, 1998
Motor vehicles per capita

Road vehicle intensities
Trends, Index 1980=100
Motor vehicles per capita

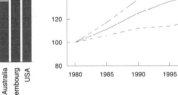

Motor vehicles per network length

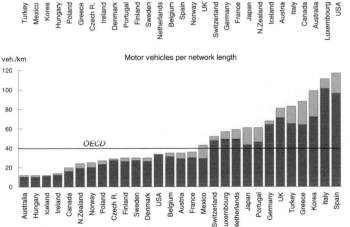

Motor vehicles per network length

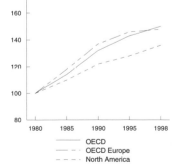

— OECD
–·– OECD Europe
–– North America

26 ROAD TRAFFIC AND VEHICLE INTENSITIES

		Road traffic						Motor vehicles in use				GDP
		Total volume		Intensity		Goods vehicles		Total stock		Private car ownership		
		billion veh-km	% change	per unit of GDP veh-km/1 000 USD	per network length 1 000 veh-km/km	Volume % change	share in total traffic, %	1 000 vehicles	% change	veh./100 inh.	% change	% change
		1998	since 1980	1998	1998	since 1980	1998	1998	since 1980	1998	since 1980	since 1980
Canada		280	36	378	307	86	35	18039	37	47	14	57
Mexico		54	28	74	169	-27	17	13891	138	10	64	46
USA	◆	4223	73	505	669	169	41	214431	38	77	18	71
Japan	◆	759	95	256	655	85	34	70818	91	40	96	65
Korea		75	763	116	715	1001	51	10468	1884	16	2423	254
Australia	◆	187	63	434	198	120	31	11262	55	49	25	82
N.Zealand		29	77	456	319	120	26	2161	38	46	11	50
Austria	◆	60	70	331	454	80	27	4709	68	48	62	49
Belgium	◆	85	76	359	580	75	8	4988	43	44	37	39
Czech R.	◆	31	46	237	239	29	14	3773	95	34	97	..
Denmark	◆	44	67	338	616	57	15	2188	33	36	31	50
Finland		45	67	405	574	49	13	2310	67	39	53	53
France	◆	476	61	373	533	85	21	32310	49	46	29	41
Germany	◆	596	47	328	908	46	11	44269	61	51	54	..
Greece	◆	59	188	400	1412	162	38	3654	189	25	186	37
Hungary	◆	33	72	319	143	-51	8	2729	132	23	146	..
Iceland	◆	2	100	259	138	28	6	158	65	52	37	58
Ireland		30	62	359	311	40	16	1379	72	33	52	132
Italy	◆	495	119	416	1603	74	12	34334	77	54	74	38
Luxembourg	◆	4	73	240	767	173	13	282	93	58	59	134
Netherlands	◆	109	61	300	863	125	17	7319	61	39	31	53
Norway		31	63	274	341	103	13	2213	58	41	35	70
Poland		153	243	481	402	187	38	10550	244	23	243	..
Portugal	◆	55	154	371	785	45	11	4250	253	32	234	62
Spain	◆	161	128	245	979	110	21	19271	115	40	99	59
Sweden		73	64	395	524	94	6	4145	35	43	24	33
Switzerland	◆	50	40	268	708	33	10	3666	51	48	36	27
Turkey	◆	50	238	122	795	170	32	5155	340	6	280	130
UK	◆	454	88	385	1221	79	16	29971	73	45	62	53
OECD		8701	77	380	618	134	31	564692	62	45	42	..

◆ *See Technical Annex for data sources, notes and comments.*

STATE AND TRENDS SUMMARY

From 1980, countries' efforts in introducing cleaner vehicles have largely been offset by growth in vehicle stocks and the rapid increase of their use. In most OECD countries road traffic growth rates exceeded economic growth.

Traffic intensities per unit of GDP and per length of network show wide variations among OECD countries. The same holds for vehicle availability per capita and vehicle density.

ROAD INFRASTRUCTURE DENSITIES 27

Road Network Density
State, 1998

km/100 km^2

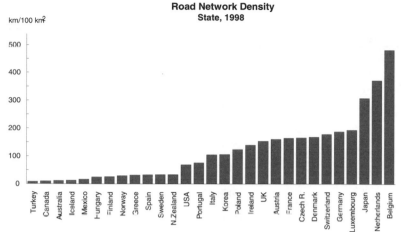

Trends in road network density
Trends, Index 1980=100

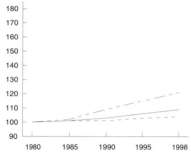

Motorways Density
State, 1998

km/10000km^2

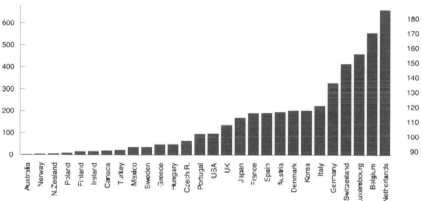

Trends in motorways density
Trends, Index 1980= 100

27 ROAD INFRASTRUCTURE DENSITIES

		Road network			Motorways			GDP
		Total length		Density	Total length		Density	
		1 000 km 1998	% change since 1980	km/100 km² 1998	km 1998	% change since 1980	km/10 000 km² 1998	% change since 1980
Canada		912	10	10	17400	112	19	57
Mexico	♦	322	51	17	6594	608	35	46
USA		6308	2	69	88613	24	97	71
Japan		1159	4	308	6356	146	169	65
Korea		105	124	106	1996	63	202	254
Australia	♦	947	17	12	1417	30	2	82
N.Zealand		92	-2	34	144	22	5	50
Austria	♦	133	25	161	1613	74	195	49
Belgium	♦	146	17	482	1682	34	556	39
Czech R.		128	129	166	498	93	64	..
Denmark		71	4	169	855	66	202	50
Finland	♦	78	4	26	473	144	16	53
France	♦	893	11	165	10300	96	190	41
Germany		656	9	188	11400	24	327	..
Greece	♦	42	12	32	601	560	47	37
Hungary	♦	229	161	25	438	110	48	..
Iceland		13	4	13	..	..	..	58
Ireland		97	5	140	117	..	17	132
Italy		309	4	105	6550	11	223	38
Luxembourg	♦	5	-2	194	118	168	459	134
Netherlands		126	16	372	2235	26	660	53
Norway		91	11	30	128	125	4	70
Poland		381	28	125	268	93	9	..
Portugal		69	34	76	870	585	95	62
Spain	♦	164	9	33	9547	394	191	59
Sweden	♦	139	8	34	1439	69	35	33
Switzerland		71	7	179	1638	40	414	27
Turkey	♦	63	5	8	1726	7092	22	130
UK	♦	372	9	154	3305	28	137	53
OECD		14090	9	42	179688	53	54	..

♦ *See Technical Annex for data sources, notes and comments.*

STATE AND TRENDS SUMMARY

Length of road network is an indicator of transport infrastructure development, which in turn is an important component of transport supply. Transport infrastructure exerts pressures on the environment through use of space and physical transformation of the natural environment (e.g. fragmentation of habitats).

Density of road infrastructure varies greatly among OECD countries (from 1 to 60). The length of motorways often grows faster than GDP.

ROAD FUEL PRICES AND TAXES 28

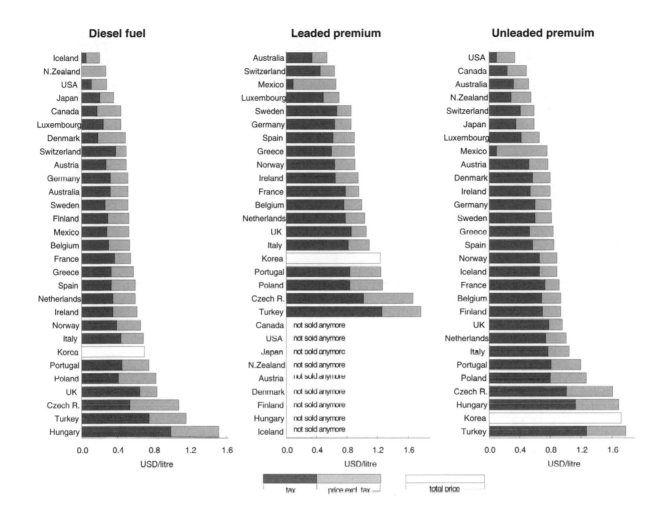

Diesel fuel

Iceland
N.Zealand
USA
Japan
Canada
Luxembourg
Denmark
Switzerland
Austria
Germany
Australia
Sweden
Finland
Mexico
Belgium
France
Greece
Spain
Netherlands
Ireland
Norway
Italy
Korea
Portugal
Poland
UK
Czech R.
Turkey
Hungary

0.0   0.4   0.8   1.2   1.6
USD/litre

Leaded premium

Australia
Switzerland
Mexico
Luxembourg
Sweden
Germany
Spain
Greece
Norway
Ireland
France
Belgium
Netherlands
UK
Italy
Korea
Portugal
Poland
Czech R.
Turkey
Canada — not sold anymore
USA — not sold anymore
Japan — not sold anymore
N.Zealand — not sold anymore
Austria — not sold anymore
Denmark — not sold anymore
Finland — not sold anymore
Hungary — not sold anymore
Iceland — not sold anymore

0.0   0.4   0.8   1.2   1.6
USD/litre

Unleaded premuim

USA
Canada
Australia
N.Zealand
Switzerland
Japan
Luxembourg
Mexico
Austria
Denmark
Ireland
Germany
Sweden
Greece
Spain
Norway
Iceland
France
Belgium
Finland
UK
Netherlands
Italy
Portugal
Poland
Czech R.
Hungary
Korea
Turkey

0.0   0.4   0.8   1.2   1.6
USD/litre

tax   price excl. tax ⌐   total price

28 ROAD FUEL PRICES AND TAXES

		Diesel				Leaded premium				Unleaded gasoline		Energy consumption by road transport		
		Price USD/litre		Taxation % of price		Price USD/litre		Taxation % of price		Price USD/litre	Taxation % of price	share of total cons.	Total Mtoe	% change since
		1980	1999	1980	1999	1980	1999	1980	1999	1999	1999	1998	1998	1980
Canada	♦	0.54	0.44	..	39	..	..	..	..	0.48	49	73	39	10
Mexico	♦	..	0.53	..	53	..	0.65	..	13	0.75	13	91	33	117
USA		0.47	0.28	15	39	0.59	..	..	..	0.34	28	81	472	36
Japan	♦	0.76	0.36	24	56	..	..	..	..	0.59	60	81	75	72
Korea	♦	1.00	0.70	..	..	3.96	1.24	..	..	1.72	..	72	18	1693
Australia	♦	..	0.52	..	62	0.53	0.54	19	62	0.52	61	79	21	52
N.Zealand	♦	0.76	0.27	2	1	0.96	..	28	..	0.55	52	50	2	40
Austria		0.96	0.50	33	55	1.05	..	42	..	0.77	68	86	6	43
Belgium		0.60	0.54	34	56	1.10	1.01	53	76	0.94	74	78	8	52
Czech R.		..	1.08	..	50	..	1.66	..	61	1.60	63	88	3	69
Denmark	♦	0.42	0.49	..	36	1.03	..	59	..	0.80	71	77	4	57
Finland		..	0.53	..	54	1.08	..	36	..	0.95	74	84	4	45
France	♦	0.75	0.55	47	67	1.07	0.96	58	81	0.92	79	84	42	49
Germany		..	0.51	..	62	..	0.86	..	74	0.81	74	86	57	41
w.Germany		0.72	..	41	..	0.83	..	49	..	..	..	..	..	..
Greece		0.76	0.58	13	57	1.77	0.91	42	67	0.84	63	71	5	126
Hungary		..	1.52	..	65	..	..	18	..	1.69	67	88	3	19
Iceland	♦	..	0.20	..	25	..	..	..	..	0.90	74	59	0	56
Ireland		0.82	0.62	28	56	1.14	0.95	48	69	0.80	68	82	3	85
Italy		0.62	0.70	8	64	1.57	1.10	61	74	1.06	73	89	37	65
Luxembourg		0.51	0.45	17	54	0.79	0.70	44	70	0.66	64	81	1	202
Netherlands		0.55	0.60	23	58	0.96	1.04	52	75	1.01	73	70	10	40
Norway		0.34	0.65	1	59	0.79	0.91	52	71	0.89	75	66	3	67
Poland		..	0.82	..	49	..	1.27	..	66	1.27	63	91	9	39
Portugal		1.02	0.76	7	60	2.70	1.25	61	67	1.20	68	86	5	159
Spain		0.70	0.60	25	56	1.41	0.90	35	69	0.86	67	79	25	131
Sweden		0.37	0.52	8	50	0.75	0.85	49	78	0.82	73	84	7	28
Switzerland		0.99	0.50	51	76	0.95	0.63	51	71	0.59	69	74	5	48
Turkey		0.95	1.16	..	64	1.63	1.79	..	71	1.78	71	81	9	90
UK		0.83	0.84	40	77	0.95	1.06	46	81	0.96	81	76	39	47

♦ See Technical Annex for data sources, notes and comments.

STATE AND TRENDS SUMMARY

Prices are a key form of information for consumers. When fuel prices rise relative to other goods, this tends to reduce demand for fuels and stimulate energy saving, and may influence the fuel structure of energy consumption.

The use of taxation to influence energy consumer behaviour and to internalise environmental costs is increasing. Taxation of unleaded fuel ranges from 13 to 81 per cent of the price. Many OECD countries have introduced tax differentials in favour of unleaded gasoline and some have imposed environmental taxes (e.g. relating to sulphur content) on energy products.

AGRICULTURE

The economic and social significance of the agricultural sector has been declining in most OECD countries for decades. Agriculture's environmental effects can be negative or positive. They depend on the scale, type and intensity of farming as well as on agro-ecological and physical factors and on climate and weather. Farming can lead to deterioration in soil, water and air quality, and to loss of natural habitats and biodiversity. These environmental changes can have important implications for the level of agricultural production and food supply, and can limit the sustainable development *of agriculture. But farming can also provide sinks for greenhouse gases, conserve biodiversity and landscapes and help prevent floods and landslides.*

The main environmental concerns *related to agriculture include nitrogen and phosphorus run-off from excessive commercial fertiliser use, intensive livestock farming and pesticides. Nitrogen and phosphorus, while major plant nutrients, are responsible for water eutrophication and related effects on aquatic life and water quality. Pesticide use adds persistent organic chemicals to ecosystems; these tend to accumulate in the soil and in biota, and residues may leach into surface and groundwaters. The general population can be exposed to pesticides through food. The main* challenge *is to progressively decrease the negative and increase the positive environmental effects of agricultural production so that ecosystem functions can be maintained and food security ensured for the world's population.*

Indicators *presented here relate to:*

- *intensity of use of nitrogen and phosphate fertilisers in agriculture, reflected through apparent consumption in tonnes of active ingredients (N and P per km^2 of agricultural land). This represents potential pressure on the environment in the absence of effective pollution abatement.*

- *Nitrogen balances, measured by the soil surface balance, is the difference between the total quantity of nitrogen inputs entering, and the quantity of nitrogen outputs leaving the soil over one year, per hectare of agricultural land.*

- *livestock densities, reflected through the number of head of cattle, pigs, sheep and goats per km^2 of agricultural land; the amount of N and P generated by livestock manure per km^2 of agricultural land is provided to complete the picture.*

- *intensity of use of pesticides in agriculture, reflected through apparent consumption or sales expressed in tonnes of active ingredients per km^2 of agricultural land. This indicator does not recognise differences among pesticides in levels of toxicity, persistence and mobility. It can be considered a first step towards a more comprehensive indicator based on an internationally agreed list of substances with appropriate weighting factors. Using km^2 of land where pesticides are actually applied as the denominator would provide important complementary information about intensity of pesticide use.*

It should be noted that these indicators describe potential environmental pressures, and may hide important sub-national variations. More information is needed to describe the actual pressure.

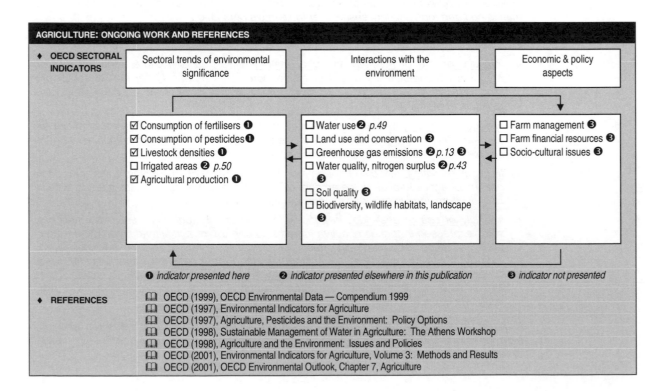

AGRICULTURE: ONGOING WORK AND REFERENCES

♦ **OECD SECTORAL INDICATORS**

Sectoral trends of environmental significance	Interactions with the environment	Economic & policy aspects

☑ Consumption of fertilisers ❶	☐ Water use ❷ *p.49*	☐ Farm management ❸
☑ Consumption of pesticides ❶	☐ Land use and conservation ❸	☐ Farm financial resources ❸
☑ Livestock densities ❶	☐ Greenhouse gas emissions ❷ *p.13* ❸	☐ Socio-cultural issues ❸
☐ Irrigated areas ❷ *p.50*	☐ Water quality, nitrogen surplus ❷ *p.43* ❸	
☑ Agricultural production ❶	☐ Soil quality ❸	
	☐ Biodiversity, wildlife habitats, landscape ❸	

❶ *indicator presented here*   ❷ *indicator presented elsewhere in this publication*   ❸ *indicator not presented*

♦ **REFERENCES**

📖 OECD (1999), OECD Environmental Data — Compendium 1999
📖 OECD (1997), Environmental Indicators for Agriculture
📖 OECD (1997), Agriculture, Pesticides and the Environment: Policy Options
📖 OECD (1998), Sustainable Management of Water in Agriculture: The Athens Workshop
📖 OECD (1998), Agriculture and the Environment: Issues and Policies
📖 OECD (2001), Environmental Indicators for Agriculture, Volume 3: Methods and Results
📖 OECD (2001), OECD Environmental Outlook, Chapter 7, Agriculture

INTENSITY OF USE OF NITROGEN AND PHOSPHATE FERTILISERS 29

Nitrogen from fertilizers per km² of agricultural land
Trends (tonnes/km²) %change 1980-98

Phosphate from fertilizers per km² of agricultural land
Trends (tonnes/km²) %change 1980-98

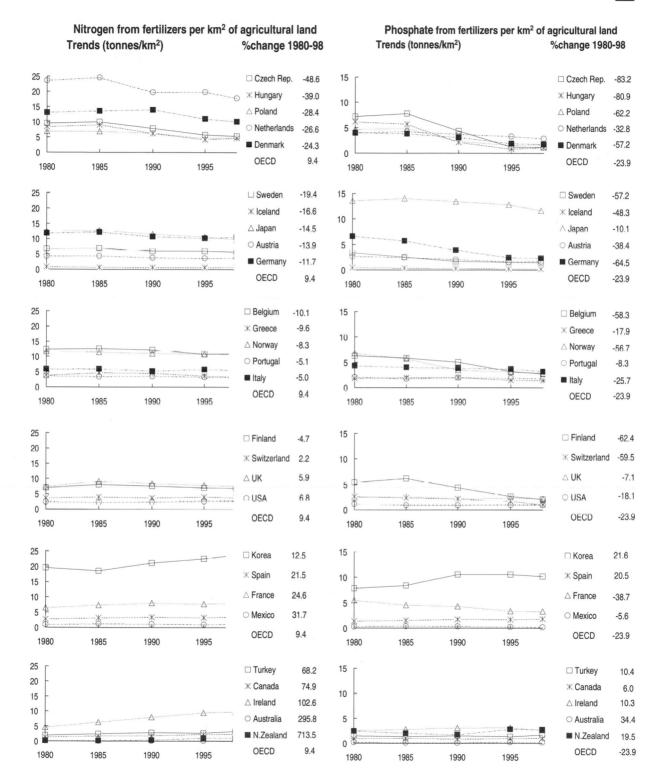

	Nitrogen		Phosphate
□ Czech Rep.	-48.6	□ Czech Rep.	-83.2
✳ Hungary	-39.0	✳ Hungary	-80.9
△ Poland	-28.4	△ Poland	-62.2
○ Netherlands	-26.6	○ Netherlands	-32.8
■ Denmark	-24.3	■ Denmark	-57.2
OECD	9.4	OECD	-23.9
□ Sweden	-19.4	□ Sweden	-57.2
✳ Iceland	-16.6	✳ Iceland	-48.3
△ Japan	-14.5	△ Japan	-10.1
○ Austria	-13.9	○ Austria	-38.4
■ Germany	-11.7	■ Germany	-64.5
OECD	9.4	OECD	-23.9
□ Belgium	-10.1	□ Belgium	-58.3
✳ Greece	-9.6	✳ Greece	-17.9
△ Norway	-8.3	△ Norway	-56.7
○ Portugal	-5.1	○ Portugal	-8.3
■ Italy	-5.0	■ Italy	-25.7
OECD	9.4	OECD	-23.9
□ Finland	-4.7	□ Finland	-62.4
✳ Switzerland	2.2	✳ Switzerland	-59.5
△ UK	5.9	△ UK	-7.1
○ USA	6.8	○ USA	-18.1
OECD	9.4	OECD	-23.9
□ Korea	12.5	□ Korea	21.6
✳ Spain	21.5	✳ Spain	20.5
△ France	24.6	△ France	-38.7
○ Mexico	31.7	○ Mexico	-5.6
OECD	9.4	OECD	-23.9
□ Turkey	68.2	□ Turkey	10.4
✳ Canada	74.9	✳ Canada	6.0
△ Ireland	102.6	△ Ireland	10.3
○ Australia	295.8	○ Australia	34.4
■ N.Zealand	713.5	■ N.Zealand	19.5
OECD	9.4	OECD	-23.9

29 INTENSITY OF USE OF NITROGEN AND PHOSPHATE FERTILISERS

		Intensity of use of commercial nitrogen and phosphate fertilizers apparent consumption per km² of agricultural land				Agricultural production		Agricultural value added
		Nitrogen		Phosphate		Crops	Total	
		tonnes/km² 1998	% change since 1980	tonnes/km² 1998	% change since 1980	% change since 1980	% change since 1980	% GDP 1999
Canada		2.4	75	1.0	6	78.4	65.0	2.5
Mexico	♦	1.2	32	0.2	-6	37.1	48.4	5.2
USA	♦	2.7	7	0.9	-18	32.3 ..	34.0	1.7
Japan		9.6	-14	11.4	-10	-15.4	-2.1	1.7
Korea	♦	22.4	13	9.3	22	39.3	68.6	5.2
Australia		0.2	296	0.2	34	149.3	57.7	3.3
N.Zealand		1.1	713	2.8	20	85.6	21.2	6.5
Austria		3.7	-14	1.7	-38	5.3	10.6	2.2
Belgium	♦	11.0	-10	2.7	-58	71.4	31.0	1.5
Czech Rep.		5.1	-49	1.2	-83	..	..	3.9
Denmark	♦	9.7	-24	1.6	-57	48.2	26.9	2.7
Finland		6.9	-5	2.1	-62	-4.5	-8.4	3.6
France	♦	8.1	25	3.3	-39	26.0	13.6	3.0
Germany		11.0	-12	2.3	-65	33.2	7.4	1.2
Greece	♦	3.3	-10	1.4	-18	20.7	15.2	7.9
Hungary	♦	4.9	-39	1.1	-81	-18.9	-19.9	5.0
Iceland	♦	0.7	-17	0.2	-48	13.9	-13.3	10.1
Ireland		9.8	103	2.8	10	17.2	29.6	3.8
Italy		5.4	-5	3.2	-26	-1.8	2.1	2.9
Netherlands		17.4	-27	2.7	-33	41.8	17.6	3.0
Norway		10.8	-8	2.9	-57	-12.7	3.1	2.3
Poland		4.9	-28	1.8	-62	24.9	2.5	3.9
Portugal		3.3	-5	1.9	-8	21.2	46.2	3.8
Spain	♦	3.5	22	1.8	21	18.3	28.4	3.9
Sweden	♦	5.3	-19	1.4	-57	-4.8	-2.9	2.0
Switzerland		3.8	2	1.1	-60	-2.1	-1.0	1.6
Turkey	♦	3.5	68	1.8	10	42.6	43.2	15.5
UK	♦	7.4	6	2.1	-7	24.1	6.9	1.0
OECD		2.2	9	0.9	-24	..	..	2.5

♦ *See Technical Annex for data sources, notes and comments.*

STATE AND TRENDS SUMMARY

Overall apparent consumption of commercial nitrogen fertiliser per unit of agricultural land since 1980 has grown in a number of OECD countries, and in the world, while consumption of phosphate fertiliser has decreased. These trends reflect developments aimed at maximising yield per hectare through specialisation and intensification. However major variations among countries exist. More recently the use of commercial nitrogen fertiliser has levelled off, and has declined in a number of countries.

Nitrogen soil surface balances˙ over the last decade show a downward or stable trend for most OECD countries, although in a few countries nitrogen surpluses have risen. The spatial variations within countries can be considerable: even in countries with relatively low national nitrogen surplus, nitrate pollution is experienced in some localities, while soil nutrient deficits occur in others.

˙ *for more information see the OECD website: www.oecd.org/agr/env/indicators.htm .*

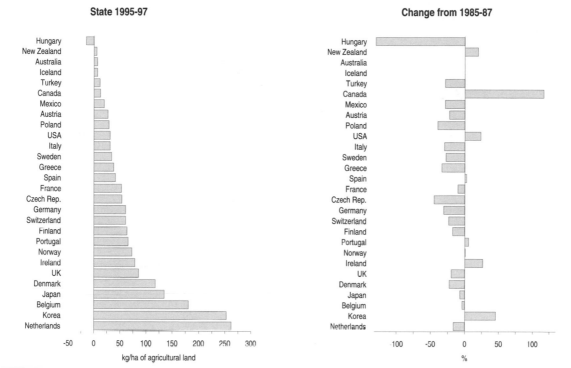

State 1995-97

Change from 1985-87

	Nitrogen input		Nitrogen output		Nitrogen efficiency (output/input)		Nitrogen balance			
	1 000 tonnes		1 000 tonnes		%		1 000 tonnes		kg/ha of agricultural land	
	1985-87	1995-97	1985-87	1995-97	1985-87	1995-97	1985-87	1995-97	1985-87	1995-97
Canada	3124	3818	2660	2843	85	74	464	976	6	13
Mexico	5429	5016	2628	2854	48	57	2801	2162	28	20
USA	27916	30596	17048	17400	61	57	10868	13196	25	31
Japan	1466	1275	690	601	47	47	775	674	145	135
Korea	652	764	267	254	41	33	385	511	173	253
Australia	8417	8667	5306	5361	63	62	3111	3306	7	7
New Zealand	3598	3455	3532	3371	98	98	66	83	5	6
Austria	411	364	288	269	70	74	123	95	35	27
Belgium	457	443	194	196	42	44	263	247	189	181
Czech Republic ♦	836	558	407	325	49	58	429	233	99	54
Denmark	716	611	280	287	39	47	435	323	154	118
Finland	318	272	129	134	41	49	189	138	78	64
France	4753	4550	2908	2965	61	65	1845	1585	59	53
Germany	4401	3442	2836	2390	64	69	1565	1052	88	61
Greece	777	653	444	457	57	70	333	195	58	38
Hungary	943	446	636	537	67	120	307	-91	47	-15
Iceland ♦	36	34	22	21	62	61	14	13	7	7
Ireland	770	878	457	480	59	55	312	397	62	79
Italy	2239	1909	1466	1424	65	75	773	485	44	31
Netherlands	1084	960	461	447	43	47	623	513	314	262
Norway	198	206	129	131	65	63	69	75	72	73
Poland	2701	1881	1808	1348	67	72	894	533	48	29
Portugal	393	384	111	120	28	31	282	264	62	66
Spain	2160	2086	926	885	43	42	1234	1202	40	41
Sweden	405	373	248	268	61	72	158	105	47	34
Switzerland	277	251	151	155	54	62	127	96	80	61
Turkey	2712	2716	2046	2216	75	82	666	500	17	12
United Kingdom	3135	2865	1319	1387	42	48	1816	1478	107	86
OECD ♦	80324	79473	49398	49126	61	62	30926	30347	23	23

♦ *See Technical Annex for data sources, notes and comments.*

31 LIVESTOCK DENSITIES

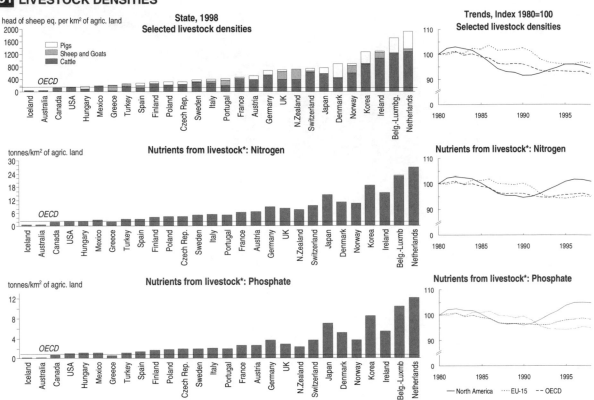

* Data refer to nutrients from cattle, sheep, goats, pigs, horses and poultry

		Selected livestock densities head of sheep equivalent per km² of agricultural land						Nutrients from livestock per km² of agricultural land		Agricultural production	
		Cattle		Sheep and Goats		Pigs		Nitrogen	Phosphate	Livestock prod.	Total
		1998	% change since 1980	1998	% change since 1980	1998	% change since 1980	tonnes/km² 1998	tonnes/km² 1998	% change since 1980	% change since 1980
Canada		117.0	10	0.9	28	17.6	20	1.9	0.8	50.4	65.0
Mexico		171.3	2	14.4	-12	14.0	-18	3.0	1.2	67.0	48.4
USA		143.1	-8	2.2	-33	14.6	-7	2.4	1.0	35.5	34.0
Japan		570.8	22	0.9	-37	200.1	9	14.2	7.0	10.5	-2.1
Korea		870.7	100	26.8	191	374.7	372	18.6	8.5	196.1	68.6
Australia		34.3	8	25.6	-7	0.6	13	0.6	0.2	32.6	57.7
N.Zealand		386.0	16	341.5	-28	3.0	2	7.5	2.3	17.6	21.2
Austria		385.3	-7	12.9	106	107.5	-1	6.5	2.7	7.0	10.6
Belgium	♦	1220.1	4	10.7	47	474.9	49	23.5	10.3	26.0	31.0
Czech Rep.		237.0	-51	3.0	-57	93.4	-24	4.6	2.0	..	..
Denmark	♦	441.3	-28	5.8	201	446.6	30	11.1	5.2	22.7	26.9
Finland		258.1	-33	5.3	33	60.2	13	4.2	1.7	-13.2	-8.4
France		396.4	-8	37.4	-5	47.0	36	6.4	2.6	8.1	13.6
Germany		527.3	-21	13.9	-19	143.1	-23	8.9	3.7	-11.3	7.4
Greece		39.2	-35	168.6	24	10.3	0	2.1	0.7	-5.4	15.2
Hungary		80.5	-54	14.8	-67	75.9	-40	2.4	1.1	-25.3	-19.9
Iceland	♦	23.6	31	25.1	-40	2.3	278	0.7	0.2	-11.9	-13.3
Ireland	♦	1055.3	45	188.9	227	41.0	127	15.3	5.4	30.7	29.6
Italy		277.7	-7	79.0	38	53.5	7	5.3	2.1	11.8	2.1
Netherlands		1280.1	-17	78.7	81	568.6	14	27.0	12.1	12.9	17.6
Norway		598.9	-5	239.0	8	66.4	-6	10.4	3.7	5.6	3.1
Poland	♦	224.3	-44	2.4	-89	103.0	-8	4.3	1.9	-14.3	2.5
Portugal		197.7	-1	168.8	27	60.6	-31	5.0	1.9	62.8	46.2
Spain		118.3	32	92.0	73	72.2	111	3.3	1.4	45.4	28.4
Sweden	♦	309.1	-1	12.5	18	67.7	-8	5.0	2.0	-0.2	-2.9
Switzerland		622.7	-10	30.4	24	94.1	-25	9.5	3.7	-6.5	-1.0
Turkey		171.1	-30	98.4	-42	0.0	-65	3.3	1.2	37.7	43.2
UK	♦	396.5	-12	255.1	109	46.7	6	8.1	2.9	-1.2	6.9
OECD		135.7	-6	28.1	-5	20.0	6	2.4	1.0	..	..

♦ See Technical Annex for data sources, notes and comments.

INTENSITY OF USE OF PESTICIDES 32

Apparent consumption of pesticides per km^2 of agricultural land

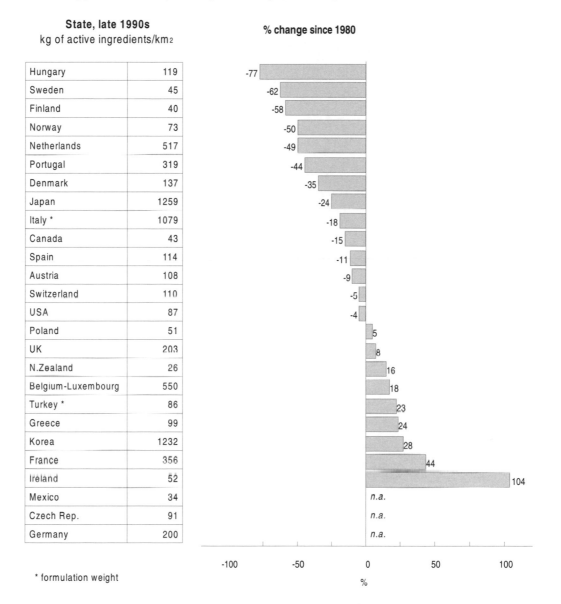

State, late 1990s kg of active ingredients/km^2		% change since 1980
Hungary	119	-77
Sweden	45	-62
Finland	40	-58
Norway	73	-50
Netherlands	517	-49
Portugal	319	-44
Denmark	137	-35
Japan	1259	-24
Italy *	1079	-18
Canada	43	-15
Spain	114	-11
Austria	108	-9
Switzerland	110	-5
USA	87	-4
Poland	51	5
UK	203	8
N.Zealand	26	16
Belgium-Luxembourg	550	18
Turkey *	86	23
Greece	99	24
Korea	1232	28
France	356	44
Ireland	52	104
Mexico	34	n.a.
Czech Rep.	91	n.a.
Germany	200	n.a.

* formulation weight

STATE AND TRENDS SUMMARY

The intensity of use of pesticides i.e. the apparent consumption of pesticides per km^2 of agricultural land has declined in a number of OECD countries since 1980, though major variations exist among and within countries. The reductions can be explained partly by changing crop prices, greater efficiency in pesticide use as a result of improvements in pest management practices and technologies, and by the use of economic and fiscal instruments. In a majority of countries, changes in pesticide use are closely correlated with fluctuations in annual crop production trends. This indicator describes potential pressure on the environment; it does not recognise differences among pesticides in levels of toxicity, persistence and mobility.

EXPENDITURE

Efforts to reduce environmental pressures imply public and private expenditure, to: i) finance pollution abatement and control at national level, and ii) provide financial and technical support for environmental protection measures in developing countries.

Indicators presented here relate to:

♦ *levels of pollution abatement and control (PAC) expenditure as a general indication of how much a country spends on controlling and reducing pressures from pollution. This expenditure is disaggregated by medium (air, water, waste) and by the sector undertaking the measures (public sector, businesses). Activities such as nature protection, natural resource preservation and water supply are excluded, as is expenditure on workplace protection, energy saving or improvement of production processes for commercial or technical reasons, though these may have environmental benefits.*

♦ *levels of official development assistance (ODA), as part of ODA supports sustainable development and, in particular, environmental protection.*

EXPENDITURE: REFERENCES

   📖 OECD (1999), OECD Environmental Data — Compendium 1999
   📖 OECD (1996), Pollution abatement and control expenditure in OECD countries
   📖 OECD (2001), Overview of environmental expenditure in NIS
   📖 OECD (2002), Pollution abatement and control expenditure in OECD countries, forthcoming

POLLUTION ABATEMENT AND CONTROL EXPENDITURE 33

OECD PAC expenditure, late 1990s

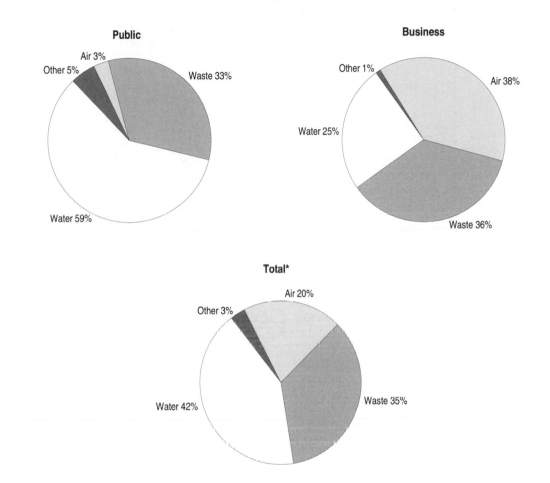

Public

Air 3%
Other 5%
Waste 33%
Water 59%

Business

Other 1%
Air 38%
Water 25%
Waste 36%

Total*

Air 20%
Other 3%
Waste 35%
Water 42%

* excluding households; based on data for 14 countries representing more than 70 per cent of the GDP of the OECD.

33 POLLUTION ABATEMENT AND CONTROL EXPENDITURE

		PAC expenditure, late 1990s or latest available year					
		as % of GDP			in USD per capita		
		Public	Business	Total*	Public	Business	Total*
Canada	♦	0.6	0.4	1.1	149	99	248
Mexico	♦	0.3	0.5	0.8	23	32	55
USA	♦	0.7	0.9	1.6	177	246	422
Japan	♦	0.9	0.6	1.6	168	115	283
Korea	♦	1.0	0.8	1.7	147	117	264
Australia	♦	0.5	0.3	0.8	120	65	184
Austria	♦	1.0	0.7	1.7	192	139	332
Belgium	♦	0.5	0.4	0.9	113	93	207
Czech Republic	♦	0.7	1.3	2.0	82	164	247
Denmark	♦	0.6	0.3	0.9	151	61	212
Finland	♦	0.6	0.5	1.1	115	104	219
France	♦	1.0	0.5	1.4	199	97	296
Germany	♦	0.8	0.7	1.5	166	144	310
Greece	♦	0.5	0.3	0.8	59	41	100
Hungary	♦	0.3	0.3	0.6	30	25	56
Iceland	♦	0.3	..	..	70	..	..
Ireland	♦	..	..	0.6	..	..	139
Italy	♦	0.5	0.3	0.9	84	51	135
Luxembourg	♦	0.7	..	..	244	..	..
Netherlands	♦	1.2	0.5	1.8	264	108	372
Norway	♦	..	..	1.2	..	..	210
Poland	♦	0.3	0.8	1.1	22	54	76
Portugal	♦	0.6	0.2	0.8	89	33	123
Spain	♦	0.5	0.3	0.8	67	40	107
Sweden	♦	0.8	0.4	1.2	140	69	209
Switzerland	♦	1.0	0.6	1.6	245	133	378
United Kingdom	♦	0.4	0.6	1.0	65	92	157

*excluding households.

♦ See Technical Annex for data sources, notes and comments.

STATE AND TRENDS SUMMARY

PAC expenditure is part of environmental protection expenditure, covering curative and preventive measures measures directly aimed at pollution abatement and control. PAC expenditure as a percentage of GDP is slowly growing as stronger pollution prevention and control polices are implemented. It now generally amounts to 1 to 2 per cent of GDP in most OECD countries. In general, the investment-related share of PAC decreases as investment programmes progress, while operating expenses' share grows. In countries with small GDP, a low level of expenditure in GDP terms means PAC is very limited.

Public sector PAC measures mainly concern sewerage, waste water treatment and the collection and disposal of municipal waste. Such measures generally represent 0.3 to 1.2 per cent of GDP. Public expenditure on water is usually large, and growing in line with efforts to ensure that most of the population is connected to sewerage and public waste water treatment. Public expenditure is generally financed by pollution taxes or charges paid by households, but most countries still fund PAC partly from the general budget.

Private sector (business) measures mostly relate to air and water pollution and hazardous waste disposal. They generally amount to 0.2 to 1.3 per cent of GDP. They mainly represent compliance with the polluter pays principle. Business also pays pollution charges to public authorities, either to offset costs of services or in relation to externalities.

OFFICIAL DEVELOPMENT ASSISTANCE 34

**Trends in Official Development Assistance, 1980-99
as % of GNP**

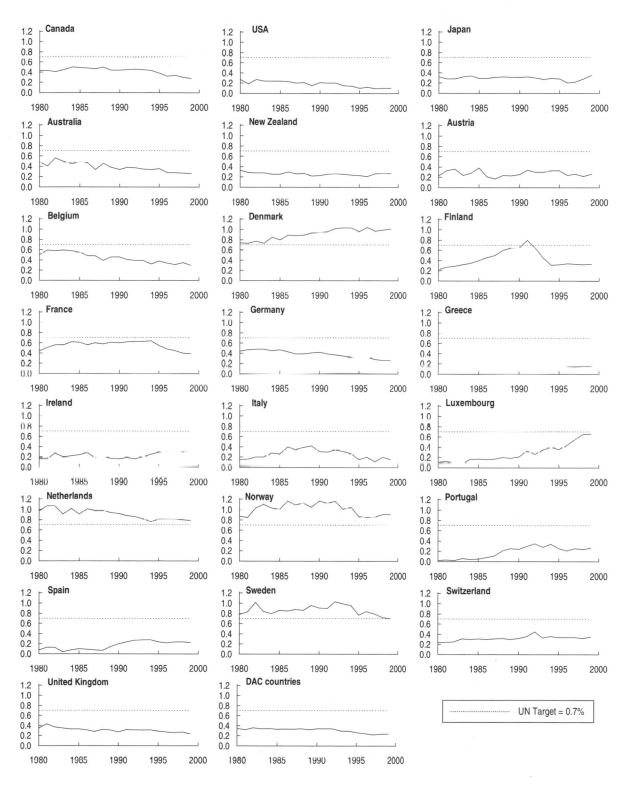

34 OFFICIAL DEVELOPMENT ASSISTANCE

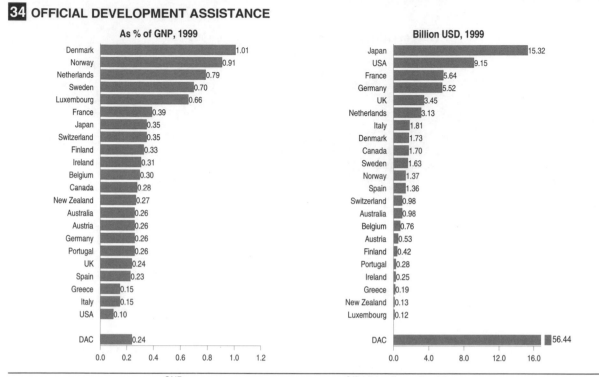

	GNP per capita 1 000 USD/cap.	Official development assistance			
		Total, 1999 million USD	as a share of GNP		
			% , 1999	absolute change since 1980	absolute change since 1992
Canada	20.2	1699	0.28	-0.15	-0.18
USA	34.3	9145	0.10	-0.17	-0.10
Japan	34.7	15323	0.35	0.03	0.05
Australia	20.2	982	0.26	-0.22	-0.11
New Zealand	13.2	134	0.27	-0.06	0.01
Austria	25.3	527	0.26	0.03	-0.04
Belgium	24.5	760	0.30	-0.20	-0.09
Denmark	32.3	1733	1.01	0.27	-0.01
Finland	24.6	416	0.33	0.11	-0.31
France	24.2	5637	0.39	-0.05	-0.24
Germany	25.5	5515	0.26	-0.18	-0.11
Greece	11.9	194	0.15	..	..
Ireland	21.1	245	0.31	0.15	0.15
Italy	20.3	1806	0.15	0.00	-0.19
Luxembourg	41.7	119	0.66	0.55	0.40
Netherlands	25.1	3134	0.79	-0.18	-0.07
Norway	33.9	1370	0.91	0.04	-0.25
Portugal	10.8	276	0.26	0.24	-0.09
Spain	15.0	1363	0.23	0.15	-0.04
Sweden	26.3	1630	0.70	-0.08	-0.33
Switzerland	38.9	984	0.35	0.11	-0.10
UK	24.4	3450	0.24	-0.11	-0.07
DAC	28.2	56442	0.24	-0.11	-0.10

STATE AND TRENDS
SUMMARY

ODA is provided to support socio-economic development of less developed countries. A large fraction of ODA aims at ensuring more sustainable development and, in particular, conserving natural resources and protecting the environment. Despite commitments made at UNCED (Rio de Janeiro, 1992), ODA is decreasing. There is no direct relation between assistance and donor wealth; the level of discrepancy is a factor of more than eight. Most countries' aid to developing countries amounts to 0.2 to 0.4 per cent of GDP. Special funding via the Global Environment Facility is directed at global environmental problems. Total aid for environmental protection is relatively small. About 10 to 25 per cent of ODA can be related to drinking water provision, river management, soil conservation, tropical forest management, nature protection and PAC.

IV. KEY ENVIRONMENTAL INDICATORS

The present report is a new product of the OECD work programme on environmental indicators. It responds to the increasing interest by OECD Member countries in a reduced number of environmental indicators selected from existing larger sets to draw public attention to key environmental issues of concern and to inform about progress made. It includes a selection of 10 key environmental indicators extracted from the OECD Core Set of environmental indicators and benefits from the experience gained in using environmental indicators in the OECD's policy and evaluation work.

The key environmental indicators were published at the occasion of the OECD meeting of Environment Ministers (Paris, 16 May 2001) and were endorsed by Ministers as a tool for use in OECD work and for public information and communication by OECD.

The key indicators are intended to give a broad overview of environmental issues in OECD countries. They will be updated at regular intervals as a free supplement to the OECD Core Set of environmental indicators and to the OECD Compendium of environmental data. Together with other indicators of the OECD Core Set, they will also contribute to follow-up work on the OECD environmental strategy.

INTRODUCTION

BACKGROUND

The OECD, with the support of its Member countries, has long been a pioneer in the field of environmental indicators with the development and publication of the <u>first international sets of environmental indicators</u> and their regular use in country environmental performance reviews.

During the 1990s, environmental indicators gained significant importance and are now widely <u>used</u> in many OECD countries. They are used in reporting, planning, clarifying policy objectives and priorities, budgeting, and assessing performance.

WHY KEY INDICATORS ?

While the indicator sets used to date have proven <u>very useful</u> in policy and reporting work, there is now increasing <u>interest in a reduced number of indicators</u> selected from these larger sets to inform civil society and to support wider communication with the public.

To respond to this demand, the OECD has identified a shortlist of key environmental indicators building on previous work and on consensus already achieved: they derive from the OECD Core Set of environmental indicators (publications 1991, 94, 98, 2001), and from the results of the OECD Rome Conference (December 1999) that discussed a first shortlist of indicators.

SELECTION CRITERIA

The selection of these indicators takes into account:

♦ Their <u>policy relevance</u> with respect to major challenges for the next decade; in particular they relate to both 1) pollution issues and 2) natural resources and assets; indicators describing sectoral trends are not considered.

♦ Their <u>analytical soundness</u>.

♦ Their <u>measurability</u>: necessary data sets are already available for a majority of OECD countries; when improvements in data availability and developments in concepts and definitions are foreseen, medium term indicators are proposed.

INTERPRETATION IN CONTEXT

The indicators selected correspond to varying degrees of policy relevance and policy priority for different countries. Like other indicators they have to be interpreted in context and be complemented with country specific information to acquire their full meaning.

A DYNAMIC PROCESS

The list of indicators presented here is <u>neither final, nor exhaustive</u>; it has to be seen together with other indicators from the OECD Core Set, and will evolve as knowledge and data availability improve.

Ultimately, the set is expected to also include key indicators for issues such as toxic contamination, land and soil resources, and urban environmental quality.

LINK TO OTHER OECD AND INTERNATIONAL WORK

The set of key environmental indicators is closely linked to other environmental indicator sets developed and used by the OECD, including indicators developed as part of the OECD-wide programme on <u>sustainable development</u> and sectoral sets of environmental indicators (e.g. the OECD set of <u>agri-environmental indicators</u>).

It further benefits from continued co-ordination with the work carried out by other <u>international organisations</u> (e.g. UNCSD, European Union).

INTRODUCTION

OECD SET OF KEY ENVIRONMENTAL INDICATORS

POLLUTION ISSUES		Available indicators*	Medium term indicators**
Climate change	1.	CO2 emission intensities	Index of greenhouse gas emissions
Ozone layer	2.	Indices of apparent consumption of ozone depleting substances (ODS)	Same, plus aggregation into one index of apparent consumption of ODS
Air quality	3.	SOx and NOx emission intensities	Population exposure to air pollution
Waste generation	4.	Municipal waste generation intensities	Total waste generation intensities, Indicators derived from material flow accounting
Freshwater quality	5.	Waste water treatment connection rates	Pollution loads to water bodies
NATURAL RESOURCES & ASSETS			
Freshwater resources	6.	Intensity of use of water resources	Same plus sub-national breakdown
Forest resources	7.	Intensity of use of forest resources	Same
Fish resources	8.	Intensity of use of fish resources	Same plus closer link to available resources
Energy resources	9.	Intensity of energy use	Energy efficiency index
Biodiversity	10.	Threatened species	Species and habitat or ecosystem diversity Area of key ecosystems

* indicators for which data are available for a majority of OECD countries and that are presented in this report

** indicators that require further specification and development (availability of basic data sets, underlying concepts and definitions).

These 10 indicators have been very useful in charting environmental progress, and their selection has benefited from the experience gained in using environmental indicators in the OECD's country environmental performance reviews.

PROSPECTS AND FUTURE WORK

OECD experience shows that environmental indicators are cost-effective and powerful tools for the monitoring and reporting of environmental progress and for the measurement of environmental performance. However, experience also shows significant lags between the demand for and the supply of environmental indicators.

GENERAL PROGRESS Continued efforts are being done by the OECD to:
- Improve the availability, quality and comparability of basic data sets.
- Link the indicators more closely to domestic goals and international commitments.
- Link the indicators more closely to sustainability issues.
- Assist in further development and use of environmental indicators in OECD Member countries, and promote the exchange of related experience with non-OECD countries and other international organisations.

SPECIFIC PROGRESS More specifically, it is planned to:
- Regularly update and publish the small set of key environmental indicators.
- Further develop concepts and data for medium term indicators (see table).
- Complement the indicators with information reflecting sub-national differences.
- Review indicator aggregation methods currently in use at national and international level, and produce aggregated indices when feasible and policy relevant (e.g. GHG emission index).

CLIMATE CHANGE

MAIN POLICY CHALLENGES

▷ *Main concerns relate to effects of increasing atmospheric greenhouse gas (GHG) concentrations on global temperatures and the earth's climate, and potential consequences for ecosystems, human settlements, agriculture and other socio-economic activities. This is because CO_2 and other GHG emissions are still growing in many countries, despite some progress achieved in de-coupling CO_2 emissions from GDP growth (weak de-coupling).*

▷ *The main challenges are to limit emissions of CO_2 and other GHG and to stabilise the concentration of GHG in the atmosphere at a level that would prevent dangerous anthropogenic interference with the climate system. This implies strengthening efforts to implement related national and international strategies and to further de-couple GHG emissions from economic growth.*

MEASURING PERFORMANCE

▷ *Environmental performance can be assessed against domestic objectives and international commitments: The main international agreement is the United Nations Framework Convention on Climate Change (1992). Its 1997 Kyoto Protocol establishes differentiated national or regional emission reduction or limitation targets for six GHG for 2008-12 and for the base year 1990.*

▷ *The indicators presented here relate to CO_2 emissions from energy use. They show emission intensities per unit of GDP and per capita for 1998, and related changes since 1980. All emissions presented here are gross direct emissions, excluding sinks and indirect effects.*

▷ *When interpreting these indicators it should be noted that CO_2 is a major contributor to the greenhouse effect. They should be read in connection with other indicators from the OECD Core Set and in particular with indicators on global atmospheric concentrations of GHG, on energy efficiency and on energy prices and taxes. Their interpretation should take into account the structure of countries' energy supply, the relative importance of fossil fuels and of renewable energy, as well as climatic factors.*

1 MONITORING TRENDS

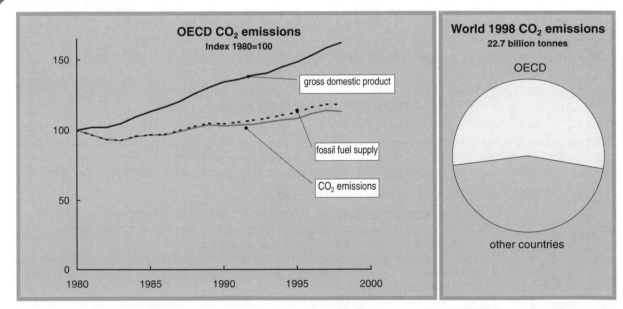

▷ *Despite wide variations in emission trends, a number of OECD countries have de-coupled their CO_2 emissions from GDP growth, but most countries have not succeeded in meeting their own national commitments. Their CO_2 emissions continued to increase throughout the 1990s, despite gains in energy efficiency (i.e. weak de-coupling). Since 1980, CO_2 emissions from energy use have however grown more slowly in OECD countries as a group than they have world-wide.*

CURRENT STATE – EMISSION INTENSITIES

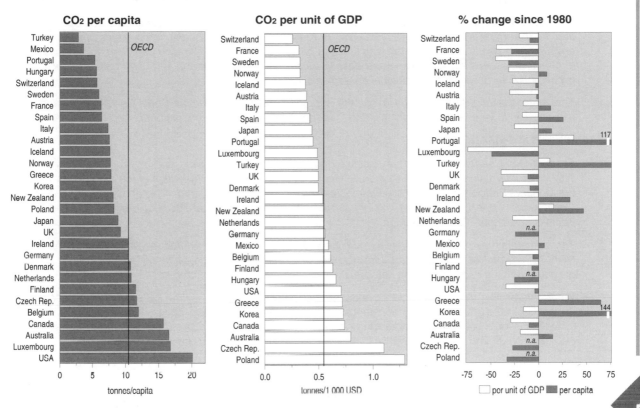

CO2 per capita

Turkey, Mexico, Portugal, Hungary, Switzerland, Sweden, France, Spain, Italy, Austria, Iceland, Norway, Greece, Korea, New Zealand, Poland, Japan, UK, Ireland, Germany, Denmark, Netherlands, Finland, Czech Rep., Belgium, Canada, Australia, Luxembourg, USA

OECD

0   5   10   15   20
tonnes/capita

CO2 per unit of GDP

Switzerland, France, Sweden, Norway, Iceland, Austria, Italy, Spain, Japan, Portugal, Luxembourg, Turkey, UK, Denmark, Ireland, New Zealand, Netherlands, Germany, Mexico, Belgium, Finland, Hungary, USA, Greece, Korea, Canada, Australia, Czech Rep., Poland

OECD

0.0   0.5   1.0
tonnes/1 000 USD

% change since 1980

Switzerland, France, Sweden, Norway, Iceland, Austria, Italy, Spain, Japan, Portugal, Luxembourg, Turkey, UK, Denmark, Ireland, New Zealand, Netherlands, Germany, Mexico, Belgium, Finland, Hungary, USA, Greece, Korea, Canada, Australia, Czech Rep., Poland

117, *n.a.*, *n.a.*, 144, *n.a.*, *n.a.*

-75   -50   -25   0   25   50   75

☐ per unit of GDP   ■ per capita

Individual OECD countries' contributions to the greenhouse effect, and rates of progress towards stabilisation, vary significantly. Over the past 20 years, CO2 emissions from energy use have continued to grow, particularly in the OECD Asia-Pacific region and North America. This can be partly attributed to energy production and consumption patterns and trends, often combined with overall low energy prices. In recent years however, annual growth rates of CO2 emissions from energy use in these regions have been slowing down.

In OECD Europe, CO2 emissions from energy use have fallen between 1980 and 1995, as a result of changes in economic structures and energy supply mix, energy savings and, in some countries, of decreases in economic activity over a few years. Recently however, CO2 emissions from energy use have been on the increase.

THE BASIS: THE OECD CORE SET OF ENVIRONMENTAL INDICATORS

Core set indicators
ISSUE – CLIMATE CHANGE

Pressures ♦ **Index of greenhouse gas emissions**
  – CO2 emissions
  – CH4 emissions
  – N2O emissions
  – PFC, HFC, SF6 emissions

Conditions ♦ **Atmospheric concentrations of GHG** ♦ **Global mean temperature**

Responses ♦ **Energy efficiency**
  – Energy intensity
  – Economic and fiscal instruments

Measurability

Data on GHG emissions are reported annually to the Secretariat of the UNFCCC. Progress has been made with national GHG inventories, but data availability remains best for CO_2 emissions from energy use.

Continued efforts are needed to further improve the completeness of national GHG inventories and their consistency over time, and to construct a GHG emission index covering the 6 gases of the Kyoto Protocol (CO2, CH4, N2O, PFCs, HFCs and SF6). At OECD level, related trends and intensities closely parallel those of CO2 emission from energy use.

Further efforts are also needed to better evaluate sinks and indirect effects and to calculate net GHG emissions.

OZONE LAYER

MAIN POLICY CHALLENGES

▷ Stratospheric ozone depletion (e.g. over the Antarctic and the Arctic oceans) remains a source of concern due to the impacts of increased ultraviolet B radiation on human health, crop yields and the natural environment. This is because of the long time lag between the release of ozone depleting substances (ODS) and their arrival in the stratosphere and despite a considerable decrease in CFC and halon production and consumption as a result of international agreements.

▷ The main challenges are to phase out the supply of methyl bromide and HCFCs (by 2005 and 2020 respectively) in industrialised countries, and to reduce international movements of existing CFCs.

MEASURING PERFORMANCE

▷ Environmental performance can be assessed against domestic objectives and international commitments. The major international agreements are the Vienna Convention for the Protection of the Ozone Layer (1985), the Montreal Protocol on substances that deplete the ozone layer (1987) and its amendments London (1990), Copenhagen (1992), Montreal (1997) and Beijing (1999). The Montreal Protocol has been ratified by 175 parties, including all OECD countries.

▷ The indicators presented here relate to the consumption (i.e. production + imports - exports) of CFCs, halons, HCFCs, and methyl bromide, as listed in Annex A, B, C and E of the Montreal protocol. Basic data are weighted with the ozone depleting potentials (ODP) of the individual substances.

▷ When interpreting these indicators it should be kept in mind that they do not reflect actual releases to the atmosphere and that individual substances vary considerably in their ozone-depleting capacity. These indicators should be read in connection with other indicators of the OECD Core Set and in particular with indicators on ground-level UV-B radiation and on atmospheric concentrations of ODS over cities.

MONITORING TRENDS

2

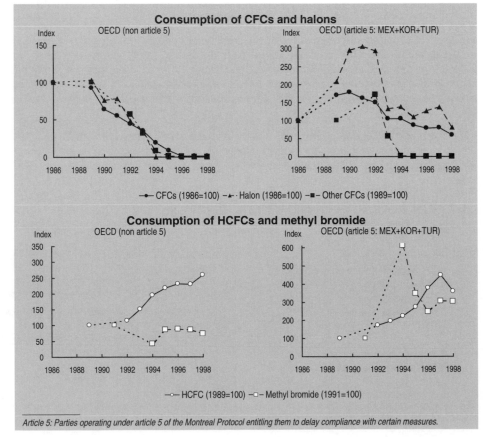

Article 5: Parties operating under article 5 of the Montreal Protocol entitling them to delay compliance with certain measures.

REGIONAL TRENDS

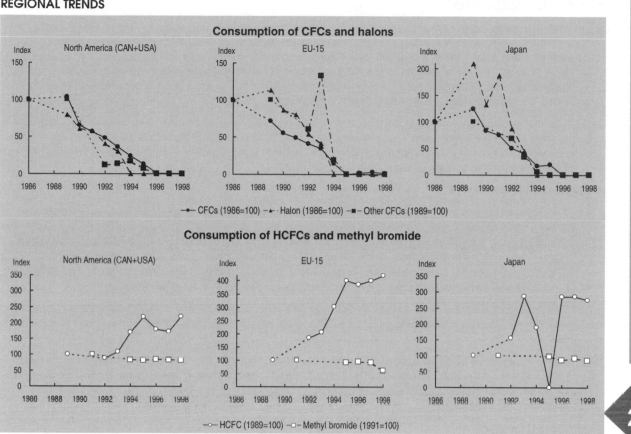

Consumption of CFCs and halons

North America (CAN+USA) — EU-15 — Japan

—•— CFCs (1986=100) —▲— Halon (1986=100) —■— Other CFCs (1989=100)

Consumption of HCFCs and methyl bromide

North America (CAN+USA) — EU-15 — Japan

—○— HCFC (1989=100) —□— Methyl bromide (1991=100)

▷ As a result of the Montreal Protocol, industrialised countries have rapidly decreased their consumption of CFCs (CFC 11, 12, 113, 114, 115) and halons (halon 1211, 1301 and 2402). The targets set have been reached earlier than originally called for, and new and more stringent targets have been adopted.

▷ Many countries reduced consumption to zero by 1994 for halons and by end of 1995 for CFCs, HBFCs, carbon tetrachloride and methyl chloroform. As of 1996, there has been no production or consumption of these substances in industrialised countries except for certain essential uses, but there are still releases to the atmosphere (e.g. from previous production or consumption).

▷ Growth rates of HCFC consumption and related concentrations in the atmosphere are still increasing. HCFCs have only 2 to 5 % of the ozone depleting potential of CFCs. Under current international agreements they will not be phased out completely for 20 years and will remain in the stratosphere for a long time thereafter.

THE BASIS: THE OECD CORE SET OF ENVIRONMENTAL INDICATORS

Core set indicators	Measurability
ISSUE – OZONE LAYER DEPLETION	Actual emissions of ODS are difficult to measure and related data are weak. Production or apparent consumption are used as a proxy. Such data are available from the Secretariat of the Montreal Protocol.
Pressures ◆ **Index of apparent consumption of ozone depleting substances (ODS)** ◆ Apparent consumption of CFCs and halons	To reflect the combined depletion capacity, the apparent consumption of each individual substance, weighted in proportion to its ozone-depleting potential relative to CFC11, should further be aggregated into a consumption index.
Conditions ◆ **Atmospheric concentrations of ODS** ◆ **Ground level UV-B radiation** ◆ Stratospheric ozone levels	
Responses ◆ **CFC recovery rate**	

AIR QUALITY

MAIN POLICY CHALLENGES

▷ *Main concerns relate to the effects of air pollution on human health, ecosystems, and buildings, and to their economic and social consequences. Human exposure is particularly high in urban areas where economic activities and road traffic are concentrated. Causes of growing concern are concentrations of fine particulates, NO_2, toxic air pollutants, and acute ground-level ozone pollution episodes in both urban and rural areas. SO_x emissions have decreased significantly in many countries and have often been successfully de-coupled from fossil fuel use and economic growth (strong de-coupling).*

▷ *The main challenges are to further reduce emissions of NO_x and other local and regional air pollutants in order to achieve a strong de-coupling of emissions from GDP and to limit the exposure of the population to air pollution. This implies implementing appropriate pollution control policies, technological progress, energy savings and environmentally sustainable transport policies.*

MEASURING PERFORMANCE

▷ *Environmental performance can be assessed against domestic objectives and international commitments. In Europe and North America, acidification has led to several international agreements among which the Convention on Long-Range Transboundary Air Pollution (1979), and its protocols to reduce emissions of sulphur (Helsinki 1985, Oslo 1994, Gothenburg 1999), nitrogen oxides (Sofia 1988, Gothenburg 1999), VOCs (Geneva 1991, Gothenburg 1999), and ammonia (Gothenburg 1999). Two other protocols aim at reducing emissions of heavy metals (Aarhus 1998) and persistent organic pollutants (Aarhus 1998).*

▷ *The indicators presented here relate to SO_x and NO_x emissions, expressed as SO_2 and NO_2 respectively. They show emission intensities per unit of GDP and per capita for the late 1990s, and related changes since 1980.*

▷ *When interpreting these indicators it should be kept in mind that SO_x and NO_x emissions only provide a partial view of air pollution problems. They should be read in connection with other indicators of the OECD Core Set and in particular with urban air quality indicators and with information on population exposure to air pollution.*

3

MONITORING TRENDS

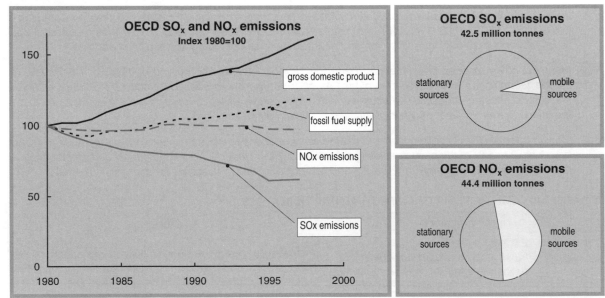

▷ *Over the past 20 years, emissions of acidifying substances and related transboundary air pollution have been considerably reduced throughout the OECD. Compared to 1980 levels, SOx emissions have decreased significantly for the OECD as a whole, showing a strong de-coupling from GDP. NOx emissions have been stabilised or reduced more recently, showing only a weak de-coupling from GDP compared to 1980.*

CURRENT STATE – EMISSION INTENSITIES

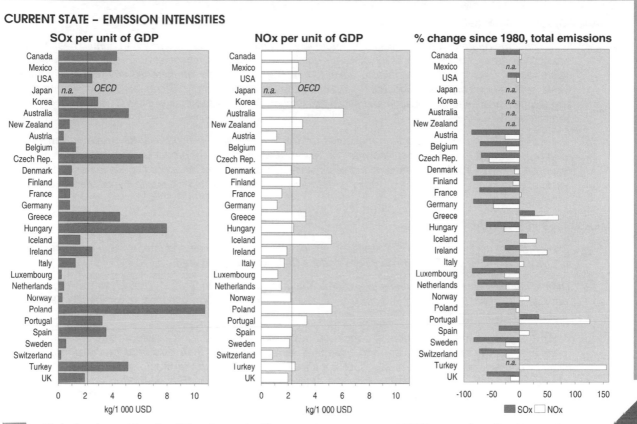

SOx per unit of GDP — kg/1 000 USD

NOx per unit of GDP — kg/1 000 USD

% change since 1980, total emissions — ■ SOx □ NOx

Countries (top to bottom): Canada, Mexico, USA, Japan, Korea, Australia, New Zealand, Austria, Belgium, Czech Rep., Denmark, Finland, France, Germany, Greece, Hungary, Iceland, Ireland, Italy, Luxembourg, Netherlands, Norway, Poland, Portugal, Spain, Sweden, Switzerland, Turkey, UK

3

> *Emission intensities for SOx show significant variations among OECD countries. Total emissions have decreased significantly in a majority of the countries. European countries' early commitments to reduce SOx emissions have been achieved, and new agreements have been adopted in Europe and North America to reduce acid precipitation even further (Gothenburg Protocol).*

> *Emission intensities for NOx and related changes over time show important variations among OECD countries. NOx emissions have been reduced in several countries over the 1990s, particularly in OECD Europe. In some European countries however, the commitment to stabilise NOx emissions by the end of 1994 to their 1987 levels (Sofia Protocol) has not been met.*

THE BASIS: THE OECD CORE SET OF ENVIRONMENTAL INDICATORS

Core set indicators	Measurability
ISSUE: ACIDIFICATION	International data on SOx and NOx emissions are available. Additional efforts are however needed to further improve timeliness and historical consistency of the data, and to improve the availability, completeness and comparability of data on other air pollutant emissions (PM10, PM2.5, VOCs, heavy metals, POPs).
Pressures ♦ **Index of acidifying substances** – Emissions of NOx and SOx	
Conditions ♦ **Exceedance of critical loads of pH** – Concentrations in acid precipitation	
Responses ♦ **Car fleet equipped with catalytic converters** ♦ **Capacity of SOx and NOx abatement equipment of stationary sources**	Information on population exposure to air pollution is scattered. Efforts are needed to monitor and/or estimate overall population exposure, and exposure of sensitive groups of the population. Data on concentrations of major air pollutants are available for major cities in OECD countries, but more work is needed to improve international comparability, and to link these data to national standards and to human health issues.
ISSUE: URBAN ENVIRONMENTAL QUALITY	
Pressures ♦ **Urban air emissions** – Urban traffic density and car ownership	
Conditions ♦ **Population exposure to air pollution** – Concentrations of air pollutants	
Responses ♦ **Economic, fiscal, regulatory instruments**	

WASTE GENERATION

MAIN POLICY CHALLENGES

▷ *Main concerns relate to the potential impact from inappropriate waste management on human health and on ecosystems (soil and water contamination, air quality, land use and landscape). Despite achievements in waste recycling, amounts of solid waste going to final disposal are on the increase as are overall trends in waste generation. This raises important questions as to the capacities of existing facilities for final treatment and disposal and as to the location and social acceptance of new facilities (e.g. NIMBY for controlled landfill and incineration plants).*

▷ *The main challenge is to strengthen measures for waste minimisation, especially for waste prevention and recycling, and to move further towards life cycle management of products and extended producer responsibility. This implies internalising the costs of waste management into prices of consumer goods and of waste management services; and ensuring greater cost-effectiveness and full public involvement in designing measures.*

MEASURING PERFORMANCE

▷ *Environmental performance can be assessed against national objectives and international agreements such as OECD Decisions and Recommendations and the Basel Convention (1989).*

▷ *The indicators presented here relate to amounts of municipal waste generated. They show waste generation intensities expressed per capita and per unit of private final consumption expenditure for the late 1990s, and related changes since 1980.*

▷ *When interpreting these indicators, it should be noted that while municipal waste is only one part of total waste generated, its management and treatment represents more than one third of the public sector's financial efforts to abate and control pollution. It should be kept in mind that waste generation intensities are first approximations of potential environmental pressure; more information is needed to describe the actual pressure. These indicators should be read in connection with other indicators of the OECD Core Set. They should be complemented with information on waste management practices and costs, and on consumption levels and patterns.*

MONITORING TRENDS

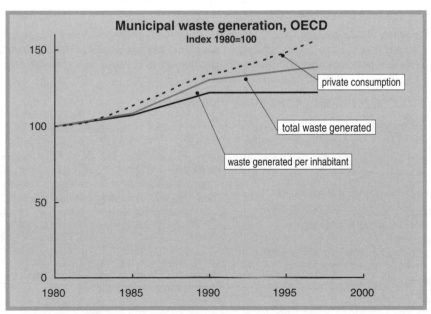

▷ *The quantity of municipal waste generated in the OECD area has risen from 1980 and reached 540 million tonnes in the late 1990s (500 kg per inhabitant). Generation intensity per capita has risen mostly in line with private final consumption expenditure and GDP, with however a slight slowdown in recent years.*

CURRENT STATE – GENERATION INTENSITIES

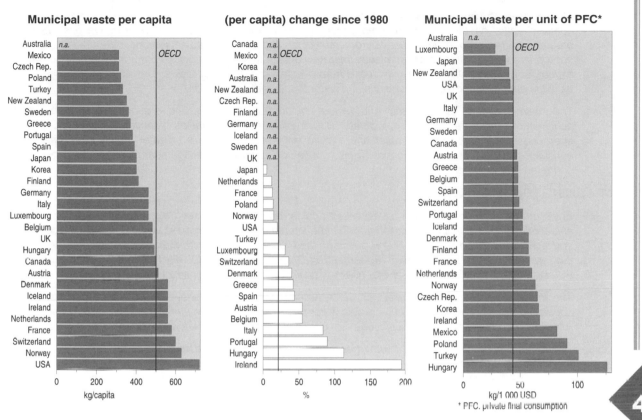

Municipal waste per capita

(per capita) change since 1980

Municipal waste per unit of PFC*

> The amount and the composition of municipal waste vary widely among OECD countries, being directly related to levels and patterns of consumption and also depending on national waste management practices.

> Only a few countries have succeeded in reducing the quantity of solid waste to be disposed of. In most countries for which data are available, increased affluence, associated with economic growth and changes in consumption patterns, tends to generate higher rates of waste per capita.

THE BASIS: THE OECD CORE SET OF ENVIRONMENTAL INDICATORS

Core set indicators	Measurability
ISSUE – WASTE	Despite considerable progress, data on waste generation and disposal remains weak in many countries. Further efforts are needed to:
Pressures ♦ **Generation of:** – **municipal waste** – **industrial waste** – **hazardous waste** – **nuclear waste** ♦ Movements of hazardous waste	♦ ensure an appropriate monitoring of waste flows and of related management practices; ♦ improve the completeness and international comparability of the data, as well as their timeliness.
Conditions Effects on water and air quality; effects on land use and soil quality; toxic contamination	More work needs to be done to improve data on industrial and hazardous wastes, and to develop indicators that better reflect waste minimisation efforts, and in particular waste prevention measures.
Responses ♦ **Waste minimisation** – Recycling rates ♦ **Economic and fiscal instruments, expenditures**	The usefulness of indicators derived from material flow accounting should be further explored.

FRESHWATER QUALITY

MAIN POLICY CHALLENGES

▷ *Main concerns relate to the impacts of water pollution (eutrophication, acidification, toxic contamination) on human health, on the cost of drinking water treatment and on aquatic ecosystems. Despite significant progress in reducing pollution loads from municipal and industrial point sources through installation of appropriate waste water treatment plants, improvements in freshwater quality are not always easy to discern, except for organic pollution. Pollution loads from diffuse agricultural sources are an issue in many countries, as is the supply of permanently safe drinking water to the entire population.*

▷ *The main challenge is to protect and restore all bodies of surface and ground water to ensure the achievement of water quality objectives. This implies further reducing pollution discharges, through appropriate treatment of waste water and a more systematic integration of water quality considerations in agricultural and other sectoral policies. It also implies an integrated management of water resources based on the ecosystem approach.*

MEASURING PERFORMANCE

▷ *Environmental performance can be assessed against domestic objectives (e.g. receiving water standards, effluent limits, pollution load reduction targets) and international commitments. Main international agreements and legislation include the OSPAR Convention on the Protection of the North-East Atlantic Marine Environment, the International Joint Commission Agreement on Great Lakes Water Quality in North America and the EU water directives. Protection of freshwater quality is an important part of Agenda 21, adopted at UNCED (1992).*

▷ *The indicators presented here relate to waste water treatment. They show the percentage of the national population actually connected to public waste water treatment plants in the late 1990s. The extent of secondary (biological) and/or tertiary (chemical) treatment provides an indication of efforts to reduce pollution loads.*

▷ *When interpreting this indicator it should be noted that waste water treatment is at the centre of countries' financial efforts to abate water pollution. It should be related to an optimal national connection rate taking into account national specificities such as population in remote areas. It should be read in connection with other indicators of the OECD Core Set, including public waste water treatment expenditure and the quality of rivers and lakes.*

MONITORING TRENDS

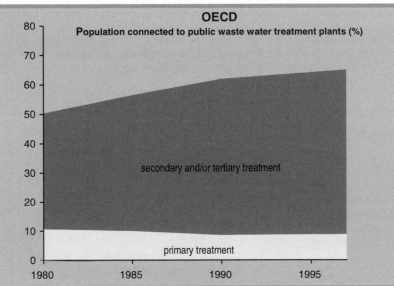

▷ *OECD countries have progressed with basic domestic water pollution abatement. The OECD-wide share of the population connected to a municipal waste water treatment plant rose from 50 % in the early 1980s to more than 60 % today. For the OECD as a whole, more than half of public pollution abatement and control expenditure relates to water (sewerage and waste water treatment), representing up to 1 % of GDP.*

CURRENT STATE – WASTE WATER TREATMENT CONNECTION RATES

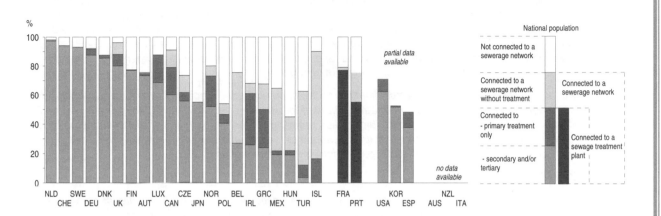

> *Due to varying settlement patterns, economic and environmental conditions, starting dates, and the rate at which the work was done, the share of population connected to waste water treatment plants and the level of treatment varies significantly among OECD countries: secondary and tertiary treatment has progressed in some, while others are still completing sewerage networks or the installation of first generation treatment plants. Some countries have reached the economic limit in terms of sewerage connection and use other ways of treating waste water from small, isolated settlements.*

> *Those countries that completed their sewer systems long ago, now face considerable investment to renew pipe networks. Other countries may recently have finished an expansion of waste water treatment capacity and their expenditure has shifted to operating costs. Yet other countries must still complete their sewerage networks even as they build waste water treatment stations.*

5

THE BASIS: THE OECD CORE SET OF ENVIRONMENTAL INDICATORS

Core set indicators	Measurability
ISSUE: EUTROPHICATION	
Pressures ♦ Emissions of N and P in water and soil → **Nutrient balance** – N and P from fertiliser use & livestock	Data on the share of the population connected to waste water treatment plants are available for almost all OECD countries. Information on the level of treatment and on treatment charges remains partial.
Conditions ♦ **BOD/DO in inland waters** ♦ **Concentration of N & P in inland waters**	More work needs to be done to produce better data on overall pollution generated covering the entire range of emission sources, on related treatment rates, and final discharges to water bodies.
Responses ♦ **Population connected to secondary and/or tertiary sewage treatment plants** – User charges for waste water treatment – Market share of phosphate-free detergents	
ISSUE: TOXIC CONTAMINATION	
Pressures ♦ **Emissions of heavy metals** ♦ **Emissions of organic compounds** – Consumption of pesticides	International data on emissions of toxic compounds (heavy metals, organic compounds) are partial and often lack comparability.
Conditions ♦ **Concentrations of heavy metals and organic compounds in env. Media**	
ISSUE: ACIDIFICATION	
Conditions ♦ **Exceedance of critical loads of PH in water**	

WATER RESOURCES

MAIN POLICY CHALLENGES

⟩ *Main concerns relate to the inefficient use of water and to its environmental and socio-economic consequences: low river flows, water shortages, salinisation of freshwater bodies in coastal areas, human health problems, loss of wetlands, desertification and reduced food production. Although at the national level most OECD countries show sustainable use of water resource, most still face at least seasonal or local water quantity problems and several have extensive arid or semi-arid regions where water is a constraint to sustainable development and to the sustainability of agriculture.*

⟩ *The main challenge is to ensure a sustainable management of water resources, avoiding overexploitation and degradation, so as to maintain adequate supply of freshwater of suitable quality for human use and to support aquatic and other ecosystems. This implies reducing losses, using more efficient technologies and increase recycling, and applying an integrated approach to the management of freshwater resources by river basin. It further requires applying the user pays principle to all types of uses.*

MEASURING PERFORMANCE

⟩ *Environmental performance can be assessed against domestic objectives and international commitments. Agenda 21, adopted at UNCED (Rio de Janeiro, 1992), explicitly considers items such as the protection and preservation of freshwater resources.*

⟩ *The indicators presented here relate to the intensity of use of water resources, expressed as gross abstractions per capita, as % of total available renewable freshwater resources (including inflows from neighbouring countries) and as % of internal resources (i.e. precipitations – evapotranspiration) for the late 1990s.*

⟩ *When interpreting this indicator, it should be noted that relating resource abstraction to renewal of stocks is a central question concerning sustainable water resource management. It should however be kept in mind that it gives insights into quantitative aspects of water resources and that a national level indicator may hide significant territorial differences and should be complemented with information at sub-national level. This indicator should be read in connection with other indicators of the OECD Core Set and in particular with indicators on water supply prices and on water quality.*

6

MONITORING TRENDS

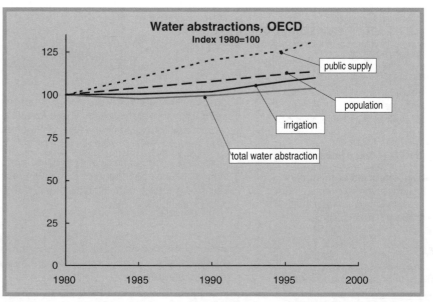

Water abstractions, OECD
Index 1980=100

⟩ *Most OECD countries increased their water abstractions over the 1970s in response to demand by the agricultural and energy sectors. Since the 1980s, some countries have stabilised their abstractions through more efficient irrigation techniques, the decline of water intensive industries (e.g. mining, steel), increased use of cleaner production technologies and reduced losses in pipe networks. However, the effects of population growth have led to increases in total abstractions, in particular for public supply.*

CURRENT STATE – INTENSITY OF USE OF WATER RESOURCES

Gross freshwater abstractions, late 1990s

| Per capita | as % of total renewable resources | as % of internal resources |

Per capita (m3/capita/year): Luxembourg, Denmark, UK, Czech Republic, Austria, Netherlands, Poland, Sweden, Ireland, Switzerland, Finland, Germany, Korea, Turkey, New Zealand, Hungary, Iceland, Norway, Belgium, France, Japan, Greece, Australia, Mexico, Italy, Spain, Portugal, Canada, USA. Scale 0 to 1500+. OECD marked.

as % of total renewable resources (%): scale 0 to 60.

as % of internal resources (%): scale 0 to 60. New Zealand 100; Hungary off-scale.

Water stress: | <10% - Low | 10-20% - Moderate | 20-40% - Medium - High | >40% - High |

6

> Indicators of water resource use intensity show great variations among and within individual countries. The national indicator may thus conceal unsustainable use in some regions and periods, and high dependence on water from other basins. In arid regions, freshwater resources may at times be limited to the extent that demand for water can be met only by going beyond sustainable use in terms of quantity.

> At world level, it is estimated that water demand has risen by more than double the rate of population growth in this century. Agriculture is the largest user of water world-wide; global abstractions for irrigation have increased by over 60 % since 1960.

THE BASIS: THE OECD CORE SET OF ENVIRONMENTAL INDICATORS

Core set indicators
ISSUE – WATER RESOURCES
Pressures ◆ **Intensity of use of water resources** (abstractions/available resources)
Conditions ◆ **Frequency, duration and extent of water shortages**
Responses ◆ **Water prices and user charges for sewage treatment**

Measurability
Information on the intensity of the use of water resources can be derived from water resource accounts and is available for most OECD countries. More work is however needed to improve the completeness and historical consistency of the data, and to further improve estimation methods.
More work is also needed to mobilise data at sub-national level, and to reflect the spatial distribution of resource use intensity. This is particularly important for countries with larger territories where resources are unevenly distributed.

FOREST RESOURCES

MAIN POLICY CHALLENGES

▷ *Main concerns relate to the impacts of human activities on forest diversity and health, on natural forest growth and regeneration, and to their consequences for the provision of economic, environmental and social forest services. The main pressures from human activities include agriculture expansion, transport infrastructure development, unsustainable forestry, air pollution and intentional burning of forests. Many forest resources are threatened by degradation, fragmentation and conversion to other types of land uses.*

▷ *The main challenge is to ensure a sustainable management of forest resources, avoiding overexploitation and degradation, so as to maintain adequate supply of wood for production activities, and to ensure the provision of essential environmental services, including biodiversity and carbon sinks. This implies integrating environmental concerns into forestry policies, including eco-certification and carbon sequestration schemes.*

MEASURING PERFORMANCE

▷ *Environmental performance can be assessed against national objectives and international principles on sustainable forest management adopted at UNCED (Rio de Janeiro, 1992). Other international initiatives are the Ministerial Conferences for the Protection of Forests in Europe (Strasbourg, 1990; Helsinki, 1993; Lisbon, 1998), which led to the Pan-European Criteria and Indicators for Sustainable Forest Management, the Montreal Process on Sustainable Development of Temperate and Boreal Forests; and the UN Forum on Forests.*

▷ *The indicator presented here relates to the intensity of use of forest resources (timber), relating actual harvest to annual productive capacity for the late 1990s. Trends in roundwood production are provided as a complement.*

▷ *When interpreting these indicators, it should be noted that relating resource abstraction to renewal of stocks is a central question concerning sustainable forest resource management. It should however be kept in mind that they give insights into quantitative aspects of forest resources and that a national average can conceal important variations among forests. They should be read in connection with other indicators of the OECD Core Set, in particular with indicators on land use changes and forest quality (species diversity, forest degradation), and be complemented with data on forest management practices and protection measures.*

7

MONITORING TRENDS

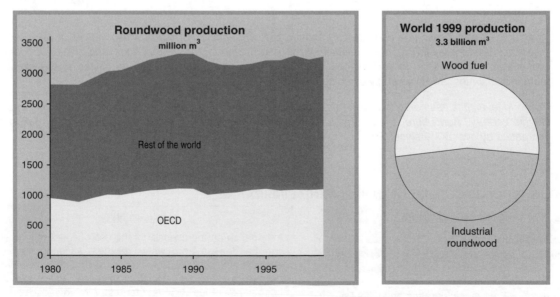

▷ *Commercial exploitation of forests and related roundwood production has been increasing over the past two decades, with some stabilisation over the 1990s, in particular in the OECD region. Over half of the roundwood produced in the world is used as a fuel, the rest for industrial production.*

CURRENT STATE - INTENSITY OF USE OF FOREST RESOURCES

harvest as % of annual growth

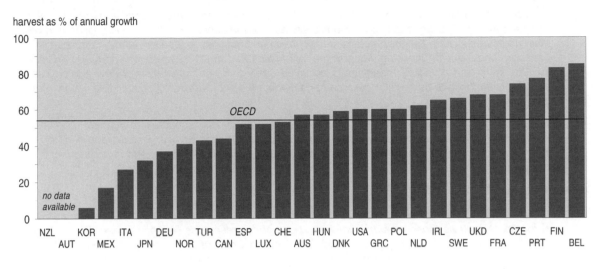

> At national levels most OECD countries present a picture of sustainable use of their forest resources in quantitative terms, but with significant variations within countries. For those countries for which trends over a longer period are available, intensity of forest resource use does not generally show an increase and has even decreased in most countries from the 1950s.

> Over the same period, the area of forests and wooded land has remained stable or has slightly increased in most OECD countries, but has been decreasing at world level due in part to continued deforestation in tropical countries.

THE BASIS: THE OECD CORE SET OF ENVIRONMENTAL INDICATORS

Core set Indicators	Measurability
ISSUE: FOREST RESOURCES	Data on the intensity of use of forest resources can be derived from forest accounts and from international forest statistics (e.g. from FAO and UN-ECE) for most OECD countries. Historical data however often lack comparability or are not available.
Pressures ♦ **Intensity of forest resource use** (actual harvest/productive capacity)	
Conditions ♦ **Area and volume distribution of forests (by biome)** (e.g. volume distribution by major tree species group within each biome, share of disturbed/deteriorated forests in total forest area)	Data on the area of forests and wooded land are available for all countries with varying degrees of completeness. Trends over longer periods are available but lack comparability due to continued improvements in international definitions.
Responses ♦ **Forest area management and protection** (e.g. % of protected forest area in total forest area; % of harvest area successfully regenerated or afforested)	More work needs to be done to monitor state and trends in the quality of forest resources and in related management and protection measures.

FISH RESOURCES

MAIN POLICY CHALLENGES

▷ *Main concerns relate to the impacts of human activities on fish stocks and habitats in marine but also in fresh waters, and to their consequences for biodiversity and for the supply of fish for consumption and other uses. Main pressures include fisheries, coastal development and pollution loads from land-based sources, maritime transport, and maritime dumping. Many of the more valuable fish stocks are overfished, and the steady trend towards increased global fish landings is achieved partly through exploitation of new and/or less valuable species. Unauthorised fishing is widespread and hinders the achievement of sustainable fishery management objectives.*

▷ *The main challenge is to ensure a sustainable management of fish resources so that resource abstraction in the various catchment areas does not exceed the renewal of the stocks over an extended period. This implies setting and enforcing limits on total catch types, levels and fishing seasons; and strengthening international co-operation.*

MEASURING PERFORMANCE

▷ *Environmental performance can be assessed against domestic objectives and bilateral and multilateral agreements such as those on conservation and use of fish resources (Atlantic Ocean, Pacific Ocean, Baltic Sea, etc.), the Rome Consensus on world fisheries, the Code of Conduct for Responsible Fishing (FAO, November 1995), the UN Convention on the Law of the Sea and its implementation agreement on straddling and highly migratory fish stocks. Within the framework of the FAO Code of Conduct for Responsible Fishing, plans are being made to address the issue of illegal, unreported and unregulated (IUU) fishing.*

▷ *The indicator presented here relates to fish catches expressed as % of world captures and changes in total catches since 1980. Fish production from aquaculture is not included. The data cover catches in both fresh and marine waters.*

▷ *When interpreting these indicators it should be kept in mind that they give insights into quantitative aspects of fish resources. They should be read in connection with other indicators of the OECD Core Set, and in particular be complemented with information on the status of fish stocks and the proportion of fish resources under various phases of fishery development. They can further be related to data on national fish consumption.*

MONITORING TRENDS

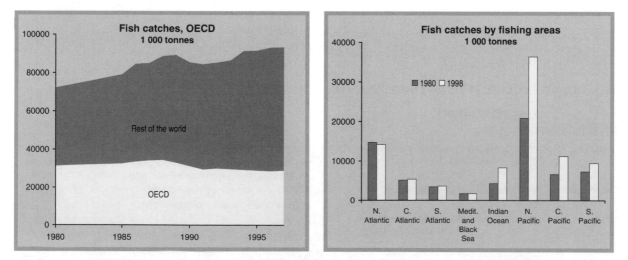

▷ *Of 441 marine stocks fished world-wide, more than 28 % are estimated to be overfished (18%), depleted (9%) or recovering (1%), while about 47 % are fully exploited. Trend analysis shows large differences among OECD countries and among fishing areas, with high increases in some areas (e.g. the Pacific and Indian Oceans) and decreases in others (e.g. the North Atlantic). Only a few of the fish stocks in areas closest to OECD countries have significant potential for additional exploitation; the North Atlantic and parts of the Pacific areas are already being overfished.*

CURRENT STATE - FISH CATCHES

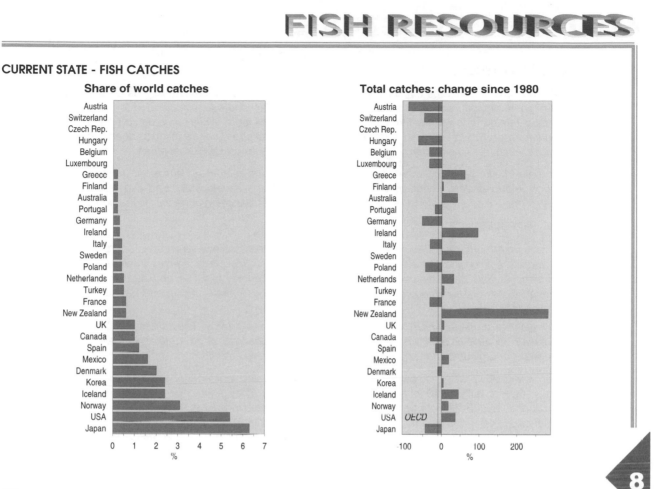

Share of world catches

Total catches: change since 1980

⇨ *The intensity of national catches per capita varies widely among OECD countries, reflecting the share of fisheries and associated industries in the economy.*

⇨ *Catches from capture fisheries are generally growing at a slower rate than 30 years ago; they are even in decline in a number of countries, whereas aquaculture is gaining in importance. While aquaculture helps to alleviate some of the stress from capture fisheries, it also has negative effects on local ecosystems and its dependence on fishmeal products adds to the demand for catches from capture fisheries.*

8

THE BASIS: THE OECD CORE SET OF ENVIRONMENTAL INDICATORS

Core set indicators
ISSUE – FISH RESOURCES
Pressures ♦ **Fish catches**
Conditions ♦ **Size of spawning stocks**   – Overfished areas
Responses ♦ **Fishing quotas** (Number of stocks regulated by quotas)   – Expenditure for fish stock monitoring

Measurability
Fish catches and production data are available from international sources at significant detail and for most OECD countries. More work needs to be done to better reflect the composition of the landings and its trophic structure.
Data on the size of major fish populations exist but are scattered across national and international sources.
More work needs to be done to better reflect the status of fish stocks, and to relate fish captures to available resources.

ENERGY RESOURCES

MAIN POLICY CHALLENGES

▷ *Main concerns relate to the effects of energy production and use on greenhouse gas emissions and on local and regional air pollution; other effects involve water quality, land use, risks related to the nuclear fuel cycle and risks related to the extraction, transport and use of fossil fuels. While some de-coupling of environmental effects from growth in energy use has been achieved, results to date are insufficient and the environmental implications of increasing energy use remain a major issue in most OECD countries.*

▷ *The main challenge is to further de-couple energy use and related air emissions from economic growth, through improvements in energy efficiency and through the development and use of cleaner fuels. This requires the use of a mix of instruments including extended reliance on economic instruments.*

MEASURING PERFORMANCE

▷ *Environmental performance can be assessed against domestic objectives such as energy efficiency targets, and targets concerning the share of renewable energy sources; and against international environmental commitments that have direct implications for domestic energy policies and strategies (e.g. the United Nations Framework Convention on Climate Change (1992), Convention on Long-Range Transboundary Air Pollution (1979)).*

▷ *The indicators presented here relate to the intensity of use of energy. They show energy supply intensities, expressed per unit of GDP and per capita, and related changes since 1980. They reflect, at least partly, changes in energy efficiency and efforts to reduce atmospheric emissions.*

▷ *When interpreting these indicators, it should be kept in mind that energy intensities reflect structural and climatic factors as well as changes in energy efficiency. They should be read in connection with other indicators of the OECD Core Set and with other energy-related indicators such as energy prices and taxes for households and industry, and the structure of and changes in energy supply. They should further be complemented with information on energy-related air and water emissions and waste generation.*

MONITORING TRENDS

9

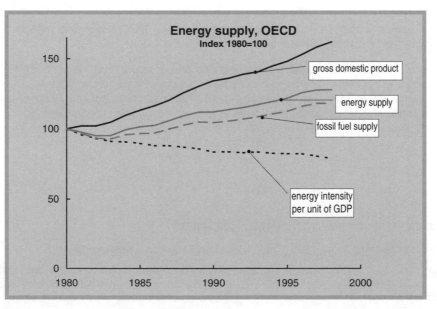

▷ *During the 1980s, energy intensity per unit of GDP generally decreased in the OECD as a consequence of structural changes in the economy and energy conservation measures. In the 1990s, energy intensity did not further improve in most countries, due to decreasing prices for energy resources (oil, gas, etc.). Progress in per capita terms has been much slower, reflecting an overall increase in energy supply and increasing energy demands for transport activities.*

CURRENT STATE - ENERGY SUPPLY INTENSITIES

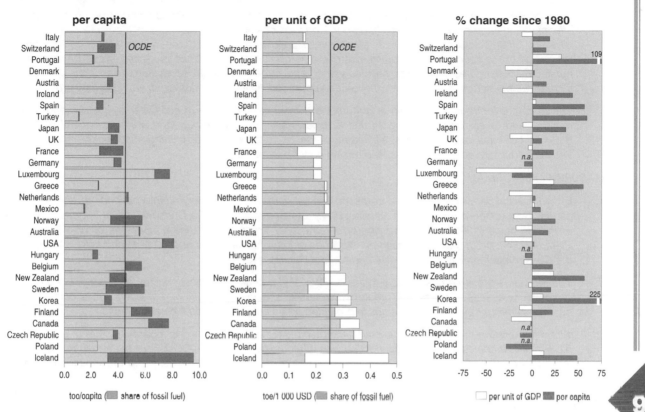

| per capita | per unit of GDP | % change since 1980 |

Variations in energy intensity among OECD countries are wide and depend on national economic structure, geography (e.g. climate), energy policies and prices, and countries' endowment in different types of energy resources.

During the 1980s and early 1990s, growth in total primary energy supply was accompanied by changes in the fuel mix: the shares of solid fuels and oil fell, while those of gas and other sources rose. This trend is particularly visible in OECD Europe. The rates of change, however, vary widely by country.

THE BASIS: THE OECD CORE SET OF ENVIRONMENTAL INDICATORS

Core set indicators	Measurability

ISSUE – CLIMATE CHANGE
 	
Responses ♦ **Energy efficiency**
  – Energy intensity
  – Economic and fiscal instruments (energy prices and taxes, expenditures)
 	
SOCIO-ECONOMIC AND GENERAL INDICATORS
  ♦ **Structure of energy supply**
 	
To be further supplemented with:
 	
The OECD set of indicators for the integration of environmental concerns into energy policies
	Data on energy supply and consumption are available from international sources for all OECD countries.
	
	More work needs to be done to further develop appropriate measures of energy efficiency (ref. IEA work).

BIODIVERSITY

MAIN POLICY CHALLENGES

▷ *Main concerns relate to the impacts of human activities on biodiversity. Pressures can be physical (habitat alteration and fragmentation through changes in land use and cover), chemical (toxic contamination, acidification, oil spills, other pollution) or biological (alteration of population dynamics and species structure through the release of exotic species or the commercial use of wildlife resources). While protected areas have grown in most OECD countries, pressures on biodiversity and threats to global ecosystems and their species are increasing. Many natural ecosystems have been degraded, limiting the ecosystem services they provide.*

▷ *The main challenge is to maintain or restore the diversity and integrity of ecosystems, species and genetic material and to ensure a sustainable use of biodiversity. This implies strengthening the actual degree of protection of habitats and species, eliminating illegal exploitation and trade, integrating biodiversity concerns into economic and sectoral policies, and raising public awareness.*

MEASURING PERFORMANCE

▷ *Environmental performance can be assessed against domestic objectives and international agreements such as: the Convention on Biological Diversity (1992), the Convention on the Conservation of Migratory Species of Wild Animals (1979), the Convention on International Trade in Endangered Species of Wild Fauna and Flora (CITES, 1973), the Convention on Wetlands of International Importance (1971) and the Convention on the Conservation of European Wildlife and Natural Habitats (1979).*

▷ *The indicators presented here relate to the number of threatened or extinct species compared to the number of known or assessed species. "Threatened" refers to species in danger of extinction and species likely to soon be in danger of extinction. Trends in protected areas are provided as a complement.*

▷ *When interpreting this indicator, it should be kept in mind that it only provides a partial picture of the status of biodiversity. It should be read in connection with other indicators of the OECD Core set and in particular with indicators on the sustainable use of biodiversity as a resource (e.g. forest, fish) and on habitat alteration. It should further be complemented with information on the density of population and of human activities.*

10 MONITORING TRENDS

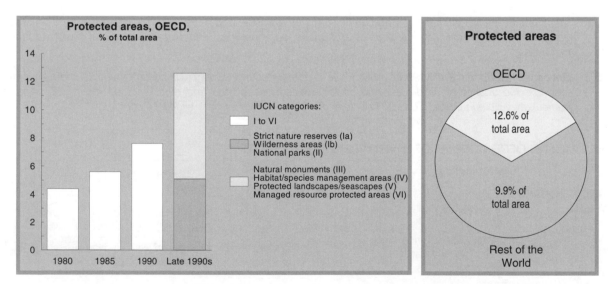

The number and extent of protected areas has increased significantly since 1980 in almost all countries, reaching 12 % of total area for the OECD as a whole. Actual protection levels, management effectiveness and related trends are more difficult to evaluate, as protected areas change over time: new areas are designated, boundaries are revised and some sites may be destroyed or changed by pressures from economic development or natural processes.

CURRENT STATE – THREATENED SPECIES

Mammals

Birds

Vascular plants

Countries listed for each chart: Canada, Mexico, USA, Japan, Korea, Australia, New Zealand, Austria, Belgium, Czech Rep., Denmark, Finland, France, Germany, Greece, Hungary, Iceland, Ireland, Italy, Luxembourg, Netherlands, Norway, Poland, Portugal, Spain, Sweden, Switzerland, Turkey, UK

% of species known

10

This Indicator shows a high percentage of species threatened; figures higher than 30 % are often reached in particular for animal species. The levels are particularly high in countries with a high population density, and a high level of concentration of human activities.

In most countries, a significant share of species are threatened not only by habitat loss or alteration inside protected areas, but also by changes in land use categories and intensity outside protected areas (e.g. agriculture, forestry, etc.)

THE BASIS: THE OECD CORE SET OF ENVIRONMENTAL INDICATORS

Core set indicators

ISSUE: BIODIVERSITY

Pressures	♦ **Habitat alteration and land conversion from natural state** to be further developed (e.g. road network density, change in land cover, etc.)
Conditions	♦ **Threatened or extinct species as a share of total species assessed** ♦ **Area of key ecosystems**
Responses	♦ **Protected areas as % of national territory and by type of ecosystem** – Protected species

Measurability

Data on threatened species are available for all OECD countries with varying degrees of completeness. The number of species known or assessed does not always accurately reflect the number of species in existence, and the definitions that should follow IUCN standards are applied with varying degrees of rigour in Member countries. Historical data are generally not comparable.

On key ecosystems, no OECD-wide data are available.

Data on protected areas are available, but not by type of ecosystem. Also, a distinction between areas protected mainly for "biological" reasons and areas protected for aesthetic or cultural reasons is not always easy.

More generally, accurate, comprehensive and comparable time-series data on wildlife populations still need to be fully developed. More needs also to be done to monitor ecosystem integrity and to develop indicators that better reflect the state of and changes in biodiversity at the habitat/ecosystem level.

IV. OECD FRAMEWORK FOR ENVIRONMENTAL INDICATORS

OECD FRAMEWORK FOR ENVIRONMENTAL INDICATORS

The OECD environmental indicators programme recognises that there is no universal set of indicators; rather, several sets exist, corresponding to specific purposes. Indicators can be used at international and national levels in state of the environment reporting, measurement of environmental performance and reporting on progress towards sustainable development. They can further be used at national level in planning, clarifying policy objectives and setting priorities.

The OECD work focuses principally on indicators to be used in national, international and global decision making, yet the approach may also be used to develop indicators at sub-national or ecosystem level. Results of this work have in turn _influenced_ similar activities by a number of countries and international organisations.

APPROACH AND RESULTS

In developing harmonised international environmental indicators, OECD countries adopted a pragmatic approach, which led in particular to:

- agreement on a common conceptual _framework_, based on a common _understanding of concepts and definitions_ and on the _pressure-state-response (PSR) model_ (Inset 1, Inset 3);
- identification of _criteria_ to help in selecting indicators and validating their choice: all indicators are reviewed according to their policy relevance, analytical soundness and measurability (Inset 2);
- _identification_ and definition of indicators (including an assessment of their measurability);
- provision of _guidance for the use_ of indicators (stressing that indicators are only one tool and have to be interpreted in context).

Those indicators for which internationally comparable data exist are regularly published and used in current OECD work, particularly in OECD environmental performance reviews.

SEVERAL TYPES OF INDICATORS

The OECD work[1] includes several types of environmental indicators, each corresponding to a specific purpose and framework:

- the OECD Core Set of environmental indicators, to keep track of environmental progress;
- several sets of sectoral indicators, to promote integration of environmental concerns into sectoral policy making: transport-environment indicators, energy-environment indicators, agri-environmental indicators[2];
- indicators derived from environmental accounting, to promote both integration of environmental concerns into economic policies and sustainable use and management of natural resources.

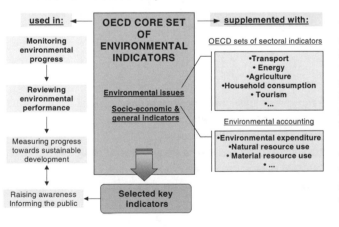

These indicator sets are closely related to each other, the OECD Core Set being a synthesis and representing a common minimum set; i.e. the most important sectoral indicators are part of the Core Set, as are major indicators derived from resource accounting.

The Core Set also provides the basis for a small set of key indicators that are mainly used for public communication purposes.

---

[1]. Work led by the OECD Working Group on Environmental Information and Outlooks.

[2]. Work led by the Joint Working Party of the Agriculture Committee and the Environmental Policy Committee.

Inset 1 **Definitions and functions of environmental indicators**

The terminology adopted by OECD countries points to two major functions of indicators:

♦ they reduce the number of measurements and parameters that normally would be required to give an "exact" presentation of a situation;

♦ they simplify the communication process by which the results of measurement are provided to the user.

TERMINOLOGY

♦ Indicator: A parameter, or a value derived from parameters, which points to, provides information about, describes the state of a phenomenon/environment/area, with a significance extending beyond that directly associated with a parameter value.

♦ Index: A set of aggregated or weighted parameters or indicators.

♦ Parameter: A property that is measured or observed.

Inset 2 **Criteria for selecting environmental indicators**

As indicators are used for various purposes, it is necessary to define general criteria for selecting indicators. Three basic criteria are used in OECD work: policy relevance and utility for users, analytical soundness, and measurability.*

POLICY RELEVANCE — An environmental indicator should:

♦ provide a representative picture of environmental conditions, pressures on the environment or society's responses;

♦ be simple, easy to interpret and able to show trends over time;

♦ be responsive to changes in the environment and related human activities;

♦ provide a basis for international comparisons;

♦ be either national in scope or applicable to regional environmental issues of national significance;

♦ have a threshold or reference value against which to compare it, so that users can assess the significance of the values associated with it.

ANALYTICAL SOUNDNESS — An environmental indicator should:

♦ be theoretically well founded in technical and scientific terms;

♦ be based on international standards and international consensus about its validity;

♦ lend itself to being linked to economic models, forecasting and information systems.

MEASURABILITY — The data required to support the indicator should be:

♦ readily available or made available at a reasonable cost/benefit ratio;

♦ adequately documented and of known quality;

♦ updated at regular intervals in accordance with reliable procedures.

These criteria describe the "ideal" indicator; not all of them will be met in practice.

Inset 3 The Pressure - State - Response (PSR) Model

The PSR model considers that: human activities exert <u>pressures</u> on the environment and affect its quality and the quantity of natural resources ("<u>state</u>"); society responds to these changes through environmental, general economic and sectoral policies and through changes in awareness and behaviour ("<u>societal response</u>"). The PSR model has the advantage of highlighting these links, and helping decision makers and the public see environmental and other issues as interconnected (although this should not obscure the view of more complex relationships in ecosystems, and in environment-economy and environment-social interactions).

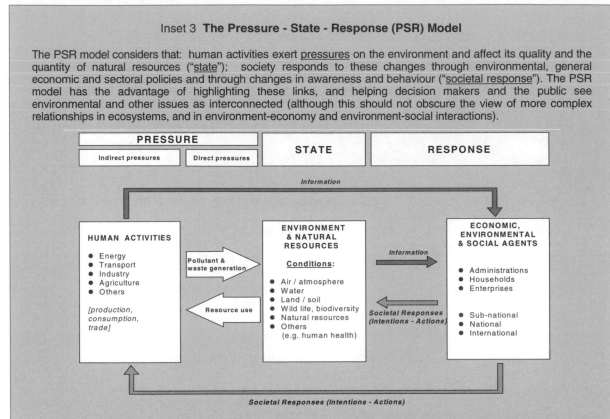

- ◆ <u>Indicators of environmental pressures</u> describe pressures from human activities exerted on the environment, including natural resources. "Pressures" here cover underlying or indirect pressures (i.e. the activity itself and trends and patterns of environmental significance) as well as proximate or direct pressures (i.e. the use of resources and the discharge of pollutants and waste materials). Indicators of environmental pressures focus on direct pressures and are closely related to production and consumption patterns; they often reflect emission or resource use intensities, along with related trends and changes over a given period. They can be used to show progress in de-coupling economic activities from related environmental pressures, or in meeting national objectives and international commitments (e.g. emission reduction targets).

- ◆ <u>Indicators of environmental conditions</u> relate to the quality of the environment and the quality and quantity of natural resources. As such they reflect the ultimate objective of environmental policies. Indicators of environmental conditions are designed to give an overview of the situation (the state) concerning the environment and its development over time. Examples of indicators of environmental conditions are: concentration of pollutants in environmental media, exceedance of critical loads, population exposure to certain levels of pollution or degraded environmental quality and related effects on health, the status of wildlife and of natural resource stocks. In practice, measuring environmental conditions can be difficult or very costly. Therefore, environmental pressures are often measured instead as a substitute.

- ◆ <u>Indicators of societal responses</u> show the extent to which society responds to environmental concerns. They refer to individual and collective actions and reactions, intended to:
    - ◆ mitigate, adapt to or prevent human-induced negative effects on the environment;
    - ◆ halt or reverse environmental damage already inflicted;
    - ◆ preserve and conserve nature and natural resources.

Examples of indicators of societal responses are environmental expenditure, environment-related taxes and subsidies, price structures, market shares of environmentally friendly goods and services, pollution abatement rates, waste recycling rates. In practice, indicators mostly relate to abatement and control measures; those showing preventive and integrative measures and actions are more difficult to obtain.

Depending on the purpose for which the PSR model is to be used, it can easily be adjusted to account for greater details or for specific features. Examples of adjusted versions are the Driving force - State - Response (DSR) model formerly used by the UNCSD in its work on sustainable development indicators, the framework used for OECD sectoral indicators and the Driving force-Pressure-State-Impact-Response (DPSIR) model used by the European Environment Agency.

THE OECD CORE SET OF ENVIRONMENTAL INDICATORS

PURPOSE AND CHARACTERISTICS

The OECD Core Set of environmental indicators is a commonly agreed upon set of indicators for OECD countries and for international use, published regularly. It is a first step in tracking environmental progress and the factors involved in it, and it is a major tool for measuring environmental performance. Characteristics of the Core Set are that:

- it is of limited size (around 50 core indicators);
- it covers a broad range of environmental issues;
- it reflects an approach common to a majority of OECD countries.

FRAMEWORK

THE PSR MODEL

Firstly, the <u>PSR</u> model provides a classification into indicators of environmental pressures, indicators of environmental conditions and indicators of societal responses (Inset 3).

MAJOR ISSUES OF CONCERN

Secondly, the Core Set structure distinguishes a number of environmental issues that reflect major environmental concerns in OECD countries. For each issue, indicators of environmental pressure, conditions and societal responses have been defined (Inset 4).

Inset 4 Structure of OECD indicators Core Set by environmental issue

Major issues	PRESSURE Indicators of environmental pressures	STATE Indicators of environmental conditions	RESPONSE Indicators of societal responses
1. Climate change 2. Ozone layer depletion 3. Eutrophication 4. Acidification 5. Toxic contamination 6. Urban environmental quality 7. Biodiversity 8. Cultural landscapes 9. Waste			
10. Water resources 11. Forest resources 12. Fish resources 13. Soil degradation (desertification, erosion)			
14. Socio-economic, sectoral and general indicators			

The first nine issues relate to the use of the environment's "sink capacity", dealing with issues of environmental quality, whereas the other issues relate to the environment's "source capacity", focusing on the quantity aspect of natural resources.

For indicators that cannot be directly associated with a specific environmental issue an additional category has been added. It relates to background variables and driving forces, such as population growth and economic growth; selected sectoral trends and patterns of environmental significance, or factors such as economy-wide environmental expenditure and public opinion. This category also provides an opportunity to further integrate indicators from sectoral sets into the OECD Core Set.

These issues depend on changing and sometimes conflicting perceptions; the list is not necessarily final or exhaustive.

SECTORAL BREAKDOWN

Thirdly, the possibility of disaggregating major indicators at <u>sectoral level</u> is considered. Data availability permitting, this is one tool for analysing environmental pressures exerted by different economic sectors and distinguishing government responses from those of the business sector or private households. Indicators at the sectoral level could be useful in reviewing the integration of environmental and sectoral policies and monitoring resource use and emission intensities in the various economic sectors. Indicators at sectoral level also facilitate the link with economic information systems and models.

KEY INDICATORS

To respond to the increasing interest by Member countries in a reduced number of indicators selected from existing larger sets to capture <u>key trends</u> and draw attention to <u>key issues</u> of common concern, as small set of key environmental indicators has been selected from the Core Set. This set has been endorsed by environment ministers of OECD countries for systematic use in the OECD's communication and policy work (see Part IV of this report).

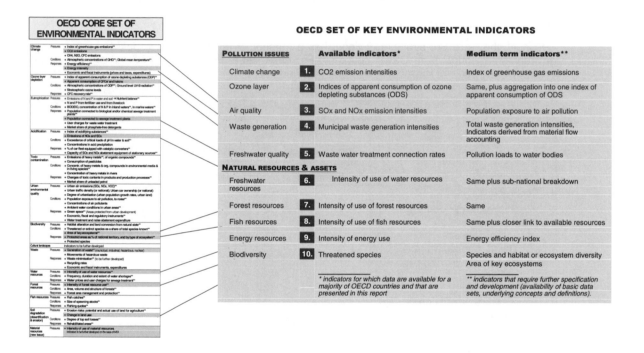

These key indicators have been very useful in charting environmental progress and their selection has benefited from experience gained in using environmental indicators in the OECD's country environmental performance reviews.

The list of key indicators is <u>neither final, nor exhaustive</u>; it has to be seen together with other indicators from the OECD Core Set, and will evolve as knowledge and data availability improve. Ultimately, the set is expected to also include key indicators for issues such as toxic contamination, land and soil resources, and urban environmental quality.

THE OECD SETS OF SECTORAL INDICATORS

PURPOSE AND CHARACTERISTICS

The OECD has been developing sets of sectoral indicators to <u>better integrate environmental concerns into sectoral policies</u>. The objective is to develop a "tool kit" for sectoral decision makers, which should facilitate the integration of environmental concerns in sectoral policy making. While limited to a specific sector and its interactions with the environment, these indicators are typically developed in larger numbers than the Core Set.

Sectoral indicator sets are not restricted to "environmental indicators" *per se* but also concern linkages between the environment and the economy, placed in a context of sustainable development. They may include environmental indicators (e.g. pollutant emissions), economic indicators (e.g. sectoral output, prices and taxes, subsidies) and selected social indicators.

FRAMEWORK

The conceptual framework adopted for sectoral indicators (Inset 5) is <u>derived from the PSR model</u>, but was adjusted to account for the specificities of the respective sectors. As defined by OECD countries, sectoral indicators have been organised along a framework that distinguishes:

♦ indicators to reflect <u>sectoral trends and patterns of environmental significance</u> (i.e. indirect pressures and/or related driving forces);

♦ indicators to reflect <u>interactions between the sector and the environment</u>, including positive and negative effects of sectoral activity on the environment (i.e. direct pressures, such as pollutant releases and resource use, and related effects and resulting environmental conditions, such as ambient concentrations of pollutants and population exposure), as well as effects of environmental changes on sectoral activity;

♦ indicators to reflect <u>economic linkages</u> between the sector and the environment, as well as <u>policy considerations</u>. This category includes environmental damage and environmental expenditure, economic and fiscal instruments, and trade issues.

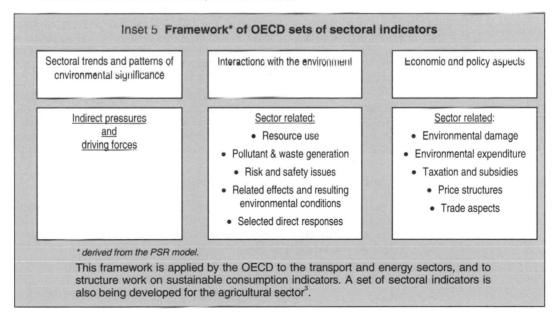

Inset 5 Framework* of OECD sets of sectoral indicators

Sectoral trends and patterns of environmental significance	Interactions with the environment	Economic and policy aspects
Indirect pressures and driving forces	Sector related: • Resource use • Pollutant & waste generation • Risk and safety issues • Related effects and resulting environmental conditions • Selected direct responses	Sector related: • Environmental damage • Environmental expenditure • Taxation and subsidies • Price structures • Trade aspects

* derived from the PSR model.

This framework is applied by the OECD to the transport and energy sectors, and to structure work on sustainable consumption indicators. A set of sectoral indicators is also being developed for the agricultural sector[3].

---

[3]. 📖 *OECD (1993, 1999), OECD Series on Environmental Indicators: Indicators for the Integration of Environmental Concerns into Transport Policies*
  📖 *OECD (1993, 2001), OECD Series on Environmental Indicators: Indicators for the Integration of Environmental Concerns into Energy Policies*
  📖 *OECD (1997, 1999, 2001), Environmental Indicators for Agriculture*
  📖 *OECD (1999), OECD Series on Environmental Indicators: Towards more sustainable Household Consumption Patterns – Indicators to measure progress*

OECD ENVIRONMENTAL ACCOUNTING

Environmental indicators are also derived from the broader area of environmental accounting, in both physical and monetary terms[4]. The OECD work focuses on physical natural resource accounts as a tool for sustainable management of natural resources, as well as on expenditure for pollution abatement and control and other environmental measures. In addition, the OECD participates in international work on environmental accounting and acts as a forum for exchanges of experiences in this field. (Inset 6)

Inset 6 **Environmental accounting: definitions and concepts**		
Environmental accounting can be defined as the systematic description of interactions between the environment and the economy by means of an accounting framework. There is no unique model for environmental accounting; approaches vary according to purpose.		
Approach	**Environmental categories taken into account**	**Characteristics**
Adjustment of national economic accounts	Valuation of: ♦ Environmental damages ♦ Environmental services ♦ Stock of natural capital	Modifies SNA framework and boundaries
Satellite accounts	Valuation of: ♦ Environmental damages ♦ Environmental services ♦ Stock of natural capital ♦ Environmental expenditure Corresponding physical flows and stocks	Complements SNA without modifying it General coherence with SNA
Natural resource and environment accounts	♦ Physical flows and stocks of natural resources ♦ Physical and monetary flows associated with anthropogenic exploitation of natural resources	Independent from and complementary to SNA

INDICATORS DERIVED FROM NATURAL RESOURCE ACCOUNTS

To progress towards a common methodology, the OECD reviewed different approaches of OECD Member countries in the field of natural resource accounting (NRA). This work resulted in the establishment of OECD pilot accounts on forests and water. The basic methodology used in the pilot accounts is simple and provides a guide to countries that are developing natural resource accounts. The format was set up to provide a tool for decision makers.

The pilot accounts propose physical input-output tables tracing the production, transformation and use of each resource throughout the economy. This provides an analytical tool with which to assess the impact of sectoral economic activity on the resource. Basic flow relations from these accounts form the input for calculating indicators of sustainable use of natural resource quantities. Examples of such indicators are: intensity of use of forest resources and intensity of use of water resources.

INDICATORS DERIVED FROM ENVIRONMENTAL EXPENDITURE ACCOUNTS

The OECD has pursued work on pollution abatement and control (PAC) expenditure for a number of years. The data thus developed are published regularly and supplement economic information from national accounts. Indicators derived from this work reflect the level of PAC expenditure compared with GDP, as well as the structure of such expenditure per environmental domain and per source sector.

---

[4]. 📕 *OECD (1996), Environmental Accounting for Decision Making - Summary Report of an OECD Seminar*
📕 *OECD (1996), Natural Resource Accounts - Taking Stock in OECD Countries*
📕 *OECD (1996), Pollution Abatement and Control Expenditure in OECD Countries*

USING ENVIRONMENTAL INDICATORS

GUIDING PRINCIPLES

When using environmental indicators in analytical and evaluation work, the OECD applies the following principles:

ONLY ONE TOOL

Indicators are only one tool for evaluation; scientific and policy-oriented interpretation is required for them to acquire their full meaning. They often need to be supplemented by other qualitative and scientific information, particularly in explaining driving forces behind indicator changes which form the basis for an assessment.

THE APPROPRIATE CONTEXT

Indicators' relevance varies by country and by context. They must be reported and interpreted in the appropriate context, taking into account countries' different ecological, geographical, social, economic and institutional features.

In the OECD environmental performance reviews, international indicators derived from the Core Set are generally used in combination with specific national indicators and data. These national indicators provide a more detailed picture of the country's situation through further sectoral and/or spatial breakdown (e.g. sub-national data) and often point at particular issues of concern.

INTERCOUNTRY COMPARISON AND STANDARDISATION

OECD focuses on national indicators for use in international work. This implies not only nationally aggregated indicators, but also an appropriate level of comparability among countries. Despite a number of achievements in this area, further work is needed on internationally harmonised definitions and concepts.

There is no single method of standardisation for the comparison of environmental indicators across countries. The outcome of the assessment may depend on the chosen denominator (e.g. GDP, population, land area) as well as on national definitions and measurement methods. It is therefore appropriate for different denominators to be used in parallel to balance the message conveyed. In some cases absolute values may be the appropriate measure, for example when international commitments are linked to absolute values.

MEASURABILITY

Measurability issues such as the quality of underlying data are important in the use of environmental indicators, and must be taken into account to avoid misinterpretation.

Measurability still varies greatly among individual indicators. Some indicators are immediately measurable, others need additional efforts before they can be published. For example, most indicators of societal responses have a shorter history than indicators of environmental pressures and many indicators of environmental conditions, and are still in development both conceptually and in terms of data availability.

TIMELINESS

Another important criterion affecting the usefulness and relevance of an indicator is the timeliness of the underlying data. The interval between the period to which data refer and the date when data are released should be as short as is practicable. Current timeliness of environmental data remains insufficient and needs improvement as a matter of priority.

LEVEL OF AGGREGATION

Most OECD indicators focus on the national level and are designed to be used in an international context. Within a country a greater level of detail or breakdown may be needed, particularly when indicators are to support sub-national or sectoral decision making or when national indicators hide major regional differences. This is particularly important when dealing, for example, with river basin or ecosystem management. The actual measurement of indicators at these levels is encouraged and lies within the responsibility of individual countries. At these levels, however, measurability and comparability problems may be further exacerbated.

ENVIRONMENTAL INDICATORS AND PERFORMANCE ANALYSIS

In the OECD context, environmental indicators are used as a tool for evaluating environmental performance. They support the analysis made in OECD country environmental performance reviews[5] and provide all reviews with a common denominator. This creates a synergy in which regular feedback is provided on the indicators' policy relevance and analytical soundness.

Using environmental indicators in environmental performance reviews implies linking these indicators to the measurement and analysis of achievements, as well as to underlying driving forces and to the country's specific conditions. Indicators can be linked to:

♦ explicit quantitative objectives (goals, targets, commitments);

♦ broad qualitative objectives concerning, for example:

  – efficiency of human activities (linked to the notions of decoupling, elasticities, integration);

  – sustainability of natural resource use and development.

It is important to recognise, however, that indicators are not a mechanical measure of environmental performance. They need to be complemented with background information, analysis and interpretation.

---

[5]. The *OECD Environmental Performance Review Programme*, assesses Member countries' performance by comparing achievements or progress with national objectives and international commitments. The reviews take into account each country's absolute levels of environmental quality and the physical, human and economic context.

📖 OECD, Environmental Performance Reviews. 4 reviews published each year. First cycle reviews published: Australia, Austria, Belgium, Belarus, Bulgaria, Canada, Czech Republic, Denmark, Finland, France, Germany, Greece, Hungary, Iceland, Italy, Ireland, Japan, Korea, Luxembourg, Mexico, Netherlands, New Zealand, Norway, Poland, Portugal, Russian Federation, Spain, Sweden, Switzerland, Turkey, United Kingdom, United States. Second cycle reviews already published: Germany, Iceland.

V. TECHNICAL ANNEX

GENERAL INFORMATION

Country region codes used are as follows:

CAN:	Canada	FIN:	Finland	NOR:	Norway
MEX:	Mexico	FRA:	France	POL:	Poland
USA:	United States	DEU:	Germany	PRT:	Portugal
JPN:	Japan	wDEU:	western Germany	ESP:	Spain
KOR:	Korea	GRC:	Greece	SWE:	Sweden
AUS:	Australia	HUN:	Hungary	CHE:	Switzerland
NZL:	New Zealand	ISL:	Iceland	TUR:	Turkey
AUT:	Austria	IRL:	Ireland	UKD:	United Kingdom
BEL:	Belgium	ITA:	Italy	DAC:	OECD Development Assistance
CZE:	Czech Republic	LUX:	Luxembourg		Committee Member countries
DNK:	Denmark	NLD:	Netherlands		

*: Data including western Germany only

➢ Country aggregates

OECD: All OECD Member countries, which include the OECD Europe — i.e. countries of the European Union (EU) plus Czech Republic, Hungary, Iceland, Norway, Poland, Switzerland and Turkey — plus Canada, Mexico, the United States, Japan, Korea, Australia and New Zealand.

OECD*: All OECD Member countries except eastern Germany.

OECD**: Partial OECD total.

➢ Signs

..; n.a.	not available	.	decimal point	%	percentage
-	nil or negligible	n. app.	not applicable	USD	US dollar

➢ Abbreviations

BOD	- biochemical oxygen demand	HCFC	- hydrochlorofluorocarbon	ODA	- official development assistance
Cap	- capita	HM	- heavy metal	PAC	- pollution abatement & control
CFC	- chlorofluorocarbon	Inh	- inhabitant	PCB	- polychlorinated biphenyls
CO	- carbon monoxide	kcal	- kilocalorie	PFC	- private final consumption
CO_2	- carbon dioxide	l	- litre	Pop	- population
CH_4	- methane	Mtoe	- million tonnes of oil equivalent	ppb	- parts per billion
DAC	- Development Assistance Committee	N	- nitrogen	PPP	- purchasing power parities
GCV	- gross calorific value	N_2O	- nitrous oxide	ppt	- parts per trillion
GDP	- gross domestic product	NO_x	- nitrogen oxides	SO_x	- sulphur oxides
GNP	- gross national product	NMVOC	- non-methane volatile organic	t	- tonne
GHG	- greenhouse gas		compounds	veh-km	- vehicle-kilometre

➢ Units

cal	- calorie (1 cal = 4.1868 joules)	kWh	- kilowatt hour	m^3	- cubic metre (1 m^3 = 1.3079 cubic
Dobson	- see Ozone Layer Depletion notes		(1 kWh = 103 Wh = 0.8598		yards)
g	- gram (1 g = 0.0353 ounces)		kilocalories)	Toe	- tonne of oil equivalent
μg	- microgram (1 μg = 10^{-6} g)	litre	- (1 l = 1 dm^3 = 0.001 m^3)		(1 Toe = 10^7 kcal = 41.868*10^9 joules)
mg	- milligram (1 mg = 10^3 g)	km	- kilometre	tonne	- metric ton
ha	- hectare (1 ha = 0.01 km^2)		(1 km = 1 000 m. = 0.6214 miles)		(1 t = 1 000 kg = 0.9842 long ton
kg	- kilogram	km^2	- square kilometre		= 1.1023 short ton)
	(1 kg = 1 000 g = 2.2046 pounds)		(1 km^2 = 0.3861 square miles)		

➢ Per capita values

All <u>per capita</u> information uses OECD and Food and Agriculture Organization (FAO) population data.

➢ Per unit of GDP values

All <u>per unit of GDP</u> information uses OECD GDP data at 1991 prices and purchasing power parties (PPPs). The use of PPPs appears preferable to the use of exchange rates in conjunction with environmental questions, as the objective of comparing measures of economic activity such as GDP is to reflect underlying volumes and physical processes as closely as possible.

PPPs are defined as the ratio between the amount of national currency and the amount of a reference currency needed to buy the same bundle of consumption goods in the two countries. In this publication, the reference currency is USD. Typically, PPPs differ from exchange rates as the latter reflect not only relative prices of consumer goods but also a host of other factors, including international capital movements, interest rate differentials and government intervention. As a consequence, exchange rates exhibit much greater variations over time than PPPs.

CLIMATE CHANGE

♦ A number of gases have <u>direct effects</u> on climate change and are considered responsible for a major part of global warming: carbon dioxide (CO_2), methane (CH_4), nitrous oxide (N_2O), chlorofluorocarbons (CFCs), hydrofluorocarbons (HCFCs), methyl bromide (CH_3Br) and sulphur hexa fluoride (SF_6). Other air pollutants, such as NMVOC, NO_x and CO, have <u>indirect effects</u> on climate change as their reactions in the atmosphere result in the production of tropospheric ozone which effectively a GHG. Sulphur-containing trace gases also play a role. A major part of these emissions stems from combustion of fossil fuels and biomass. Other sources are industrial processes, agriculture and changes in land use.

CO_2 EMISSION INTENSITIES

Data sources: IEA-OECD

♦ Data refer to <u>gross direct emissions</u>; CO_2 removal by sinks, indirect emissions from land use changes and indirect effects through interactions in the atmosphere are not taken into account.

♦ Data refer to CO_2 emissions from <u>fossil fuel combustion</u>. Anthropogenic emissions by other sources (industrial processes, biomass burning) are not included.

♦ Data are estimates based on the default methods and emission factors from the *Revised 1996 IPCC Guidelines for National Greenhouse Gas Inventories* and on the IEA-OECD data for total primary energy supply.

♦ Oil and gas for non-energy purposes such as feedstocks in the chemical and petrochemical industries are excluded.

♦ Oil held in international marine and aviation bunkers is excluded at national level; world emissions include marine and aviation bunkers, amounting to 398 million tonnes and 322 million tonnes in 1998.

♦ Further details on calculation methods and conversion factors can be found in *IEA-OECD (2000), CO_2 Emissions from Fuel Combustion ,1971-1998*.

♦ For details on fuel supply and energy prices see Energy notes.

♦ Energy prices: % change refer to 1980-98 period.

MEX • Energy prices: % change refer to 1981-98 period.

OECD• Emission intensities and GDP change since 1980: data exclude Czech Republic, Hungary and Poland.

GREENHOUSE GAS CONCENTRATIONS

Data sources: World Resources Institute (WRI), *World Resources 2000-2001, People and Ecosystems: The Fraying Web of Life* based on data from CDIAC (Carbon Dioxide Information Analysis Center).

♦ Although gas concentrations at any given time vary among monitoring sites, the data reported reflect global trends. CO_2 data refer to Mauna Loa, Hawaii ($19°32'$ N, $155°35'$ W). Data for other gases are from values monitored at Cape Grim, Tasmania ($45°41'$ S,

$144°41'$ E) under the Atmospheric Lifetime Experiment (ALE) and Global Atmospheric Gases Experiment (GAGE).

♦ Total gaseous chlorine concentrations: calculated by multiplying the number of chlorine atoms in each of the chlorine-containing gases (carbon tetrachloride ($CCl4$), methyl chloroform ($CH3CCl3$), CFC-11 ($CCl3F$), CFC-12 ($CCl2F2$), CFC-22 ($CHClF2$), and CFC-113 ($C2Cl3F3$)) by the concentration of that gas.

♦ For further details, please refer to the above-cited WRI publication.

OZONE LAYER DEPLETION

OZONE DEPLETING SUBSTANCES

Data sources   Ozone Secretariat/UNEP Nairobi; OECD

♦ <u>CFCs:</u> Annex A Group I substances (chlorofluorocarbons).

♦ <u>Halons:</u> Annex A Group II substances (halons).

♦ <u>Other CFCs:</u> Annex B Group I, II and III substances (other fully halogenated CFCs, carbon tetrachloride and methyl chlorotorm).

♦ <u>HCFCs:</u> Annex C Group I substances (hydrochlorofluorocarbons).

♦ <u>Methyl bromide:</u> Annex E.

♦ Data are weighted with the ozone depleting potentials of the substances.

♦ Regional totals include OECD Secretariat estimates.

♦ Dotted lines (graphics) refer to data not available.

OECD• Excludes Mexico, Rep. Korea and Turkey (Article 5 countries).

STRATOSPHERIC OZONE

Data sources: Column ozone: WOUDC (World Ozone and Ultraviolet Radiation Data Center). Global ozone levels: Ozone Processing Team of NASA/Goddard Space Flight Center.

♦ Data refer to <u>total column ozone</u> (i.e. tropospheric plus stratospheric ozone) in Dobson units. Stratospheric ozone represents the majority of total column ozone, e.g. comprises on average about 90% of total column ozone in Canada. <u>Dobson unit:</u> measure used to estimate the thickness of the ozone layer. 100 Dobson units represent a quantity equivalent to a 1-mm-thick layer of ozone at 0 degrees Celsius and at a pressure of 1013 hectopascal (sea level).

♦ Ozone levels over selected cities: data presented are annual averages of daily values taken from the WOUDC database calculated by the OECD Secretariat.

♦ Global ozone levels: data are annual averages generated from daily ozone measurements. Ozone was measured by the Total Ozone Mapping Spectrometer (TOMS) on the Nimbus-7 (1979-1992), the Meteor-3 (1992-1994) and the Earth Probe (1996-2000) satellites, referring to latitudes between 70 ° N and 70 ° S. At latitudes above 70 °, ozone data are not collected during the winter months and there is increasing seasonal and interannual variability.

AIR QUALITY

SO_x AND NO_x EMISSIONS

Data sources: OECD, UN/ECE

♦ Man-made emissions only. SO_x and NO_x: given as quantities of SO_2 and NO_2 respectively.

♦ Excludes emissions from international transport (aviation, marine).

♦ Data may include provisional figures and Secretariat estimates.

♦ % change: change with respect to latest available year from 1990 on.

♦ For further details, please refer to *OECD Environmental Data — Compendium 1999*.

♦ National objectives: current reduction targets as submitted by the Parties to the Convention on Long-Range Transboundary Air Pollution.

CAN • SO_x: SO_2 only.

USA • SO_x: SO_2 only.

KOR • SO_x: SO_2 only, excluding industrial processes. NO_x NO_2 only. Break in time series in 1990 due to a change in emission coefficient of industrial fuel combustion.

AUS • Data from Australia's National GHG Inventory. NO_x: excl. land use changes and forestry. Incl. large amounts of emissions from prescribed savannah burning.

NZL • SOx: SO2 only. Emissions from energy sources only.
AUT • Data based on UNECE/CLRTAP 98 reporting. SOx: SO2 only. NOx: national objectives refer to the 1992 Ozone Act and to the years 1996, 2001 and 2006.
CZE • SOx: SO2 only.
DNK • Data based on CORINAIR inventories and UNECE format. Fluctuations in emissions due to import/export of electricity.
FIN • Change in estimation methodology in 1992.
FRA • Change in estimation method. in 1990. Since 1990: UNECE format; emissions from nature included. SOx: SO2 only.
DEU • SOx: change in estimation methodology in 1991.
GRC • SOx 1990-97: SO2 only.

HUN • SOx: SO2 only.
ISL • IPCC 1995 methodology. SOx: SO2 only.
IRL • Emissions from industrial processes are excluded.
NLD • Change in estimation methodology in 1990.
PRT • Break in time series in 1990. Since 1990 data include Madeira and Azores Islands. SOx: Pre-1990 data refer to SO2 only.
SWE • SOx: SO2 only. NOx: NO2 only. Data for 1985-89 (SOx) and 1987-89 (NOx) not directly comparable with other years.
TUR • Secretariat estimates.
UKD • SOx: SO2 only.
OECD • Secretariat estimates.

URBAN AIR QUALITY (SO2 AND NO2)

Data sources: OECD

CAN • Measurement temperature:15.6°C.
JPN • Fiscal year. Measurement temperature 20°C.
FIN • Measur. temperature 20°C. NO2: traffic sites near city centre.
FRA • Paris (SO2): Paris agglomeration.
ISL • SO2:1990: mean concentrations for the months 09 to 12. NO2: station near busy street corner and unusually close to traffic in 1995; mean concentrations for the months – 1990: (07-10), 1991: (03-12), 1992 (2-4, 6-8, 10-12), 1993 (1-3).

LUX • NO2: data refer to city centre.
NLD • fiscal year
PRT • SO2: in 1992 six UV Fluor. stations were incorporated. NO2: data after 1991 refer to more than one station.
ESP • The number of monitoring stations differs from year to year. Madrid: city centre.
SWE • Monitoring period from October to March. Stockholm: number of monitoring stations changed during the series.
UKD • Fiscal year. Measur. method follows British Standard 1747 Part. 3.

		SO2		
	Cat. (a)	City or area	Measurement method	No. Stn. (b)
Canada	A	Montreal	UV Fluor.	7-8
	B	Hamilton	UV Fluor.	3-4
Mexico	A	Mexico City	..	..
USA	A	New York	UV Fluor.	15
	A	Los Angeles	UV Fluor.	6
Japan	A	Tokyo	Conduct. c.	1
	B	Kawasaki	Conduct. c.	1
Korea	A	Seoul	UV Fluor.	20
	A	Pusan	UV Fluor.	9
Austria	A	Wien	UV Fluor.	14
	B	Linz	UV Fluor.	7
Belgium	A	Brussels	UV Fluor.	8-6
	B	Antwerpen	UV Fluor.	12-8
Czech. R.	A	Praha	UV Fluor./manual	24-27
	A	Brno	UV Fluor./manual	9-16
Denmark	A	København	KOM Imp. F.	6-1
Finland	A	Helsinki	UV Fluor./Cuol.	2
France	A	Paris	UV Fluor.	7-46
	B	Rouen	UV Fluor.	3-9
Germany	A	Berlin	UV Fluor.	13
	A	München	UV Fluor.	5
Greece	A	Athens	Pulsed fluor.	4-5
Hungary	A	Budapest	UV Fluor./W.Gaeke	..
	B	Miskolc	UV Fluor.	..
Iceland	A	Reykjavik	UV Fluor.	1
Luxemb.	A	Luxembourg	UV Fluor.	2
Netherl.	A/B	Rotterdam	..	..
Poland	A	Lódz	Colorimetry	12
	C	Warszawa	Colorimetry	6
Portugal	A	Lisboa	UV Fluor.	7
Spain	A	Madrid	UV Fluor.	14-10
Sweden	A	Göteborg	UV Fluor./Ion.c.	5-3
	B	Stockholm	UV Fluor.	2
Switzerl.	A	Zurich	UV Fluor. c.	1
	B	Basel	UV Fluor. c.	1
Turkey	A	Ankara	H2O2/Conduct.	7-8
UK	A	London	Acid.Titr.c./UV Fluor.	11
	B	Newcastle	Acid. Titr. c.	1

		NO2		
	Cat. (a)	City or area	Measurement method	No. Stn. (b)
Canada	A	Montreal	Chem.	3-10
	B	Hamilton	Chem.	2-4
Mexico	A	Mexico City	..	..
USA	A	New York	Chem.	5
	A	Los Angeles	Chem.	15
Japan	A	Tokyo	Saltzman	1
	B	Kawasaki	Saltzman	1
Korea	A	Seoul	Chem.	20
	A	Pusan	Chem.	9
Austria	A	Wien	Lumin.	12
	B	Linz	Lumin.	7
Belgium	A	Brussels	Chem. c.	4-6
	B	Antwerpen	Chem. c.	2-1
Czech. R.	A	Praha	Chem./manual	19-23-25
	A	Brno	Chem./manual	7-10
Denmark	A	København	Chem.	3-1
Finland	A	Helsinki	Chem.	2
France	A	Paris	Chem.	6-19
	B	Rouen	Chem.	3-6
Germany	A	Berlin	Chem.	13
	A	München	Chem.	5
Greece	A	Athens	Chem.	4-5
Hungary	A	Budapest	Chem./Saltz.	..
	B	Miskolc	Chem.	..
Iceland	A	Reykjavik	Chem.	1
Luxemb.	A	Luxembourg	Chem.	1
Netherl.	A/B	Rotterdam	..	..
Poland	A	Lódz	Saltzman	4-3
	C	Warszawa	Saltzman	3-2
Portugal	A	Lisboa	Sod.Ars./Chem.	1-11
Spain	A	Madrid	Chem.	6-14
Sweden	A	Göteborg	Chem. c.	1-3
	B	Stockholm	Chem. c.	2
Switzerl.	A	Zurich	Chem. c.	1
	B	Basel	Chem. c.	1
Turkey	A	Ankara	Chem.	2-1
UK	A	London	Chem. c.	1

(a) Categories: A - city in which a notable portion (5-10%) of national population is concentrated; B - industrial city in which a significant number of inhabitants is considered to be exposed to the worst level of pollution in 1980; C - city with residential and service functions and with intermediate pollution level.
(b) Number of monitoring stations may change over the years.

WASTE

MUNICIPAL WASTE

Data sources: OECD

♦ Municipal waste is waste collected by or on the order of municipalities. It includes waste originating from households, commercial activities, office buildings, institutions such as schools and government buildings, and small businesses that dispose of waste at the same facilities used for municipally collected waste. Household waste is waste generated by the domestic activity of households. It includes garbage, bulky waste and separately collected waste. National definitions may differ.

♦ Values per capita are rounded.

♦ Change since 1980, italics: household waste only.

♦ Management of municipal waste: categories may overlap because residues from some types of treatment (incineration, composting) are landfilled; categories do not necessarily add up to 100% since other types of treatment may not be covered.

CAN • Data refer to 1996; municipal w.: all w. disposed of, except construction and demolition w., even if not collected by municipalities; includes flows diverted for recycling or composting; Mun. w.: excl. 976 289 t of sewage sludge; hous. w.: excludes hazardous w.; management: includes construction and demolition waste (4 881 443 t.) and sewage sludge (976 289 t).

MEX • Landfill: includes open landfill and illegal dumping.

USA • Data refer to 1996; landfill: after recovery and incineration.

JPN • Municipal w.: data refer to 1994 and exclude w. from institutions such as schools and hospitals; management data refer to 1993.

KOR • Data refer to 1996.

NZL • Data refer to 1995; household waste: excludes 150 480 t of construction and demolition w. which are included in national definition.

AUT • Data refer to 1996; municipal w.: excludes construction site w., which is included in national definition; data on management refer to amounts of hous. w. landed to facilities.

BEL • Municipal w.: aggregate of 1995 data for Brussels and 1996 data for Flanders and Wallonia; data on management refer to Flanders only and include 330 000 t of construction waste.

CZE • Data refer to 1996 (municipal and hous. w.) and 1994 (management); data on management refer to about 80% of municipal w. generated.

DNK • Data refer to 1997; municipal w. data come from a new survey done in treatment plants (excl. about 9 000 t of w. from hospitals); data on management refer to household waste only.

FIN • Data refer to 1994; data on management are expert estimates and might include some w. from demolition sites and from sewerage and water treatment.

FRA • Data refer to 1995 and include DOM; municipal w.: includes 5.2 million tonnes of "Déchets industriels banals" and 700 000 t of w. from hospitals; hous. w.: includes bulky w.; data on management refer to household (excluding bulky w.) w. only.

DEU • Data refer to 1993; municipal w. includes separate collection for recycling purpose conducted outside the public sector (about 11 million tonnes in 1993); this particularly concerns packaging material (paper, glass, metals, plastics) collected by the Duale System Deutschland; excl. w. directly brought to disposal sites by the generator and street cleaning w..

GRC • Traditional w. collection only.

HUN • Data refer to 1996; municipal w. refers to transported amounts; includes w. from households, offices, firms and services.

IRL • Data refer to 1995; household w.: include estimated arisings from household not served by waste collection; management: data refer to the total municipal waste collected.

ITA • Management data refer to 1995.•

LUX • Municipal w.: excludes separate collection; household w.: data refer to 1994; management data refer to 1996.

NLD • Municipal w.: includes separate collection for recycling purposes, solid w. from sewerage and small amount of mixed building and construction w.; household w.: includes w. paper collected by schools, churches, sport clubs; management data refer to 1996.

NOR • Figures are based on a enquiry covering all local authorities and treatment plants (include about 90 000 t of construction and demolition waste); per capita: amounts adjusted to population served by municipal waste services.

PRT • Estimated data.

ESP • Data refer to 1996.

SWE • Data refer to 1994.

CHE • Data refer to 1996; municipal w.: includes separately collected waste for recycling (1.7 million tonnes).

TUR • 1995 data; per capita: amounts collected in municipalities served by w. service (72% of the population in 1995) as a share of total population..

UKD • Data refer to 1996-97 financial year; household w.: incl. hous. hazardous w. and clinical w., street clean. w. and litter, w. taken to civic amenity sites for disposal or recycling; management: data refer of households w. in England and Wales.

OECD • Rounded figures. Data do not include eastern Germany, Korea , Czech Rep., Hungary and Poland.

INDUSTRIAL / NUCLEAR / HAZARDOUS WASTE

Data sources: OECD

♦ Industrial waste refers to waste generated by the manufacturing industry. National definitions often differ. Rounded data.

♦ Nuclear waste refers to spent fuel arisings in nuclear power plants. The data are expressed in tonnes of heavy metal. It should be noted that these data do not represent all radioactive waste generated.

♦ Hazardous waste refers to waste streams controlled according to the Basel Convention on Transboundary Movements of Hazardous Wastes and their Disposal (see Annex IV of the convention for complete definition and methods of treatment, movement and disposal). National definitions often differ, and caution should be exercised when using these figures. Imports, exports: should refer to actual amounts moved, but may in some cases refer to total authorisations (notifications).

MEX • Ind. w.: 1990 data.

USA • Haz. w.: data based on national law.

JPN • Ind. w.: 1994 data ; Nuc. w.: for fiscal year; Light Water Reactor fuel and Heavy Water Reactor fuel only.

KOR • Ind. w.: 1996 data including ISIC 01-02 ,10-14, 40 and 41; Nuc. w.: Light Water Reactor fuel and Heavy Water Reactor fuel only. Haz. w.: data based on national law.

AUS • Ind. w.: refers to 1993 and to Queensland only; haz. w.: Victoria only.

NZL • Ind. w.: 1995 data including waste from all economic activities. Haz. w. production: includes special and potentially hazardous w.

AUT • Ind. w.: 1993. Austrian classification refers not to economic sectors but to waste streams. Data may not be comparable to those of other countries; haz. w.: data based on national law.

BEL • Ind. w.: total based on Brussels 1994, Flanders 1995 and Wallonia 1995; haz. w.: production: notified amounts for Brussels and Wallonia; extrapolated amounts for Flanders. Movements: Wallonia and Flanders only; does not account for movements between regions.

CZE • Ind. w.: 1996 estimated amounts including hazardous waste.

DNK • Ind. w.: 1997 data; haz. w. according to the European Waste Catalogue.

FIN • Ind. w.: 1992 estimates for dry weight based on wet weight figures; haz. w.: Ind. haz. w. only; data based on national law.

FRA • Ind. w.: 1995 data. A detailed breakdown by ISIC sector is not available. Data may not be comparable to those of other countries; includes hazardous and non-hazardous w.; data may cover other ind. sectors; haz. w.: amounts to be managed: excludes internal treatment by private enterprises.

DEU • Ind. w.: 1993 data; haz. w.: movements: w. going to final disposal only; data based on national law.

GRC • Ind. w.: 1997 data including liquid w; haz. w.: exports: PCB waste only.

HUN • Ind. w.: 1995 data excluding haz. w.; waste from privatised enterprises may not be fully covered; haz. w.: data based on national law; according to Basel definition, haz. w. amounted to 1 253 kt in 1996; movements: 1993 data.

ISL • Ind. w.: 1997 data; mostly waste from slaughterhouses.

IRL • Ind. w.: 1995 data; haz. w.: data based on national law.

ITA • Ind. w.: 1995 data; may include some mining & quarrying waste.

LUX • Ind. w.: 1990 data for special industrial waste, mainly liquid waste assimilated in industrial waste water; haz. w.: data based on national law.

NLD • Ind. w.: 1996 data; haz. w.: all waste defined as special waste in Dutch legislation including contaminated soil.

NOR • Ind. w.: 1996 data; haz. w.: production: all waste defined as special waste in Norwegian regulations. Data are estimates

based on a special study carried out in 1995. If European Waste Catalogue relevant hazardous w. is included, production is 640 kt; movements: exclude aluminium salt slags (49 kt imported in 1993).

POL • Ind. w.: 1997 data covering most industrial and energy sources; haz. w.: special waste, not fully consistent with Basel definition.

ESP • Ind. w.: 1992 data; haz. w.: data based on national law.

SWE • Ind. w.: rough estimates for 1993; sector specific waste; haz. w.: notified amounts.

CHE • Ind. w.: 1996 data referring to recovered/landfilled industrial waste; excludes special waste; haz. w.: all waste defined as special waste in Swiss legislation. Amount generated according to Basel Convention: 462 kt in 1993, 504 kt in 1994.

TUR • Ind. w.: 1994 data referring to 2006 firms with more than 25 employees.

UKD • Ind. w.: includes 6 Mt from basic metal industries. The remaining 50 Mt is a broad estimate valid for any 12 month period in the late 1980s; haz. w.: refer to fiscal year. Only waste going to final disposal must be notified (under 1988 transfrontier shipments of hazardous waste regulations).

OECD • Ind. w.: rough Secretariat estimates.

WASTE RECYCLING

Data sources: OECD, Fédération Européenne du Verre d'Emballage (Brussels), Confederation of European Paper Industries (Brussels), FAO

♦ Recycling is defined as reuse of material in a production process that diverts it from the waste stream, except for recycling within industrial plants and the reuse of material as fuel. The recycling rate is the ratio of the quantity collected for recycling to the apparent consumption (domestic production + imports - exports).

♦ Table: data may refer to the years immediately preceding or following the columns' header; 1997: or latest available year; data prior to 1993 were not taken into account.

CAN • Glass: packaging glass only.

MEX • Recycling rates are based on amounts of waste generated and refer to municipal waste only.

USA • Data refer to the material diverted from the municipal waste stream; recycling rates are based on amounts of waste generated.

JPN • Glass: returnable bottles are excluded; data refer to reuse of glass as cullet compared to national production of glass bottles.

AUS • Paper: data refer to newsprint, cardboard, and paper packaging; definitions of recycling vary according to the material collected (e.g. may include amounts incinerated to divert them from landfill).

NZL • Glass: packaging glass only.

BEL • Paper: data refer to waste recycled (includes net imports for recycling) as % of apparent consumption; waste collected as % of apparent consumption in 1997: 44%.

FRA • Glass: amounts collected as a percentage of apparent consumption (FEVE).

DEU • 1980, 85, (and 90 for glass): western Germany; latest year: total Germany; glass: recycling rate is based on total sales.

NLD • Glass: glass collected in bottle banks as % of sale of products in disposable glass on domestic market.

NOR • Glass: excludes considerable amounts of glass recovered before entering the waste stream (deposit/reuse of bottles).

TUR • Paper: data refer to waste recycled (include net imports for recycling) as % of apparent consumption.

UKD • Glass: Great Britain only; glass collected in bottle banks and from industrial sources (bottlers and packers) and flat glass.

WATER QUALITY

RIVER QUALITY

Data sources: OECD

♦ Measurement locations are at the mouth or downstream frontier of rivers.

♦ Data: refer to three year averages around 1980, 1985, 1990 and 1997.

♦ Nitrates: total concentrations unless otherwise specified.

CAN • Nitrates: Saskatchewan: NO2 + NO3.

DNK • Nitrates: NO2 + NO3.

FRA • Seine: station under marine influence. Rhône: since 1987 data refer to another station. Nitrates Loire and Seine: dissolved concentrations.

DEU • Nitrates: dissolved concentrations.

ITA • Po: until 1988: Ponte Polesella (76 km from the mouth); since 1989: Pontelagoscuro (91 km from the mouth).

NLD • Nitrates Rijn-Lobith: dissolved concentrations.

ESP • Guadalquivir: from 1990 onwards data refer to another station closer to the mouth and farther away from Sevilla influence. Nitrates: dissolved concentrations.

UKD • Nitrates: when the parameter is unmeasurable (quantity too small) the limit of detection values are used when calculating annual averages. Actual averages may therefore be lower.

WASTE WATER TREATMENT

Data sources: OECD

♦ Total served: national population connected to public sewage treatment plants. Includes: primary treatment - physical and mechanical processes which result in decanted effluents and separate sludge (sedimentation, flotation, etc.); secondary treatment - biological treatment technologies, i.e. processes which employ

anaerobic or aerobic micro-organisms; tertiary treatment - advanced treatment technologies, i.e. chemical processes.

♦ Sewerage connection rates: refers to population connected to public sewage network with or without treatment.

♦ Late 1990s: data refer to 1997 unless otherwise specified. Data prior to 1992 have not been considered.

CAN • Data refer to 1981 and 1994. Secondary usually includes private treatment & waste stabilisation ponds. Tertiary: secondary with phosphorus removal.

MEX • Late 1990s: 1993 data.

USA • Data refer to 1982 and 1992. Primary: may include ocean outfalls and some biological treatment. Tertiary: includes 2-3% of non-discharge treatment, e.g. lagoons, evaporation ponds. Excludes rural areas served by on-site disposal systems.

JPN • Late 1990s: 1996 data. Secondary: may include primary treatment and some tertiary treatment.

KOR • Late 1990s: 1996 data.

AUT • Late 1990s: 1995 data. Among the 24.5% of population not connected to public sewerage, 23.4% are connected to private or independent treatment.

BEL • Late 1990s: Secretariat estimates for 1995.

CZE • Late 1990s: data on waste water treatment by category are country estimates.

DNK • Late 1990s: 1996 data. The 12.6% of population not connected to public sewerage are connected to private or independent treatment.

FIN • Secondary: 50-80% removal of BOD; tertiary: 70-90% removal of BOD. Late 1990s: 1993 data.

FRA • Late 1990s (1995 data): in % of dwellings. Among the 21% of population not connected to public sewerage, 10% are connected to private or independent treatment.

DEU • 1980 data refer to 1979 and to w. Germany only. Late 1990s: 1995 data.

GRC • In 1993 a new waste water plant in Athens city started working; data include connections still under construction.

HUN • Late 1990s: 1996 data. Among the 55% of population not connected to public sewerage, 19% are connected to private or independent treatment.

ISL • Late 1990s: 1999 data. Among the 10% of population not connected to public sewerage, 6% are connected to private or independent treatment.

LUX • Late 1990s: 1995 data. The 12.5% of population not connected to public sewerage are connected to private or independent treatm.

NLD • Late 1990s: 1996 data. Tertiary: incl. dephosphatation and/or disinfection.

NOR • Late 1990s: 1999 data. The 20% of population not connected to public sewerage are connected to private or independent treatment.

PRT • 1980 and late 1990s: 1981 and 1999 data.

ESP • Late 1990s: 1995 data. Total public treatment in 1997: 45% in accordance with 91/271/EEC Directive.

SWE • Late 1990s: 1994 data. Primary: may include removal of sediments. Secondary: chemical or biological treatment. Tertiary: chemical and biological plus complementary treatment.

CHE • Late 1990s: 1995 data.

TUR • Late 1990s: 1995 data. Data result from an inventory covering municipalities with an urban population of over 3 000, assuming that the sewerage system and treatment facilities serve the whole population of the municipalities.

UKD • Late 1990s: 1996 data. Data refer to England and Wales and to financial year (April to March). Primary: removal of gross solids. Secondary: removal of organic material or bacteria under aerobic conditions. Tertiary: removal of suspended solids following secondary treatment.

OECD• Secretariat estimates, not taking into account Australia. 1980: include w. Germany only; data cover 23 OECD Member countries (Mexico, Korea, Australia, Czech Rep., Hungary and Poland were not taken into account).

PUBLIC EXPENDITURE ON WATER

Data sources: OECD

♦ Data refer to public pollution abatement and control (PAC) expenditure (see Expenditure item) at current prices and purchasing power parities for the latest available year. PAC activities for soil and water comprise collection and purification of waste water, combating of pollution in the marine environment, prevention, control and monitoring of surface water pollution, combating of pollution of inland surface waters, prevention and combating of thermal pollution of water, abatement of groundwater and soil pollution, and regulation and monitoring. Excludes the supply of drinking water.

CAN • Expenditure: according to the financing principle; estimated 1994 data.

MEX • Partial 1997 data.

KOR • Trial 1997 estimate by the Bank of Korea.

CZE • Investment only (1996).

DNK • 1996 data; include subsidies and transfers to private sector.

HUN • Investment only (1996).

LUX • 1997 estimate.

POL • Investment only (1997).

SWE • Data refer to municipalities only.

WATER RESOURCES

INTENSITY OF USE OF WATER RESOURCES

Data sources: OECD, FAO, World Resources Institute (WRI)

♦ Abstractions: accounts for total water withdrawal without deducting water that is reintroduced into the natural environment after use.

♦ Abstractions as % of available resources: data refer to total abstraction divided by total renewable resources, except for total, where the internal resource estimates were used to avoid double counting.

♦ Renewable water resources: net result of precipitation minus evapotranspiration (internal) plus inflow (total). This definition ignores differences in storage capacity, and represents the maximum quantity of fresh water available on average.

♦ Inflow: water flows from neighbouring countries. Includes underground flows.

♦ Water stress (source: CSD, "Comprehensive Assessment of the Freshwater Resources of the World") is based on the ratio of water withdrawal to annual water availability.

  ♦ Low (less than 10 per cent): generally there is no major stress on the available resources.

  ♦ Moderate (10 to 20 per cent): indicates that water availability is becoming a constraint on development and significant investments are needed to provide adequate supplies.

  ♦ Medium-high (20 to 40 per cent): implies the management of both supply and demand, and conflicts among competing uses need to be resolved.

  ♦ High (more than 40 per cent): indicates serious scarcity, and usually shows unsustainable water use, which can become a limiting factor in social and economic development.

National water stress levels may hide important variations at subnational (e.g. river basin) level; in particular in countries with extensive arid and semi-arid regions.

♦ Freshwater abstractions by major sector

  ♦ "Public water supply" refers to water supply by waterworks, and may include other uses besides the domestic sector.

  ♦ "Irrigation" refers to self supply (abstraction for own final use).

  ♦ "Others": include industry and electrical cooling (self supply).

  ♦ Freshwater abstractions data: refers to 1997 or latest available year (data prior to 1990 have not been considered).

♦ Cultivated land: refers to arable and permanent crop land.

CAN • 1980 and late 1990s: 1981 and 1995 data. Abstractions by major uses: 1991 data.

MEX • Data include Secretariat estimates for electrical cooling - 1980: based on electricity generation in power stations.

USA • Late 1990s: 1995 data. Abstractions by major uses: 1990 data.

JPN • Mid-1990s: Secretariat estimates based on 1990 and 1994 data.

KOR • Partial totals excluding electrical cooling. Abst. for public supply: data refer to domestic supply.

AUS • In Australia the intensity of use of water resources varies widely among regions; one third of the country is arid, one third semi-arid and the high rainfall areas in the north are far from the densily populated areas in the south. 1980: 1977 data adjusted for an average climatic year. Late 1990s: estimated data.

NZL • Partial totals excl. industrial and electrical cooling. 1980: composite total based on data for various years. Late 1990s: 1993 estimates.

AUT • Partial totals. Irrigation and industry no cooling: groundwater only. Electrical cooling (includes all industrial cooling): surface water only. Late 1990s: 1993 data.

BEL • Data include Secretariat estimates. Late 1990s: 1994 data.

CZE • Data refer to 1997.

DNK • 1980: 1977 data. Late 1990s: 1996 data, groundwater only (major part of total freshwater abstractions, e.g. 95-99% for 1995).

FIN • Partial totals. Late 1990s: 1994 data excluding all agricultural uses. Abst. by major uses: irrigation: 1992 data.

FRA • 1980 and Late 1990s: 1981 and 1994 data.

DEU • Excluding agricultural uses other than irrigation. Late 1990s: 1995 data which include national estimates. Change since 1980: ratios for total Germany compared to ratios for western Germany (1979).

GRC • Partial totals. Excluding agricultural uses besides irrigation. Includes data for public water supply which refer only to data from 42 out of 75 great water distribution enterprises.

HUN • Late 1990s: 1996 data.

ISL • Fish farming is a major user of abstracted water. Abst. for public supply: includes the domestic use of geothermal water.

IRL • Late 1990s: 1994 data; totals include 1980 data for electrical cooling. Abstractions by major uses: irrigation includes other agricultural abstractions.

ITA • Excluding agricultural uses besides irrigation. 1980: including 1973 estimates for industrial cooling.

LUX • Late 1990s: annual average of the 1990-95 period.

NLD • Partial totals excluding all agricultural uses. 1980 and Late 1990s: 1981 and 1996 data.

NOR • Late 1990s: estimates for 1994 including 1978 data for industry.

POL • Totals include abstractions for agriculture, which include aquaculture (areas over 10 ha) and irrigation (arable land and forest areas greater than 20 ha); animal production and domestic needs of rural inhabitants are not covered.

PRT • Late 1990s: 1996 data (INAG estimates).

ESP • Excluding agricultural uses other than irrigation. Groundwater: excluding industry.

SWE • 1980: include data from different years. Late 1990s: 1995 data.

CHE • Partial totals excluding agricultural uses. Late 1990s: 1994 data.

TUR • 1980: partial totals; excluding agricultural uses other than irrigation and electrical cooling.

UKD • Partial totals. England and Wales only. Data include miscellaneous uses for power generation, but exclude hydroelectric power water use.

OECD • Rounded figures, including Secretariat estimates. Abstractions as % of available resources: calculated using the estimated totals for internal resources (not total resources as for countries), and considering England and Wales only. Abstractions by major uses, trends: estimates based on 19 countries representing about 85% of total OECD abstractions.

IRRIGATION

CAN • Abst. for irrigation: 1991 data.

USA • Abst. for irrigation: 1990 data.

JPN • Irrigated land: rice irrigation only.

KOR • Abst. for irrigation includes other agricultural abstractions. Irrigated land: rice irrigation only.

AUT • Abst. for irrigation includes other agricultural abstractions.

BEL • Data for Belgium include Luxembourg.

DNK • Abst. for irrigation: 1995 data.

FIN • Abst. for irrigation: 1992 data.

FRA • Abst. for irrigation: Secretariat estimates; includes other agricultural uses, but irrigation is the main use.

HUN • Irrigated land: excl. complementary farm plots & individual farms.

IRL • Abst. for irrigation: irrigated area is negligible.

SWE • Abst. for irrigation: data are estimates for dry year.

UKD • England and Wales only.

OECD • Do not include the Czech Republic.

WATER PRICE

Data sources: IWSA (International Water Supply Association), 1999, International Statistics for Water Supply

♦ Prices calculated on the basis of a family of four (two adults and two children) living in a house with garden rather than an apartment. Where there are water meters, the price is based on annual consumption of 200 m³. Where supply is normally unmeasured the average price has been used (Norway and UK). Prices at current exchange rates. VAT is not included. 1996 data have not been reported on the figure.

ISL • 1996 data.

NOR • Unmeasured data: refer to the average price.

TUR • 1996 data.

UKD • Unmeasured data: refer to the average price.

FOREST RESOURCES

INTENSITY OF USE OF FOREST RESOURCES

Data sources: OECD, FAO, national statistical yearbooks

♦ Annual growth: gross increment.
♦ Late 1990s: 1997 or latest available year.
♦ Data exclude Iceland as there is no traditional forestry in this country.

CAN • Late 1990s: 1994 data.

USA • 1980 and 90 are estimates. Late 1990s: 1992 data.

JPN • 1980s: 1985 data. Growth: national forest; % change since 1985; 1995 data: Basic Plan for Forest Resources.

AUS • 1980s: 1985 data. Harvest and growth: % change since 1985. Late 1990s: TBFRA 2000 data (reference year: 1994).

NZL • Data refer to planted production forests only. Growth of natural forests is considered to be near zero with a growth rate equal to mortality. Harvest from natural forests is less than 3 % of harvest. 1980s: 1985 data.

AUT • Growth: 1980 and 1990 data refer to 1971-80 and 1986-90.

BEL • 1980s: 1985 data. 1990: 1992 data, Wallonia only. Late 1990s: TBFRA 2000 data not comparable to previous years. Harvest: period 1986-95; estimations based in annual public forest harvest extrapolated to total forest. Annual growth: 1982-97, and net annual growth (natural losses excluded); estimations based on data for Wallonia extrapolated to the rest of the country.

DNK • 1980 data are Secretariat estimates. Growth late 1990s (1996 data): expected mean annual volume increment for 1990-2000.

FIN • Growth late 1990s: refer to 1981-96 data.

GRC • 1990: 1992 data.

ITA • 1990: 1991 data.

LUX • 1980s: 1985 data. Growth % change since 1985; 1990: based on 1989 harvest. Harvest late 1990s: 1995 data. Growth late 1990s: 1992.

NLD • Data refer to total exploitable forest. 1980s: 1985 data. Late 1990s: break in time series (TBFRA 2000 data).

POL • Data refer to TBFRA 2000 definitions. Data refer to the 1st January. Harvest: decrease in 1990 was a result of decreased demand for wood in the economic transition period.

PRT • Late 1990s: TBFRA 2000 data for 1995; break in time series due to a change in definitions; data refer to Portugal Continental, Açores and Madeira Islands.

ESP • Growth and intensity of use 1980: Secretariat estimate.

SWE • 1980 and 1990 data refer to 1971-80 and 1986-90. Annual growth late 1990s: data refer to 1992-96 to TBFRA 2000; break in time series. Data refer to total forest including other wooded land and trees outside the forests.

TUR • Data are provisional.

OECD • Secretariat estimates; excludes eastern Germany (in 1980), Korea and Iceland.

GROWING STOCK

♦ Data include exploitable and non-exploitable forests.
♦ Data refer to 1997 or latest year available.

CAN • % change: 1981-94 period.

FOREST AND WOODED LAND

Data sources: OECD, FAO

♦ Data include Secretariat estimates.

CAN • Numerical differences between successive national inventories do not necessarily reflect real changes. Accordingly forest in Canada has been considered as constant, taking into account the most recent figure available (1991).

MEX • 1970, 1997: data refer to the Mexican inventories 1961-85 and 1994 which were made with different methodologies and classifications. 1980 and 1990: Secretariat estimates. Data exclude scrubs, perturbed areas and other vegetation types of the Mexican inventory.

USA • Includes low productivity forest land (less than 1.4 m³/ha/year).

JPN • Data refer to areas under the management of the Minister of Forestry; 1980, 1990, 1997 data refer to 1981, 1991, 1995.

AUT • 1970, 1980, 1990 and 1997 data refer to 1961-70, 1971-80, 1986-90 and 1992-96 forest inventories.

BEL • % of land area: TBFRA 2000 data; trend: cadastre figures.

DNK • Change in definition in wooded area; comparison requires caution. Accordingly 1990 and 1997 data are Secretariat estimates referring to 1976 data.

MEX • % change: estimate for 1980-94.
JPN • % change: 1980-95.
KOR • % change: 1980-97.
BEL • TBFRA 2000 data.
CZE • % change: 1980-97.
FIN • % change: 1980-86/97.
FRA • % change: 1980-97.
HUN • % change: 1980-97.
ITA • % change: 1980-95.
NOR • % change: 1980-94/97.
POL • % change: 1980-97. Data refer to TBFRA 2000 definitions. Data refer to the 1st January.
ESP • % change: estimate for 1980-95.
TUR • % change: 1980-97 (provisional).
UKD • % change: 1980-97; estimates at 31 March.

FORESTRY PRODUCTS AS % OF NATIONAL EXPORTS OF GOODS

BEL • Belgium and Luxembourg.
LUX • Belgium and Luxembourg.

FIN • 1997 figures are based on National Forest Inventory 1986-97. Includes all the wooded land (forest and scrub land) where the annual potential wood production exceeds 0.1 m³/ha.

FRA • Trend: Secretariat estimates.

DEU • Trend: data refer to western Germany only.

GRC • Data refer to Agriculture and Livestock Census (according to 1992 national forest inventory: 65 130 km²).

ISL • Data refer to land outside arable areas.

ITA • Since 1986 some agricultural land has been reclassified as forest land; since 1990 Mediterranean maquis included in mixed forest.

LUX • Inventory methodology changed between 1980 and 1990.

NOR • Trend: data include Secretariat estimates.

POL • Data refer to the public ground register.

PRT • % of land area: TBFRA 2000 data for 1995; data refer to Portugal Continental, Açores and Madeira Islands.

SWE • % of land area: TBFRA 2000 data for 1992-96; trend: according to National Forest Inventories.

OECD • Include Secretariat estimates.

FISH RESOURCES

FISH CATCHES AND CONSUMPTION

Data sources: FAO

♦ Total catches: data refer to capture fisheries in inland and marine waters, including freshwater fish, diadromous fish, marine fish, crustaceans, molluscs and miscellaneous aquatic animals; excludes aquaculture.

♦ Marine catches: include marine fish, crustaceans, and molluscs.

♦ World marine fish resources by phase of fishery development: the figure illustrates the process of intensification of fisheries since 1950 and the increase in the proportion of world resources which are subject to declines in productivity. The resources refer to the top 200 species-area combinations for marine fish, selected for analysis on the basis of average landings over the whole time period. These 200 major resources account for 77% of world marine fish production. The process of development of a fishery is schematically represented in the figure next column. The relative rate of increase during the development process, which varies significantly as the maximum long-term yield is approached, reached and "overshot" has been used here to provide a rough assessment of the state of marine resources.

For further details, please refer to: "Review of the state of world fishery resources: marine fisheries", FAO, Rome 1997.

♦ Fish consumption: Total food supply = production - non-food use + imports - exports + stock variations. Data refer to 1997 or latest available year; OECD total excludes Czech Republic.

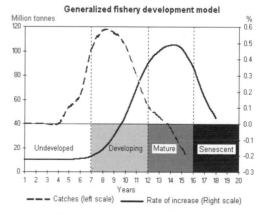

Generalized fishery development model

BEL • Data include Luxembourg.
DNK • Excludes Greenland and Faroe Islands.

BIODIVERSITY

THREATENED SPECIES

Data sources: OECD

♦ Threatened species: "Threatened" refers to the sum of species "critically endangered", "endangered" and "vulnerable" (new IUCN categories), or to the sum of species "endangered" and "vulnerable" (old IUCN categories).

♦ "Critically endangered": species is facing an extremely high risk of extinction in the wild in the immediate future.

♦ "Endangered": species is not "critically endangered" but is facing a very high risk of extinction in the wild in the near future.

♦ "Vulnerable": species is not "critically endangered" or "endangered" but is facing a high risk of extinction in the wild in the medium-term future.

♦ When interpreting these tables, it should be borne in mind that the number of species known does not always accurately reflect the number of species in existence; and that the definitions are applied with varying degrees of rigour in countries, although international organisations such as the IUCN and the OECD are promoting standardisation.

CAN • 1997 data. Mammals: indigenous sp.; fish: of which 177 fresh water sp.; all reptile and amphibian species are declining somewhat due to urbanisation and agriculture.

MEX • Excludes extinct species; birds: resident and migratory species; fish: freshwater and marine species.

USA • Including Pacific and Caribbean islands.

JPN • Mammals: of which 179 indigenous species; birds: includes species that are occasionally present; fish: freshwater and brackish water species; reptiles, amphibians: of which 97 and 61 indigenous species.

KOR • Mammals, birds, fish: excludes extinct species.

NZL • Indigenous species only; mammals: land-breeding and marine mammals.

AUT • Indigenous species only; threatened mammals: includes extinct and/or vanished species; birds: breeding species on national territory; fish: freshwater only.

BEL • Data refer to Flanders; extinct species are excluded.

CZE • Data refer to indigenous species and include extinct species.

DNK • Data exclude extinct species; fish: freshwater only; known species of vascular plants: indigenous species only.

FIN • Excludes extinct species; mammals: indigenous species only; fish: excl. introduced species and occasionally present marine fish; vascular plants: resident wild sp., subspecies, varietis and independent hybrids.

FRA • Metropolitan France; extinct species are excluded; mammals: of which 112 indigenous species; birds: number of breeding pairs; fish: marine and freshwater species.

DEU • Mammals: indigenous species out of 87 known species; birds: number of breeding species out of 255 known species; fish:

freshwater only; reptiles and amphibians: indigenous species; vascular plants: indigenous species out of 3319 known species.

GRC • Fish: freshwater only; vascular plants, threatened: incl. eight extinct species.

HUN • Threatened: protected and highly protected species; fish: freshwater species, of which 2 indigenous species; "Threatened" fish: includes indeterminate species; vascular plants: of which 2 433 indigenous species.

ISL • Birds: breeding species only; about 335 species have been recorded one or more times on national territory; fish: freshwater only.

IRL • Mammals: excluding marine mammals; because total of known species includes some sp. for which status is not evaluated, threatened % is underestimated; birds: resident sp., regular visitors and passage migrants.

ITA • Fish: freshwater only.

LUX • Birds: breeding species only.

NLD • Excl. extinct species; birds: breeding species only; fish: freshw. only.

NOR • Excludes extinct species; mammals: indigenous terrestrial species; the status of the 26 known species of marine mammals is uncertain; birds: breeding species on national territory; fish: 45 freshwater sp. (of which 9 introduced), 150 marine sp.; reptiles and amphibians: indigenous species; vascular plants: native species only; about 2 800 species (incl. introduced ones) are known.

POL • Mammals: indigenous species only (out of 90 species); birds: breeding species only (total number of species recorded so far in Poland: 418); fish: freshwater indigenous species, excluding lampreys (out of 67 freshwater species); vascular plants: of which 1 950 indigenous species.

PRT • Fish: freshwater species only.

ESP • Threatened: endangered and vulnerable; fish: freshwater only.

SWE • Mammals, birds: of which 60, 243 indigenous species; fish: freshwater species only.

CHE • Excludes extinct species; mammals: indigenous species; birds: all breeding species on national territory; fish: indigenous species of Pisces and Cyclostomata; reptiles and amphibians: indigenous species.

TUR • Fish: freshwater sp. only; marine sp.: 400-450 (estimated number).

UKD • Great Britain only; mammals: terrestrial and marine species, excluding cetaceans; 41 of species known are native; "threatened" refers to national standard; birds: total number of native species recorded in Britain and Ireland on the British Ornithologists' Union list A; "threatened": globally threatened and rapidly declining birds of conservation concern; fish (of which 37 indigenous): freshwater fish, including those that leave the sea to breed in fresh water (e.g. salmon); reptiles and amphibians: indigenous species; vascular plants: approximate figures; species known: includes 800 microspecies.

PROTECTED AREAS

Data sources: OECD, World Conservation Monitoring Centre, IUCN

♦ Major protected areas: IUCN management categories I-VI:
   ♦ Ia: strict nature reserves, managed mainly for science;
   ♦ Ib: wilderness areas, managed mainly for wilderness protection;
   ♦ II: national parks, managed mainly for ecosystem protection and recreation;
   ♦ III: natural monuments, managed mainly for conservation of specific natural features;
   ♦ IV: habitat/species management areas, managed mainly for habitat and species conservation through management intervention;
   ♦ V: protected landscapes/seascapes, managed mainly for landscape/seascape conservation and recreation;
   ♦ VI: managed resource protected areas, managed mainly for the sustainable use of natural ecosystems.

♦ For further details on management categories please refer to "Guidelines for Protected Area Management Categories", IUCN, 1994.

♦ See also the Recommendations established at the IVth World Congress on National Parks and Protected Areas.

♦ National classifications may differ.

MEX • As of 1997 there were 107 national protected areas under the National System of Natural Protected Areas (SINAP), with a total size of 117 340 km².

USA • Includes Alaska. Excludes American Samoa, Guam, Minor Outlying Islands, Northern Mariana Islands, Puerto Rico and Virgin Islands.

AUS • Excludes the Great Barrier Reef Marine Park totalling 344 800 km² (cat. VI); national data.

DNK • Excludes Greenland: one national park of 972 000 km², one national reserve of 10 500 km².

FRA • Excludes non-metropolitan France.
HUN • Total size: 1999 national data; number of sites and breakdown by categories: IUCN data.
LUX • Total size: national data; number of sites and breakdown by categories: IUCN data.
NLD • Excludes the Netherlands Antilles.
NOR • Includes Svalbard, Jan Mayen and Bouvet islands.

PRT • Includes Azores and Madeira.
ESP • Includes Baleares and Canaries.
TUR • Total size: 1998 national data; number of sites and breakdown by categories: IUCN data.
UKD • Excludes Bermuda, British Virgin Islands, Cayman Islands, Falkland Islands, St. Helena and Dependencies, South Georgia and the South Sandwich Islands, Turks and Caicos Islands.

GDP AND POPULATION

GROSS DOMESTIC PRODUCT

Data sources: OECD.

♦ Gross Domestic Product: expressed at 1991 price levels and purchasing power parities.
♦ Value added: late-1990s: 2000 or latest available year; agriculture: also includes hunting, forestry and fishing; industry: includes mining and quarrying, manufacturing, gas, electricity and water, and

construction; value added excludes financial intermediation services indirectly measured.
DEU • % change GDP - % change population: refer to western Germany only.
OECD • % change GDP - % change population: includes western Germany only; % change GDP - % change population: excludes Czech Republic, Hungary and Poland.

POPULATION GROWTH AND DENSITY

Data sources: OECD

♦ Population: all nationals present in or temporarily absent from a country, and aliens permanently settled in the country.

♦ Unemployment rate: commonly used definitions.

CONSUMPTION

PRIVATE FINAL CONSUMPTION EXPENDITURE

Data sources: OECD

♦ Private final consumption expenditure: the sum of (i) the outlays of resident households on new durable and non-durable goods and services less their net sales of second-hand goods, scraps and wastes; (ii) the value of goods and services produced by private non-profit institutions for own use on current account; expressed at 1991

price levels and purchasing power parities. Consumption patterns: data refer to 1999 or latest data available.
DEU • Change since 1980 refer to western Germany only.
OECD • Change since 1980: includes western Germany only and excludes Czech Republic, Hungary and Poland.

GOVERNMENT FINAL CONSUMPTION EXPENDITURE

Data sources: OECD

♦ Government final consumption expenditure: the value of goods and services produced by governments for their own use on current account; expressed at 1991 price levels and purchasing power parities.

DEU • Change since 1980 refers to western Germany only.
OECD • Change since 1980: includes western Germany only and excludes Czech Republic, Hungary and Poland.

ENERGY

ENERGY SUPPLY

Data sources: IEA-OECD

♦ see IEA (1997-98) *Energy Balances of OECD Countries* for conversion factors from original units to Toe for the various energy sources.

♦ Total primary energy supply: indigenous production + imports - exports - international marine bunkers and ± stock changes. Primary energy comprises hard coal, lignite and other solid fuels, crude oil and natural gas liquids, natural gas, and nuclear, hydro, geothermal and solar electricity. Electricity trade is also included.
♦ Solid fuels: coal, combustible renewables and waste.

ENERGY PRICES AND TAXES

Data sources: IEA-OECD

♦ see IEA (2001), *Energy prices and taxes, first quarter, 2001*
♦ Oil: light fuel oil only.
♦ Oil and electricity: USD using current exchange rates.
♦ Natural gas: USD per 10^7 kcal (GCV basis) using current exchange rates.

♦ Real energy end-use prices: refers to real energy end-use prices for industry and households. % change refer to 1980-99 period.
MEX • Energy prices: % change refers to 1981-99 period.
USA • Electricity prices: exclude taxes.
AUS • Electricity prices: exclude taxes.

TRANSPORT

ROAD TRAFFIC

Data sources: OECD, International Road Federation (IRF), national yearbooks

♦ Traffic volumes are expressed in billions of kilometres travelled by road vehicle; they are usually estimates and represent the average annual distance covered by vehicles, in kilometres, multiplied by the number of vehicles in operation. In principle, the data refer to the whole distance travelled on the whole network inside the national boundaries by national vehicles, with exception of two- and three-wheeled vehicles, caravans, and trailers.
♦ Data include Secretariat estimates.
USA•• Traffic by local and urban buses is excluded.
JPN • Traffic by light vehicles is excluded.
BEL • Including motor vehicles with 2 or 3 wheels (about 1%)

CZE • Excludes buses.
DEU • Except for military vehicles, traffic by special vehicles is included.
GRC • Data refer to inter-city traffic only.
ISL • Traffic by local and urban buses is excluded.
ITA • Traffic by three-wheeled goods vehicles is included.
NLD • Traffic by trams and subways is included.
ESP • Data refer only to traffic on motorways and national roads.
SWE • Data include traffic by Swedish passenger cars abroad. Traffic by goods vehicles with a load capacity under 2 tonnes is excluded. Up to 1988, only the public network is included; after 1989, the total network is taken into account.
TUR • Data refer only to traffic on motorways and national roads.
UKD • Data refer to Great Britain only.

MOTOR VEHICLES

Data sources: OECD, European Conference of Ministers of Transport (ECMT), IRF, American Automobile Manufacturers' Association, national yearbooks

♦ Total stock includes passenger cars, goods vehicles, buses and coaches. Data refer to autonomous road vehicles with four or more wheels, excluding caravans and trailers, military vehicles, special vehicles (for emergency services, construction machinery, etc.) and agricultural tractors.
♦ Private car ownership is expressed as passenger cars per capita. Data refer to passenger cars seating not more than nine persons (including the driver), including rental cars, taxis, jeeps, estate cars/station wagons and similar light, dual-purpose vehicles.
♦ Data describe the situation as of 31 December of the year.
USA • Passenger cars includes other 2-Axle 4-Tire vehicles.

JPN • Total stocks include three-wheeled vehicles.
AUS • Private car ownership includes utility vehicles.
AUT • Includes Kombi.
BEL • Data are reported on 1 August of the reference year.
CZE • Includes delivery vans.
DNK • Passenger cars includes vans under 2 tonnes.
FRA • Data are reported on 1 January.
DEU • Passenger cars includes motor vehicles for mixed use.
HUN • Change in methodology in 1996.
LUX • Data are reported on 1 January of the reference year.
NLD • Data are reported on 31 July of the reference year.
PRT • The definition of commercial vehicles changed in 1990.
CHE • Data are reported on 30 September of the reference year.
UKD • Total stocks include special purpose vehicles.

ROAD INFRASTRUCTURE

Data sources: OECD, ECMT, IRF, national yearbooks

♦ Roads refer to motorways, main or national highways, secondary or regional roads, and others. In principle, the data refer to all public roads, streets and paths in urban and rural areas, but not private roads.
♦ Motorways refer to a class of roads differing from main or national, secondary or regional, and other roads.
♦ Data describe the situation as of 31 December of the year.
♦ Data include Secretariat estimates.
MEX • Road network: break of time series in 1994. Motorways refer to toll roads.
AUS • Road network: roads types taken into account changed after 1980.
AUT • Road network: about 100 000 km of private roads are excluded.
BEL • Including not paved municipal roads.

FIN • Road network: urban streets are excluded.
FRA • Road network: excludes certain rural roads. Motorways include about 1 200 km of urban motorways.
GRC • Road network: excl. other roads (estim. at 75 600 km in 1995).
HUN • Change in methodology in 1997.
LUX • Change in methodology in 1996.
ESP • Road network: motorways, national and secondary roads only. Excludes other roads estimated at 175 000 km in 1995. Motorways: certain two-lane roads are included.
SWE • Road network: private roads are excluded. Motorways: excludes access and exit ramps.
TUR • Road network: national and provincial roads only. Village roads are excluded (320 055 km in 1995).
UKD • Data refer to Great Britain only. Motorways: excl. slip roads.

ROAD FUEL PRICES AND TAXES

Data sources: IEA-OECD

♦ see IEA (2001), *Energy Prices and Taxes, First Quarter 2001*
♦ Taxes: includes taxes that have to be paid by the consumer as part of the transaction and are not refundable.
♦ Diesel fuel: diesel for commercial use.
♦ Leaded premium: 1999 or latest available year. Data prior to 1996 have not been considered.
♦ Unleaded gasoline: unleaded premium (95 RON) except as noted.
♦ Prices: expressed in USD at 1995 prices and PPPs.
♦ Total energy consumption by road traffic: all fuels used in road vehicles (including military) as well as agricultural and industrial highway use; excludes gasoline used in stationary engines, and diesel oil in tractors that are not for highway use.

CAN • Diesel: 1980 data refer to 1981. Unleaded gasoline: unleaded regular (92 RON).
MEX • Unleaded gasoline: unleaded regular (92 RON).
JPN • Unleaded gasoline: unleaded regular (91 RON).
KOR • 1980 data refer to 1981.
AUS • Unleaded gasoline: unleaded regular (91 RON).
NZL • Unleaded gasoline: unleaded regular (91 RON).
DNK • Unleaded gasoline: unleaded premium (98 RON).
FRA • Up to February 1985 prices were kept within a set range. Figures before 1985 refer to maximum price for Paris. Figures after 1985 refer to average price for all of France.
ISL • Data from Statistics Iceland.

AGRICULTURE

INTENSITY OF USE FROM NITROGEN AND PHOSPHATE FERTILISERS

Data sources: OECD, FAO, International Fertilizer Industry Association, national statistical yearbooks, UN/ECE, UNEP

♦ Use of nitrogen and phosphate fertilisers: data refer to the nitrogen (N) and phosphoric acid (P_2O_5) content of commercial fertilisers, and relate to apparent consumption during the fertiliser year (generally 1 July to 30 June) per unit of agricultural land.

♦ Agricultural land: refers to arable and permanent crop land and permanent grassland. "Arable l." refers to all land generally under rotation, whether for temporary crops or meadows, or left fallow. "Permanent crops l." comprises those lands occupied for a long period that do not have to be planted for several years after each harvest. "Permanent grassland" includes land used for five years or more for herbaceous forage, either cultivated or growing wild.

♦ Data includes estimates.

♦ Phosphate fert.: includes ground rock phosphates.

MEX • Fertiliser year: calendar year.
USA • Includes data for Puerto Rico.
KOR • Fertiliser year: calendar year.
BEL • Data for Belgium include Luxembourg.
 Phosphate fert.: excludes other citrate soluble phosphates.
DNK • Fertiliser year: August-July.
FRA • Phosphate fert.: fertiliser year: May-April.
GRC • Fertiliser year: calendar year.
HUN • Fertiliser year: calendar year.

NITROGEN BALANCES

Data sources: OECD

♦ Nitrogen balance: the annual total quantity of inputs includes mainly livestock manure and chemical fertilisers. The annual total quantity of outputs includes mainly crops and forage. The indicator provides information on the potential loss of nitrogen to the soil, the air, and to surface or groundwater. However, nitrogen loss through the volatilisation of ammonia to the atmosphere from livestock housing and stored manure is excluded from the calculation.

LIVESTOCK DENSITIES

Data sources: OECD, FAO, UN/ECE

ISL • Fertiliser year: calendar year.
ESP • Fertiliser year: calendar year.
SWE • Fertiliser year: June-May. Nitrogen fert.: data include forest fertilisation.
TUR • Fertiliser year: calendar year.
UKD • Fertiliser year: June-May.

AGRICULTURAL PRODUCTION

Data sources: OECD, FAO

♦ Data refer to indices of agricultural production based on price-weighted quantities of agricultural commodities produced for any use except as seed and feed. The commodities covered are all crops and livestock products originating in each country.

♦ Data may differ from national data due to differences in concepts of production, coverage, weights, time reference and methods of calculation.

BEL • Data for Belgium include Luxembourg.

AGRICULTURAL VALUE ADDED

Data sources: OECD

♦ Data also includes hunting, forestry and fishing.

♦ Data refer to 1999 or latest year available.

♦ Nitrogen efficiency: in agriculture, measures the physical nitrogen input/output ratio.

CZE • Data for the period 1985-92 refer to the Czech part of the former Czechoslovakia.
ISL • The 1995-97 average refer to 1995.
OECD • Excluding Luxembourg.

♦ head of sheep equivalent: based on equivalent coefficients in terms of manure: 1 cattle= 6 sheep; 1 sheep=1 goat=1 pig.

Coefficients used to estimate nitrogen from livestock		
	kg of dry matter per year	Coefficients for N content in excrement (% of dry matter)
Cattle	1 500	5.0
Horses	1 200	4.4
Sheep and goats	250	3.0
Pigs	250	4.4
Poultry (hens)	15	5.3

Source: IEDS-UN/ECE

Coefficients used to estimate phosphate from livestock		
	kg of dry matter per year	Coefficients for P_2O_5 content in excrement (% of dry matter)
Cattle	1 500	1.8
Horses	1 200	1.4
Sheep and goats	250	0.6
Pigs	250	2.5
Poultry (hens)	15	3.5

Source: IEDS-UN/ECE

BEL • Data for Belgium include Luxembourg.
DNK • Sheep and goats: sheep only.
ISL • 1997 national data (goats: 1996 data).
IRL • Sheep and goats: sheep only.

POL • Sheep and goats: sheep only.
SWE • Sheep and goats: sheep only.
UKD • Sheep and goats: sheep only.

INTENSITY OF USE OF PESTICIDES

Data sources: OECD, FAO, national statistical yearbooks, European Crop Protection Association

♦ Unless otherwise specified, data refer to active ingredients.

♦ Unless otherwise specified, data refer to total consumption of pesticides, which include: insecticides (acaricides, molluscicides, nematocides and mineral oils), fungicides (bactericides and seed

treatments), herbicides (defoliants and desiccants), and other pesticides (plant growth regulators and rodenticides).

CAN • Survey coverage has varied greatly (different active ingredients, registrants and products); survey trends may therefore not reflect actual trends but simply changes in the survey coverage. 1994: refer to agriculture uses only (non-agricultural uses excluded). % change since 1980: base year refer to 1984.
USA • Data refer to agricultural pesticides only.

JPN • Data refer to national production of pesticides.
KOR • % change since 1980: base year refer to 1986.
NZL • % change since 1980: base year refer to 1985.
BEL • Data include Luxembourg.
CZE • Data refer to agricultural pesticides and sales of chemical pesticides. Include: animal repellents, additives, adhesives and other pesticides.
DNK • Sales for use in plant production in open agriculture. % change since 1980: base year refer to 1981.
FIN • Data include forest pesticides and refer to sales.
FRA • Data refer to quantities sold to agriculture.
DEU • Data refer to sales.
GRC • Data refer to sales. % change since 1980: base year refer to 1986.
ITA • Data refer to formulation weight.

NLD • Data refer to sales of chemical pesticides. Data include soil disinfectants, which correspond to about the half of the total consumption. % change since 1980: base year refer to 1984.
NOR • Data refer to sales.
POL • Data include animal repellents and other pesticides.
PRT • Data refer to sales.
ESP • Data refer to sales. % change since 1980: base y. refer to 1986.
SWE • A special sales tax has been applied to pesticides since 1987. Another tax was applied in 1995. Data refer to sales.
CHE • Data refer to sales and have been estimated to represent 95 per cent of the total market volume; Liechtenstein included.
TUR • Formulation weight. Powdered sulphur and copper sulphate excluded.
UKD • Great Britain only. Data include sulphuric acid, which represents approx. 40% (1995) of the total.

EXPENDITURE

POLLUTION ABATEMENT AND CONTROL EXPENDITURE

Data source: OECD

♦ Pollution abatement and control (PAC) expenditure according to the abater principle. PAC activities are defined as purposeful activities aimed directly at the prevention, reduction and elimination of pollution or nuisances arising as a residual of production processes or the consumption of goods and services. Excludes expenditure on natural resource management and activities such as the protection of endangered species, the establishment of natural parks and green belts and activities to exploit natural resources (such as the supply of drinking water).

♦ Total expenditure: the sum of public and business expenditure (excluding households); values in USD per capita: at current prices and purchasing power parities.

CAN • 1995 data; public: includes subsidies to private sector; in principle, does not include fees from the private sector; data include estimates.
MEX • Total: Secretariat estimate for 1995; public: partial figure.
USA • 1994 data.
JPN • 1990 data; total includes Secretariat estimate.
KOR • Trial estimate by the bank of Korea for 1997.
AUS • 1996 data.
AUT • 1994 data. Excludes expenditure concerning protection of nature and landscape and R&D; estimates were made in such a way as to eliminate double counting of fees for waste water and waste.
BEL • Total: Secretariat estimate for 1996.

CZE • Total: Secretariat estimate for mid-1990s; public and business: based on shares in investment.
DNK • Total: Secretariat estimate for 1996: public: includes subsidies and transfers to private sector.
FIN • 1997 data; business: ISIC 10 to 40 only.
FRA • 1996 data.
DEU • 1995 data.
GRC • 1995 data.
HUN • 1996 data referring to investment only.
ISL • Public sector: 1998 expenditure on waste, waste water and general environmental monitoring only.
IRL • Total: Secretariat estimate for 1998.
ITA • 1989 data including Secretariat estimate.
LUX • 1997 data.
NLD • 1995 data.
NOR • Secretariat estimate for 1990.
POL • 1995 data referring to investment only.
PRT • 1998 data including receipts from by-products; excluding this amounts, expenditure for public and business sectors would reach 0.9% of GDP.
ESP • Total: Secretariat estimate for 1991.
SWE • 1991 data.
CHE • Public: 1992 data; business and total: 1993 data.
UKD • 1990 data.

OFFICIAL DEVELOPMENT ASSISTANCE

Data source: OECD-DAC

♦ Data refer to loans (except military loans), grants and technical co-operation by the public sector to developing countries. Data cover

OECD Development Assistance Committee (DAC) Member countries. The new System of National Accounts (SNA) tends to depress donors' ODA/GNP ratios in the mid-1990s.

MEMBERS OF THE WORKING GROUP ON ENVIRONMENTAL INFORMATION AND OUTLOOKS[*]
1999/2000

Chair: Ms. Anne Teller

♦ AUSTRALIA	Mr. A. Haines (Vice-Chair) Mr. B. Harrison	♦ KOREA	Mr. J. Choi Ms. Y.S. Kim
♦ AUSTRIA	Ms. E. Milota Mr. W. Schober	♦ LUXEMBOURG	Mr. J.P. Feltgen
		♦ MEXICO	Mr. R. Lopez-Perez Mr. A. Yanez
♦ BELGIUM	Ms. A. Teller (Chair)		
♦ CANADA	Mr. M. Lemire Mr. D. O'Farrell	♦ NETHERLANDS	Mr. P. Klein Mr. C. Vijverberg
♦ CZECH REPUBLIC	Mr. E. Lippert (Vice-chair)	♦ NEW ZEALAND	Mr. D. Brash
♦ DENMARK	Mr. P. Etwil Ms. A. Ladefoged	♦ NORWAY	Mr. O. Nesje Mr. F. Brunvoll
♦ FINLAND	Mr. L. Kolttola Mr. J. Muurman	♦ POLAND	Ms. L. Dygas-Ciolkowska Ms. D. Dziel
♦ FRANCE	Mr. T. Lavoux (Vice-chair)	♦ PORTUGAL	Mr. G. Espada
♦ GERMANY	Ms. J. Burkhardt Mr. O. Angermann	♦ SPAIN	Mr. F. Cadarso
		♦ SWEDEN	Ms. E. Hoglund-Davila Ms. M. Notter
♦ GREECE	Ms. M. Peppa		
♦ HUNGARY	Mr. E. Szabo	♦ SWITZERLAND	Mr. P. Glauser Mr. T. Klingl
♦ ICELAND	Ms. E. Hermannsdottir		
♦ IRELAND	Mr. L. Stapleton (Vice-Chair)	♦ TURKEY	Mr. M. Gürcü Ms. A. Tokel
♦ ITALY	Ms. R. Calicchia Mr. P. Soprano	♦ UNITED KINGDOM	Mr. J. Custance
		♦ UNITED STATES	Mr. P. Ross (Vice-Chair)
♦ JAPAN	Mr. Y. Moriguchi (Vice-Chair)	♦ CEC	Mr. U. Wieland Mr. P. Bosch

---

OECD SECRETARIAT

Ms. M. LINSTER
Ms M. BAGHERZADEH, Ms. F. ZEGEL

Consultants: Ms. M.J. SANTOS

---

[*] former Working Group on the State of the Environment.

OECD PUBLICATIONS, 2, rue André-Pascal, 75775 PARIS CEDEX 16
PRINTED IN FRANCE
(97 2001 09 1 P) ISBN 92-64-18718-9 – No. 52079 2001